WEST MEETS EAST

Charles L. Freer

Trailblazing Asian Art Collector

Helen Nebeker Tomlinson

Helen N. Tomlinson

West Meets East: Charles L. Freer, Trailblazing Asian Art Collector

Author photo by Richard B. Barton
Web design by Thomas Barton

For more information, please contact:
Mascot Books
620 Herndon Parkway, Suite 320
Herndon, VA 20170
info@mascotbooks.com

Library of Congress Control Number: 2019904772

CPSIA Code: PRFRE0919A
ISBN-13: 978-1-64543-013-1

Printed in Canada

To John, Laura, and Will
for their initiative, compassion,
and serendipity.

AUTHOR'S NOTE

Until after World War II, scholars typically divided the world into two cultures: Occidental (west) and Oriental (east). The art Freer and his contemporaries labeled Oriental, we call Asian today. Place names have also changed: Peking to Beijing, Ceylon to Sri Lanka, Constantinople to Istanbul, and some have changed spelling: Racca to Rakka to Raqqa, Kioto to Kyoto, and Tokio to Tokyo. Chinese dynasty names have altered from T'ang to Tang, Sung to Song, and Ch'ing to Qing. The reader will find these names used interchangeably.

CONTENTS

PART THREE: ADVENTURES IN ART

PART FOUR: ENTREPRENEUR'S LEGACY

PROLOGUE

In Charles Freer, two natures coexisted: a homespun country boy and a worldly connoisseur. Even his physical appearance suggested his dual natures. Large laborer's hands and feet offset his tall, slender patrician frame. Warm, twinkling brown eyes defied the severity of his oval face, his long, narrow nose, and thin mouth. Among close friends he was a delightful raconteur, noted for his wit and love of intrigue; business associates, however, found him serious and demanding.

Freer carried a walking stick, and often an unlit cigar tilted from his mouth. A high celluloid collar accentuated his smug air, but he was a gentleman to the core, a modest man. His full, sandy beard, mustache, and thinning hair, all meticulously clipped, hinted at a redhead's quick temper kept under careful control. He was the kind of man young nephews remembered more with respect than with love. "When Uncle Charlie was around, everyone shaped up, toed the mark." Yet except during startling moments of rage, he was a soft-spoken man. He shunned both the public and publicity. As one contemporary wrote of him:

> It is believed he has not spoken in the first person to the public… He is the most retiring man in the

> world. You could bury Freer in cut glass goblets in the whispering gallery at Washington and he'd get out without a tinkle.[1]

In Freer's Gilded Age, like our own, great disparity of wealth separated classes, economic depressions devastated industries, and the political system roiled in drama. Change was in the air, and Charles Freer caught the gold rings it offered. He aimed for uncrowded fields. Rather than face off with the Vanderbilts building railroad lines, he earned a fortune manufacturing the freight cars essential to those lines and compounded it by investing in pharmaceuticals. Ignoring the European masterpieces for which his contemporaries J. P. Morgan and Henry Clay Frick competed, he pioneered collecting in the field of ancient Oriental art, a field practically unknown to Americans in 1900. As both business tycoon and art connoisseur, he was well aware that perseverance, not fate or family, had gained him position, polish, and respect.

Hardly the "effete aesthetic" as claimed by some who have written about him, Freer was a man of physical endurance. He relaxed by hiking in the mountains. On business trips he traveled regularly over at least two-thirds of the United States, moving from bumpy railroad trains to jerky hack cabs with an energy that would stagger the modern, jet-sped businessman. On vacations he sailed rough seas for weeks; climbed over mammoth ancient ruins for hours; rode native transportation, whether mule, camel, or wheelbarrow, all with little need to spare a day for rest. He shepherded his touring parties through bandit-infested valleys, over precipitous mountain paths, and through steaming jungles. When necessary to accomplish his goals, Freer energetically persevered. He also could be a hypochondriac; he feared the debility of illness and took care to avoid it.

In his prime he traveled throughout the world, cultivated important people (if he liked them), gathered rare artworks, and created the Smithsonian's Freer Gallery of Art. A retired millionaire at forty-five years old; a personal confidant of expatriate American artist James McNeill Whistler; a welcome guest in the most elite circles of art connoisseurs in Paris, London, Tokyo, and Shanghai; a respected amateur upon whom art scholars throughout the world called for advice, he cut a low-profile but powerful figure. To gather rare art treasures, he traveled the world from Aleppo to Peshawar, from Cairo to Calcutta, from the Nile to the Himalayas, and from the wild north coast of Japan to the remote Li valley of China. He ferreted out treasures secretly to avoid alerting competitors to the caves, temples, or dealers he discovered. Yet to fellow collectors or students he deemed "the right sort," he shared information and contacts generously. As his legacy, he left 9,717 works of art and a generously endowed world-class museum.

Fortunately for a biographer, the very private Mr. Freer kept meticulous records. My research started with the rich storehouse of his personal papers in the Freer Gallery Archives. His diaries are cryptic businessman's journals with occasional pithy comments, a guide to his priorities, his movements and the people he met. His Letterbooks retain copies of the formal, dictated letters written from his office between 1890 and 1910. The most intimate insights for this biographer, however, came from letters to his friends, often handwritten during his travels. In many cases, their letters of reply are also on deposit. Vouchers, inventory lists, and memoranda provided details on his collection. Manuscripts at the Library of Congress and the Detroit Public Library gave me the perspective of his associates. My research next led to France and Japan to place Freer in the context of worldwide activities in Oriental art, and I traveled in his footsteps to India, Japan, and China to experience the places he explored albeit years later and at airplane speed.

Freer's complex personality made my writing journey a fascinating one. At first, I found him a fussy bachelor, then a stiff, demanding tyrant, and finally a big-hearted and vulnerable man of dedication and discernment. The Victorian gentleman became such a presence in our family that my children dubbed him "Chuckie," a term of endearment that might have delighted—or perhaps offended—him.

One hundred years after his death, it's time for Charles Freer to be an acknowledged public figure. The uncommon capitalist left not only a farsighted national art museum; he also created an extraordinary life. The story that follows traces his journey from his birth in New York's Catskill Mountains to his memorial in Koetsu-ji, Japan, in pursuit of adventure, purpose, and beauty.

PART ONE: ROAD TO RICHES

— 1 —

LEAVING KINGSTON

1854–1879

THE REMARKABLE EVOLUTION OF CHARLES Lang Freer would have seemed unimaginable when he was born in rural Kingston, New York, on February 25, 1854. The town was one of two small villages. Rondout was built along the sheltered banks of the Rondout Creek close to the Hudson River. Row houses and an occasional market or saloon lined the few rutted dirt roads that ran parallel to the water. Behind that village rose a steep bluff and a high plateau where the village of Kingston opened to farmland beyond. Homes, schools, library, markets, and livery stables crowded its main streets. When Freer was a boy, the old plank road connecting the two villages was updated to a gaslit street. A horse-drawn trolley ran from the Rondout ferry to the center of Kingston. Pigs still roamed freely. When the villages merged in 1872, the population was 20,000.

A mile or two beyond Kingston, the Catskill Mountains formed a majestic green backdrop for the village and its surrounding farmlands. For the young boy, they offered a ready escape and inspired his passion for nature. As an adult Freer never lost his love for the hills he had roamed as a child. His taste in art gravitated first to tonalist paintings reminiscent of the blue, mist-shrouded horizons he knew from early-morning hikes.

Class distinction struck Freer at an early age. Young Charlie, as his family called him, grew up in a small frame house close to Broadway where railroad tracks would soon cross. As he struggled with his family's meager means, he observed the more prosperous citizens in their stately brick mansions along a gently curving boulevard called Albany Avenue. The quietly ambitious boy hungered for their financial security and education.

The roots of Kingston and the Freer family were planted deep in America's past. In July 1675, a group of French Huguenots, Calvinists driven from Catholic France by religious persecution, sailed into the area; among them was a young man named Hugo Freer. These Frenchmen moved inland from Kingston in 1677, bought land from friendly Native Americans and established their own community. Hugo Freer signed as one of the twelve patentees of their New Paltz settlement. A bit of a loner, he lived apart from the group and "continued to be troublesome and vexatious as ever." That independent streak he passed down to his most famous descendant.[1]

Charlie grew up fast in the quiet backwater of Kingston; his father's financial failures and his own lack of an education propelled him to a lifetime of seeking new opportunities. His grandfather, Jan Freer, had set an example; in addition to running a farm, Jan and his father operated a mill, and he owned the Eddyville Ferry. The town across Rondout Creek from Eddyville was called Freersville. In 1826 Jan built an impressive stone house where he and his wife lived until their deaths nearly fifty years later. They provided each of their ten children with a solid education and a model of success.

Only their ambitious grandson would emulate Jan's drive; none of their own children made a notable mark or much of an effort.[2]

Freer's father, Jacob, complacent and slow, had graduated from Kingston Academy, the private school that educated Kingston youth in Latin, logic, geometry, and history. At twenty-seven, he wed nineteen-year-old Phoebe Townsend, the daughter of a well-respected Hyde Park family. Unable to match the prosperity and productivity of his father, Jacob struggled to meet the demands of his expanding family. Emma, their first child, arrived less than a year after their 1845 marriage. Their second child died at the age of two, and six more children were born to the couple at regular three-year intervals. The last child died in infancy.

Jacob provided his children a modest home, a minimal education, and an uninspiring example. For much of his life, he worked as a jockey or horse breaker, and for a short time, he owned a livery stable. At one point, he might have tried farming. Relatives claimed he ran an inn in his later years. By 1871, however, the city directory listed his occupation as a laborer, and the following year it listed no occupation at all. By then, illness had left him partially paralyzed; he remained an invalid until his death in 1875.[3]

Freer's letters and papers never mention his parents by name. There is no question, however, that he felt more respect and affection for his mother's side of his family. He lost contact with his father's large family; no record remains of letters, visits, or exchanges of gifts with them. In the Townsends, however, he found a refinement that shaped his life and an emotional connection tethered by tragic loss. Phoebe, the strength of the family, died suddenly, six months after the death of her youngest child. Only forty-two years old in 1868, she left behind a brood of six children ages six to twenty-three. Whatever the influence of his mother while she lived, her death was a traumatic change for fourteen-year-old Charlie.

The children held the family together. Emma Frances, whom the family called "Frank," assumed her mother's responsibilities. She was the eldest child and the only girl. She took care of the home, the boys, and her father. A tall woman, on the stout side, fastidious, and very religious, she devoted her life to the family she had inherited from her mother. She worked as a seamstress, but money was scarce. George, at seventeen the oldest of five boys, settled down as a carriage smith. A tall, young man inclined to be serious and often crabby, he was too old to be mothered by Emma and too independent to shepherd all those younger brothers; he took responsibility for himself but little more. Like Emma, he spent his entire life in Kingston. It fell to Charlie to provide the paternal support and financial bulwark for his siblings, a responsibility the remarkably successful adult Charles carried throughout his life.

After Phoebe's death, Charlie did not return to school, nor did he continue working on the nearby farm. A quiet, sensitive boy galled by his family's strained circumstances, he took his first full-time job in a cement factory. Less than two years later, John C. Brodhead, a dealer in "Groceries, Provisions, etc.," hired him as a clerk. Brodhead, a prominent man in Kingston, served as county treasurer and lived in a fine brick home on Albany Avenue. Under Brodhead's scrutiny, Charlie tabulated accounts, handled money, and received orders. The quick teenager proved his ability with figures and earned a reputation as an honest, reliable worker. For the ambitious boy, such training was invaluable.

On May 27, 1870, the same year that young Charlie started with Brodhead, the first railroad train steamed into Kingston. Thomas Cornell, owner of a large steamboat, was president of the Rondout and Oswego Railroad. Brodhead was the vice president and construction supervisor. Their train ran on thirty-two miles of track from the Hudson River through the Catskill Mountains. The black machine overwhelmed many of the rural inhabitants with its noise, smoke, and treacherous speeds. For Charlie, it stretched space and time beyond Kingston and into the future, and it promised employment.[4]

Frank J. Hecker, an ambitious twenty-six-year-old, arrived that year as superintendent of the railroad's operations. His office was on the second floor above Brodhead's store; Charlie probably waited on him and peppered him with questions. Of sturdy, hardworking German stock, Hecker had an erect posture and penetrating eyes that gave him an aura of authority. He had left public school before he was eighteen to clerk under General G. M. Dodge in the closing years of the Civil War. When Dodge became chief engineer of the Union Pacific Railroad, Hecker followed him to the Wyoming Territory. He then made his move to Kingston from the desolate town of Cheyenne through a connection with Cornell.

Within months, Cornell resigned as president of the railroad, and Brodhead took over. In 1872, Charlie moved upstairs to clerk in Hecker's office. The new railroad grew steadily; Hecker soon made the teenager his paymaster. He would later recall with an air of paternalism, "I first met the boy...when, at the age of 16, he clerked in the general store." It was the beginning of a partnership that continued for the next half century.[5]

For a keen young man like Charlie, Frank Hecker modeled a demanding leader; he brooked no nonsense from workers, no hint of cheating or dishonesty. He was also ambitious and quick to seize financial opportunities. In 1874, with Abel A. Crosby, he bought the patent for a railroad car coupler. The following year he bought the patent for an invention that improved the efficiency of plows unloading gravel from flatcars. Already married and the father of a young family, he had traveled the United States and had gained experience as well as contacts in the railroad industry. By contrast, Charlie had never been outside Kingston. Hecker attracted powerful friends and inspired loyal employees, tactics the observant Freer would later mimic with scholars and art dealers. In Hecker, he found the first of three important mentors who would dramatically impact his future.[6]

Operating a fledgling railroad in Kingston presented constant challenges. Revenues dropped thirty percent in the Panic of 1873. In 1875, the railroad, now running seventy-five miles of track, was auctioned back to its founder, Thomas Cornell, who reorganized it as the Ulster and Delaware Railroad. Vanderbilt's New York Central line posed new competition. Train accidents and derailments were frequent. In 1876, when fire destroyed the railroad shops and a crucial bridge, arson by dismissed employees was suspected. The experience was a revelation to the naïve Charlie. Railroading was not for the faint of heart.[7]

Amid the perpetual chaos, Hecker prospected for new opportunities. Through a New York merchant who summered in the Catskills, he met James F. Joy, president of the Michigan Central Railroad. The "Joy roads" stretched trains throughout the Midwest. Joy invited the enterprising superintendent to Detroit to meet Christian H. Buhl, a railroad speculator and president of the Detroit & Eel River & Illinois Railroad. Impressed by the go-getter, Buhl offered him the position of general superintendent of the Eel line in Logansport, Indiana. Hecker, eager to become a part of Joy's network, accepted.[8]

Before leaving Kingston, Hecker received the traditional watch. Freer probably wrote the letter that bore his own signature (now the more businesslike "Charles") and those of the other employees paying tribute to their departing superintendent. Like his mentor, Charles hoped for grander prospects and longed to venture beyond Kingston. His father had died a year earlier, and the earnest twenty-two-year-old assumed responsibility for his parents' family. Determined to provide his younger brothers with the education he had missed, he needed a better position and more money. He remained in Kingston, anticipating a call from Hecker.

On August 15, 1876, Frank Hecker arrived in Logansport, Indiana, home of the spur railroad. His predecessor was ill and perhaps had been incapacitated for some time, for the railroad was in disarray. Hecker sent Buhl his evaluation of the repair status of the line and stiffened the policy regarding free passes. Within the first month, he dismissed the accountant. Charles Freer replaced him.[9]

Like many fledgling lines popping up across the United States, the Eel covered limited territory, depended on good local harvests, fought price wars, and ran on dilapidated equipment. An acquaintance of Freer's later described the railroad prize that had drawn him west as a "rust-eaten, rotten timbered neighborhood mistake," boasting equipment characterized by "two teakettles, which Freer passionately asserted were engines." The Eel had thirty miles of track, sixteen freight cars, six passenger cars, and two locomotives. It "wobbled through Mexico and Chile," two remote towns in Indiana, and picked up passengers at any cornfield crossroads.[10]

The new superintendent may have inherited a weak line; but three years later, his report to the president listed "11 engines, 260 freight cars, 5 cabooses, 5 passenger cars, and 1 baggage car." Hecker worked an eighteen-hour day and expected the same commitment from others. Always a gentleman, fair but with the highest standards, he made many friends along the line and, as the local press reported, almost as many enemies, "the penalty of his energy." Charles kept the books and made the payments for the Eel. Ensconced in his own office at the dingy railroad station, he earned $90 a month, the same rate as the chief clerk. Only Hecker and the yardmaster earned more. He shared a room with another young Eel employee, Walter Osmer, who later recalled, "from boyhood Freer had a passion for beautiful surroundings. For half his life, he could not gratify it."[11]

Charles concentrated on business and maintained a record of every aspect of the fledgling Eel River Railroad. The business of running a railroad in Indiana involved not only moving freight, mail, and passengers, but also negotiating line crossings, maintaining track, and outwitting numerous competitors. Hecker upgraded the "rust eaten" Eel by purchasing freight cars, primarily from Buhl's Detroit associates James and Hugh McMillan at the Michigan Car Company, thereby shrewdly cementing business contacts in Detroit. After his first year in the Indiana outpost, a restless Frank Hecker wrote to James Joy, stating frankly that eventually he would like to leave Logansport. In reply Joy offered paternal support but left him there.[12]

By 1879, route competition, rate fluctuations, and the specter of a takeover by a bigger line constantly threatened the Eel. Rumors spread that Vanderbilt interests were quietly buying Eel stock. The Wabash, Saint Louis & Pacific Railroad, controlled by the ruthless Jay Gould, successfully diverted traffic from the Eel to its line, and absorption appeared imminent. Hecker, ever aggressive and buoyed by the annual mid-July to mid-August farm shipments, advised Buhl and Joy to make the inevitable sale of the Eel line by September 1, predicting that the minute a takeover became final, cooperation from friends and employees would diminish and the Eel "would fizzle, where as if we can turn over [now],we will go out with a snap to our whip."[13]

The Wabash line did take over the Eel by leasing the line for 99 years. With Joy's assurance that the new ownership of the Eel would not jeopardize their jobs, Hecker and Freer remained at their posts, but it was a trying period for Charles. He became ill, a reaction to stress he would experience often in his career. Retreating to the mountains in Canada for a month, he tried to regain his strength and spirit in quiet days of fishing and trapping in the woods. Hecker handled the finances and ran the line. The new management left him alone. Accustomed to close supervision under Buhl, he chafed at a lax attitude, ascribing it to the typical pattern of large, rich companies. He should have been suspicious of their indifference. On October 31, the Wabash canceled all employee contracts.[14]

Charles left no record of his reaction to their sudden termination. He had gained three years of valuable experience but had accumulated little money. The thought of admitting failure and returning to Kingston and his struggling siblings was a gloomy one. The alternative prospect of continuing to cast his lot with Hecker offered greater promise. Hecker had personal contacts and modest savings. Freer's assets included working skills and reliability. Together the two men explored opportunities outside Logansport.

Christian Buhl assured Frank Hecker he would have no difficulty finding a comparable position "in railroading or outside," that "an active man need not be idle long." He proposed financing a project that Hecker could manage: combining an old steam forge, then sitting idle in Detroit, with a wheel foundry to make railroad cars. By then Freer and Hecker had learned a harsh lesson in running railroads. The instability of the railroad industry in the 1880s demanded manipulation, secrecy, and corruption to survive.

A business of their own that they could control and run on their own terms was more to their taste.[15]

Friends in Kingston tried to entice them to return. But now their dreams were bigger. The forge that Buhl proposed buying had failed in the Panic of 1873. Hecker and Freer were confident they could succeed. They had experience in the railroad industry and strong financial backers in Detroit. Like the pioneers who supplied shovels to the miners in the California gold rush, they would supply freight cars to the railroad lines. Betting their future on what remained of a bankrupt railroad car plant, they moved to the burgeoning frontier town of Detroit.[16]

— 2 —

DETROIT INDUSTRIALIST

1879–1889

When Charles Freer disembarked from the train at the crowded Detroit station, he found himself in a bustling western city of just over 100,000 inhabitants. Its wide streets were cluttered with horse-drawn buggies, hack cabs, and scurrying pedestrians. Horses pulled trolleys along a few of the main avenues. Cedar blocks, not cobblestones, paved the streets of lumber land's largest city, creating occasional problems: in a downpour, the blocks floated, and during hot, dry spells, they caught on fire. The nascent entrepreneur rented rooms at a boarding house on Jefferson Avenue and confidently assumed he could find a backer to stake him to a claim in the car business. He was a modest man, but he did not lack assurance.

Detroit, gutsy and strong in 1880, matched the ambitions of the two young partners. When the Erie Canal opened in 1825, it reduced the cost of shipping goods from $32 to $1 per ton for each 100 miles. It also funneled thousands of Americans and Europeans west. When the Civil War imposed immense material demands on the divided nation and Congress authorized subsidies for a transcontinental railroad in 1863, the state's new railroad industry exploded. Detroit's location connected commerce from the Atlantic coast to the western territories, and its land provided an abundance of raw material. As an important hub for the railroads, Michigan served their needs as she had earlier served the demands of the fur trade. The vast forests that formerly harbored animal pelts now provided acres of lumber, a perfect warehouse for railroad supplies.[1]

Immigrants nurtured the city's population growth. By the 1890s nearly half of the adults were foreign born, mostly German and Irish, but many were Italian and Polish as well. Foundries and machine shops hummed with immigrant workers, many doing backbreaking work casting iron stoves and 570-pound railroad wheels. The city's Democratic majority faced a Republican dominance in the rest of the state; but so long as abundant jobs and a minimal standard of living continued, Detroit's denizens did not challenge the system that fed them, a system rigged by the captains of industry to secure their position at the top.[2]

New Detroit entrepreneurs nipped at the established heels of Joy and Buhl. Smart men like John Newberry and James McMillan quickly concluded that supplying the railroad industry could be more lucrative and less precarious than owning major railroads. They saw Michigan forests turned into rolling stock: lines of cars snaking behind the smoking locomotives. In 1864, they organized the Michigan Car Company, the company that had supplied new cars for the Eel Railroad in Logansport. Newberry, a maritime lawyer, helped organize the Republican Party in Michigan. With fellow Republican congressional leaders, he forced a change in tariff rates to favor local car manufacturers so the United States car industry could compete effectively against the British.[3]

James McMillan was only seventeen years old when he left his family and school in Canada and struck out for Detroit. Within a few years, he joined Newberry in a partnership that controlled car building as well as steamship building. By 1888 James McMillan was a United States senator and captained the small group of businessmen who unofficially ran Detroit politics. The McMillan men, including James's brothers William and Hugh, soon ran the Michigan Telephone Company, founded the Edison Electric Company, and managed the Street Light Company.[4]

In that frontier environment, economic development depended on cooperation more than competition. Newberry, McMillan, Buhl, and Joy formed the core of Detroit's social order after the Panic of 1873, along with Russell Alexander Alger, a lawyer and former Civil War general who became a railroad president and the world's largest dealer in pine lumber. The personification of Michigan's slogan "Pine and Politics," he was later governor of Michigan and a U.S. senator. These men—the ruling class of Detroit—interlocked economically, consolidated politically, and bonded socially, including through marriages.[5]

They were the powerful men who brought Hecker and Freer to Detroit. Buhl had proposed the idea of taking over a freight car building shop and with his family provided the major investment in the enterprise. Their syndicate of friends funded the business. Alger not only invested his own money but also signed for a $5,000 loan to enable Freer to buy himself a share in the company. The McMillan brothers, owners of the city's major car company, accepted the newcomers into their fast-expanding industry.[6]

Hecker and Freer secured a charter for the Peninsular Car Works in December 1879. Buhl's son Theodore D. Buhl assumed the title of president, although he was not active in its management.

Hecker took the post of vice president and general manager; Freer became assistant treasurer. With a five-year lease on a freight car plant and a steam forge built near the Detroit River, they started their company. With a capital investment of only $100,000, their 300 employees produced 1,440 cars in the first year. Within months, the company bought a defunct car plant in Adrian, Michigan, and operated it separately as the Adrian Car Company. Their output of wooden freight cars, box cars, coal-and-coke cars, logging cars, and refrigerator cars grew more than fourfold in the second year to 6,014. Just as Hecker had shown progress despite depressing problems on the beleaguered Eel River Railroad, he doggedly pushed the young company.[7]

While Frank Hecker managed the technical aspects of plant production, raw materials, personnel, and delivery of the cars, Charles Freer concentrated on accounting, pricing, and sales. He competed with discretion, relying on conservative calculations before bidding on prospective contracts. National competition might be fierce and price margins tight, but he preferred to lose an order rather than bid an insufficient margin. Profit, patience, orderly process, and gentlemanly relations were his bywords. He gained confidence fast, secure in his meticulous attention to detail and in his unflinching skill as a tough bargainer.

By 1883 the two partners recapitalized their company. Explaining why they bought out the Buhl family, Hecker wrote many years later,

> A difference of opinion arose over the views expressed by Mr. Freer, who had worked closely with me in the management of the business, and myself, and those held by Mr. C. H. Buhl.

The differences may have been over their ambitious plan to build a new, modern plant. The Buhls took their money and exited with no hard feelings. Alger, Joy, and Allan Sheldon (an organizer of the Eel Railroad) invested $50,000 each in the new Peninsular Car Company. Now the two entrepreneurs were firmly in control of their company, with Hecker as president and Freer as secretary/treasurer. They owned $100,000 and $50,000 respectively of the new $300,000 capital stock.[8]

That same year, Hecker turned over management of the company to Freer and departed for a lengthy vacation to California. Through letters, Charles reported twice a week to Hecker. Although General Alger and T. D. Buhl both offered advice and consultation, he made it clear that their help was seldom needed.

In fact, Freer thrived on the challenge. The sales game suited his calculating mind. Shipping costs and price wars constantly complicated his plans. The percentage of failure was high, and bids were made and lost, but a single successful contract netted heady profits and kept the plant churning out cars for months. He prized the pursuit, the sense of personal control and accountability, just as he would later use them in his pursuit of art. In his letters to Hecker, he catalogued his failures as carefully as his victories. He lost one bid to a competitor who was on the buyer's railroad line and, therefore, faced no freight expense. However, on a promising order involving 1,000 boxcars for Mr. Vanderbilt, he made a careful study of the drawings, submitted his bid, and pacified the middlemen, who were "sore" because they had not been consulted on the specifications. Despite dealing with three separate "soreheads," Freer reported that he was "nicely treated" by all. His bid of $580 per car delivered to the Vanderbilt road included a $20 per car margin, a tidy $20,000 profit. Selling was his sport.[9]

Plant accidents disrupted production weekly if not daily, creating a dramatic staccato against the harmony of steady production and shipment. Stimulated by the dynamics of the business, Freer's interest in the game flagged when a venture became either routine or beyond his control. He handled accidents with a cool, detached efficiency. Once, when a supervisor was boiling paint, it exploded and destroyed the boiling house. The men acted quickly in getting a hose and water, but the hose was too short to save the building. Freer commended their action, ordered more hose the next day, and had the house rebuilt of brick. Another time he blithely reported another "little scorch" and confidently stated that "the little trouble occasioned prevented us from getting rusty."[10]

Freer could also be callous. He dispatched with one accident in which one of the foundry drivers was knocked off the coal car he was unloading, struck the back of his neck, and died. With the assistance of a Dr. Douglass, Freer closed the matter for a total of twenty-five dollars. "Have the widow's receipt in full and we are entirely free from any future trouble in the case," he reported to Hecker, assuring him that "no particular loss was suffered."[11]

Freer's flip efficiency is appalling to us today, but few of his peers in the 1880s, given the era's rampant power disparity and social discrimination, would have considered the aspects of the man's accident any differently. Like unreasonable competition, accidents were disorderly and annoying but not monumental concerns. He admitted the loss of life was sad, but the man was a "Polander of the lowest type" who with his wife and child "lived more like brutes than human beings." The man's relatives, he wrote Hecker, took a mercantile view of the matter; their only concern was the money, "and you can judge of their estimate of the fellow by the amount paid."[12]

Freer was concerned with careful management of the industrial process, not with human relations, especially human relations that crossed class and ethnic boundaries. Quality labor, however, he valued as a critical part of the machinery. He took great pride in good workers. Happily, he announced finding "an A.1. pine inspector" as a "perfect Bonanza." The man could handle 5,000 feet of pine more quickly than his predecessor managed to handle 2,000 feet, and in addition he put "some life in our yard laborers." Occasionally, scarcity of labor presented a problem. In the spring of 1883, some carpenters threatened to leave, lured away by the higher wages offered by house builders. Ten days later Freer offered a few men an advance of five to ten cents a day, and their carpenter force stabilized.[13]

After Hecker returned from California in May of 1883, Charles had his own opportunity to go west. Thomas Fletcher Oakes, vice president of the Northern Pacific Railroad, invited him to meet with some cattlemen to discuss a recently patented railroad stock car. They traveled in Oakes's private car accompanied by his bodyguards to Miles City, Montana, an adventure into the Wild West Freer obviously relished. Even among seasoned miners, copper territory was infamous for its lawlessness and violence, for the Judith Basin, and Calamity Jane. Years later he remembered only that "there were no nights for an entire month." He concluded his long trip with a stay in San Diego, where he later recalled riding horseback and chasing coyotes. In all his adventures, whether the object was railroad cars, wild animals, or artworks, he relished the pursuit as much as the capture.[14]

Meanwhile, their new Detroit plant, positioned away from the congestion by the river, began to receive freight and ship cars by rail from all points on the compass. One of the first in the city to install an independent electric light plant, it also boasted extraordinary fire safety precautions and advanced water and sewage systems. The Republican *Detroit Free Press* reported that the "New Works" employed 700 men and praised in detail the multiple buildings, foundries, machine shops, and their efficient operations. The current output of fifteen cars per day promised to rise to thirty.[15]

Success had come to Charles Freer at frontier speed. At the age of twenty-nine, he had proved himself in every sense a partner equal to the older Frank Hecker. Seven years after they took over the bankrupt forge, their company had nearly caught up with the McMillans' Michigan Car Company in both sales and production. By the end of their first decade in business, they employed an average of 1,350 men, and their annual output value had risen to $4,000,000. Their gamble on Detroit had paid off handsomely, but success made strenuous demands. Freer traveled frequently: by train to New York for a week, returning to Detroit for a few days, then setting off again for Chicago, St. Louis, Baltimore, or by boat to Toledo and Cleveland. Constitutionally unable to let details slide or projects remain incomplete, he devoted his time in Detroit and en route to business.[16]

For over ten years his life had been intimately tied to that of Frank Hecker. In business and financial matters, they maneuvered in tandem and reacted in harmony. They had joint accounts at clubs, invested together in companies, and sent gifts in both names. In their private lives, however, they traveled different paths. The gregarious Hecker gravitated to political and civic activities; he was appointed police commissioner. Each summer he and his socially ambitious wife sailed with their five teenage children aboard his yacht *Halcyon* to their cottage on Mackinac Island. Their life in Detroit revolved around cotillions, receptions, and musicals; their home on Jefferson

Avenue became a center for Detroit society.

The mentor relationship with Hecker concealed Freer's contribution. The more aggressive older man absorbed the public attention and captained the company. Hecker, although a loyal partner, could be condescending. Freer never challenged Hecker, always granting him deference, yet he quietly chafed in Hecker's shadow. Freer yearned for an identity expressive of his more sensitive personality.

Since arriving in Detroit, he had rented rooms, first boarding at 1061 Jefferson, then from 1885 to 1892 lodging with the widow of Andrew McLaughlin on Alfred Street. He had no household staff and probably few belongings. Yet in less than a decade, the new tycoon had the beginnings of a fortune. His social stature rose with his income. The *Dau's Blue Book* included Hecker in 1881 and Freer in 1885. Giving no business association or other information, it provided a social service for the calling-card crowd. Detroit's contemporary historian, Charles Moore, claimed that while New York City had its "400," Detroit had its 1,000. The society was open, he wrote, requiring neither family money nor culture, only that the knocker not be "pushy." Freer, certainly not the pushy sort, had made it to the top.[17]

His private life outside business centered on hiking in the mountains and participating in men's clubs. He was a founding member of the Detroit Club, a private sanctuary where men could gather to discuss business. Its original membership of 100 grew fast to 200 and then to 430, but the men were generally of the "right sort." In 1888, he joined Witenagemote, the younger men's answer to the prestigious and rather stodgy Prismatic literary club. Offering Freer a smaller, more challenging circle than the Detroit Club, Witenagemote held lively monthly meetings in which journalists, artists, and other men interested in the creative arts took turns lecturing or preparing programs to enlighten the entire group. The brief note "My night at Witenagemote," was a frequent entry in Freer's diary and a well-honored social commitment.

His freedom from financial constraint erased a tension lingering from his boyhood. Never again would he or his family struggle for economic security. To each sibling he meted out the necessary support. George, the oldest of the brothers, at first kept a distance from his successful younger brother. After accepting help from Charles to purchase a livery stable and build a new home, he maintained his independence. Emma, the quiet de facto matriarch, remained at the family home, content in her life as an unmarried seamstress. She had worked hard for the "boys;" Charles saw to it that she lived comfortably and with security.[18]

Of his three younger brothers, Will was the most different from him in temperament. A huge, jolly man weighing nearly 250 pounds, he moved to Detroit, accompanied by a mangy dog, and happily accepted his brother's favors, including a job at the Adrian Car Company. When his wife died in 1887 shortly after the birth of their daughter, Charles bought him a farm near Kingston so Will could start a new life more suited to his temperament: breeding horses. Richard, a short, thin, even-tempered man, traveled out of Kingston as a shoe salesman. Charles set him up in his own shoe store in Philadelphia. His untimely death in 1891 left Charles with additional responsibility for his five children. Watson, the baby of the family, a good-looking, well-built teenager with intelligence and a pleasant disposition, inspired his brother's greatest hopes. Thanks to Charles, Watson graduated from Kingston Academy and moved to Detroit as a member of the Peninsular Car Company management team.[19]

Now a trim, balding man in his early thirties, Charles Freer looked mature beyond his years, his beard and mustache precisely groomed and his eyes intent behind a pince-nez. Financial success in Detroit had cured the family "sore" in Freer's background, but it exposed another. In neither Kingston nor Logansport had he felt the consequences of his truncated education. A hard worker, he had overcome his deficiencies by learning on the job. The men who ruled Detroit, however, had private education and even college behind them. Among them, Freer was an anomaly: poorly educated and bereft of family connections or support.

Desperate to gain parity with his sophisticated peers, he embarked on a quest for a cultural patina. He first spent money on fine clothes. As meticulous in his dress as in his bookkeeping, Freer engaged tailors in New York City and later in London. He requested suits, simply but beautifully cut, that reflected his well-ordered, unpretentious personality. On the other hand, his new prosperity allowed him to give vent to an inherent perfectionism. He would return a shirt for adjustment if the collar rose one-eighth of an inch too high.[20]

Next, he bought books to educate himself, not merely leather-bound volumes to adorn a library, but books to read: poetry by Violet Fane and the novels of Trollope. He devoured books on art, history, and philosophy. By 1888, he valued his inventory of books at $3,215, close to the value of his nascent art investments, $4,248.[21]

Freer found his niche in the art world. It offered an intellectual challenge he could master as well as the beauty he cherished. It gave him an avenue to assuage his outsider's longing, an expertise to mask his lack of education. In the end, his legacy exceeded that of his peers. It was what he did with his money that set him apart.

— 3 —

APPRENTICE IN ART
1882–1889

IN THE YEARS BEFORE CHARLES Freer arrived in Detroit, art was mostly a curiosity there. Local Detroit organizations held art loan exhibitions in union or young men's halls, featuring the "old, new, curious, rare, expensive, and desirable." Miscellaneous items overwhelmed the fine arts of paintings and drawings. *The Art Treasures of America*, a three-volume compendium published between 1879 and 1882, listed the 150 most important private art collections scattered throughout the country; none were in Detroit. Despite the influx of men from the East Coast, little of the eastern cultural polish glossed Detroit society.[1]

During the 1880s, Detroit's leaders awakened to the civic importance of the arts. The McMillan crowd entertained traveling artists and gallery owners who hawked artworks on their circuit tours from the East Coast to the frontier towns. The city's elite filled their grand homes with miscellaneous *objets d'art*. The very existence of art in the homes of men like Alger and McMillan evidenced their culture and erudition. Freer craved that kind of environment. He observed what his peers bought and hung on their walls, but he quietly went his own way in his own time.

His eagerness for education led him to lectures by traveling art experts. Francis Seymour Haden, a respected London doctor equally renowned as a painter-etcher, stopped in Detroit in 1882. The "toplofty" British gentleman, incidentally, was the brother-in-law of American artist James McNeill Whistler. Earlier the same year, Oscar Wilde, a more glittering wit, had discoursed on aesthetics in Detroit. In 1883, Frederick Keppel, a New York dealer of etchings and prints, arrived in Detroit with a large portfolio. These were Freer's first classes in art education. He made his first art purchase from Keppel and began to frequent the curio shops of Lower Manhattan on his business trips to New York. Amid the clutter in their shops, those dealers offered him valuable information. Thus began his apprenticeship in art collecting.[2]

Keppel was a curious man. His pet crow accompanied him on trips to Europe, sported with the seagulls on the ocean, and flew about his open window in London. The Irish farmer had immigrated to New York City and opened a bookstore. He bought etchings and sold them at such a handsome profit that in 1868 he sailed to Europe to buy more prints. For forty years thereafter, he made annual trips to Paris and London and, in the process, became an American authority on etchings and engravings. Freer responded to the quirky dealer and capitalized on his expertise. Their relationship was close but always formal, based on respect, trust, and service.[3]

Contemporary European etchings were a logical first step for the beginning collector. They appealed to his naïve eye and practical nature; they were inexpensive, portable, and refined. For three to five dollars, he could own an etching by Johan Barthold Jongkind or Maxime Lalanne. Freer absorbed analytical information eagerly; like railroad cars, the print was tangible. He could verify specifications, count on continued supply, and secure the maker's accountability to minimize the risks of his investment.

Initially his selections on art purchases sprang from a gut feeling, an emotional connection. He bought what he called "Dutch scenes," familiar landscapes reminiscent of his Ulster county boyhood haunts. The Dutch artist Charles Storm van's Gravesande captured his attention. Keppel had met the artist during his European trip in 1883 and brought his prints to Detroit that same year. He offered to sell "some rarities" that, he assured Freer, the artist "would not have parted with for my general trade."[4]

Freer began to correspond with Gravesande. Establishing a personal connection with his favorite artists was an early hallmark of his collecting process. He bought more confidently from an artist with whom he could share ideas and reactions. The artist verified for him the signature on works he had purchased and advised him on the states of the proofs and their dates.

Through Keppel, Freer established correspondence with other artists in Europe. From London, Keppel wrote that Haden had allowed him to take a set of etchings that the artist had saved for one of his own sons: *Etudes a l'Eau Forte*, a set then out of print for several years. Freer requested that the artist sign the prints, but Haden declined to sign any proofs in the set. He wrote a dedication to Freer instead. The arrogant Dr. Haden could be as prickly and stubborn as his brother-in-law Whistler.[5]

Knowing that Freer wanted to be discerning and discriminating, that he cared for quality, not quantity, Keppel wrote, "I have left no stone unturned to find the best things that are for sale in Europe." In turn Freer made certain the dealer met his prominent Detroit friends who might be interested in art. In a postscript to a letter in 1888, Keppel asked to be remembered "cordially to Mr. Hecker, and to my other kind friends in Detroit."[6]

Keppel's greatest contribution to Freer's future was an offhanded introduction. One day in early November 1886, as Freer was rummaging through the prints at Keppel's shop on Fifth Avenue, the dealer introduced him to Howard Mansfield, a young lawyer who had already gathered an impressive collection of etchings, including 300 by Whistler. Mansfield later described their first meeting:

> Mr. Keppel met me at the door and said, 'There is a man in my back room who has as good an eye for a print as anyone who comes into the place…' Two days later, after Mr. Freer had dined with me, we went to my bachelor apartment in West 36th Street for the evening to look at prints.

When Freer was comfortably seated and nursing an unlit cigar, Mansfield suggested they examine his Whistler prints together:

> Well, said [Freer], I would like to see your Whistlers; for I have heard about Whistler and read about Whistler, and I have seen some of his etchings in the print shops, and I would like to know why anyone in the world should make any fuss over Whistler as an artist.[7]

After they pored over the first portfolio of prints, Mansfield wrote that he returned to the room with a new portfolio: "I found Mr. Freer walking the floor and uttering large adjectives." By the end of the evening, a newly converted Freer left Mansfield with the parting comment "I have no words to express my admiration for the genius of this man [Whistler]."[8]

Shortly after his meeting with Mansfield, Freer bought Frederick Wedmore's catalogue of Whistler etchings and began an earnest study of the genius he had ignored. From Edward Kennedy of Wunderlich Gallery, he bought Whistler's prints and copies of the artist's *10 O'Clock Lecture*. A year later, he acquired proofs of all twenty-six etchings from Whistler's Venice, Second Series from the New York dealer Roland Knoedler. In 1888, he added Whistler dry points as well proofs from the Naval Review Set and from the French Sets. When the Grolier Club held its 1889 Whistler exhibition, the important lenders were Mansfield, the sugar baron Horace Havemeyer, and Charles Freer. The young Detroit industrialist had become a force in the print world.[9]

In Mansfield, Freer found a kindred spirit. The thirty-seven-year-old New Yorker had served as counsel for the New York West Shore and Buffalo Railroad Company from 1881 to 1884 before establishing his own law firm. As their collections grew, Freer and Mansfield shared their discoveries in the print market, buying duplicates for each other, notifying each other of available proofs. Freer acknowledged Mansfield's supremacy: "I doubt if there is now any finer collection of Whistler's prints to be seen anywhere."[10]

Freer also assembled an almost complete collection of Gravesande prints. His ambition was not to corner the market in a capitalist sense but to complete a comprehensive body of work in an aesthetic sense. Much like the pleasures we derive today from museum exhibitions tracing a single artist's evolution over time, Freer's collection gave vivid evidence of Gravesande's evolving skill and inspiration.

Meanwhile, Detroit marched forward with its own cultural ambitions. The city leaders hosted by far the grandest Art Loan Exhibition in the fall of 1883. The idea was conceived by James Scripps, the powerful publisher of the *Detroit Evening News*, whose collection was included, along with those of James McMillan, Alger, Joy, the Buhls, and a few others.

Encouraged by the public response to this exhibition, Senator Thomas Palmer pledged $10,000 toward the construction of a permanent museum if another $40,000 could be subscribed from other parties. Forty citizens pledged $1,000 each. Hecker and Freer did not participate; their funds were fully committed to their new plant. The Detroit Museum of Art was chartered in 1885. That year, among a very long list of modest donations for the museum building, the Hecker and Freer names finally appeared. The first exhibition under the auspices of the new museum opened May 30, 1886, in Merrill Hall. This time Freer contributed seventeen etchings, and Hecker lent three etchings. When the new museum opened in September 1888, Palmer was installed as its first president, James McMillan as vice president, and Scripps and his newspaper's advertising manager, William Brearley, as trustees. Although the city could finally boast of an institution that "stimulated talent, quickened genius, improved taste and excited new desires for the beautiful," all was not roses in the Detroit art world.[11]

Freer had a frosty relationship with James Scripps, who was a rebel in a city run by the elite cadre of Republican industrialists. As the owner and editor of the *Detroit Evening News*, he directed his sheet's appeal to the masses rather than to the moneyed classes, undercutting other papers by charging two cents a copy rather than five cents. Broadcasting his reform ideas, he stood staunchly independent of political parties and private interests. None of these traits endeared him to the smoothly oiled McMillan machine. The political lines that paralleled the city's economic and social ties had drawn boundaries in the newspaper world as well. The morning competitor *Detroit Free Press*, supported by Freer's friends, was run by the "iron- bottomed conservative" William Quinby, a man more suited to the capitalists' needs, their aspirations, and their sense of right.[12]

Scripps bucked the establishment, and the Detroit Museum of Art became his vehicle for social and civic recognition. One of the new museum's first major gifts came from Scripps. In the increasingly elitist Freer's eyes, the newspaperman was catering to the masses rather than focusing on uplifting them. His antipathy to Scripps's populism was reinforced by Whistler's *10 O'Clock Lecture*, published in 1885, which Charles read to a meeting of the Witenagemote Club in 1888. Whistler pretentiously exclaimed: "'The many' have elbowed 'the few'—and the gentle circle of Art swarms with the intoxicated mob of mediocrity…and catastrophe is upon us!" Charles Freer aspired to be counted among "the few." Wary of institutions, especially ones over which he exercised little influence, and of Scripps's leadership in the museum, Freer's relationship with the Detroit Museum of Art was guarded.[13]

An intriguing influence on Freer came indirectly from Frederick A. Stearns, who, in 1889, made the second major gift to the new museum. In port city bazaars from Alexandria to Tokyo, he had bought 7,000 Japanese items, 1,500 artifacts from China, and 1,000 from Korea. Typical of most early Oriental collections, few have artistic merit; they are now consigned to storage or ethnological study. At that time, however, the Stearns gift claimed distinction as "one of the largest and most representative collections in the United States of the art of Japan and Korea." His exhibit of

"Kakemonos" (hanging scrolls) drew popular attention for their "novelty and quaintness." Stearns, an acquaintance to whom Freer addressed letters "Dear Sir," had exposed the ever-curious Charles to a wider world of art. Visiting lecturers further piqued his interest: the famed Professor Edward S. Morse spoke on Japanese pottery, and others discussed Egyptology as well as "Cannibals of Australia." Freer's purported first purchase of fine Oriental art was in 1887, a Japanese folding fan. Different from Stearns's curios, the simplicity of a single elegant crane painted on the fan signaled Freer's developing aesthetic taste.[14]

By the 1890s Freer had very nearly depleted Keppel's warehouse and exhausted his resources. The disciplined collector then began a lifelong practice of culling inferior early purchases. He returned prints to the dealers from whom he had purchased them originally. Weeding was an emotional and difficult process of letting go; sometimes he faltered. Hoping to delete some of his Haden prints, Freer wrote wistfully to John Jordan, Keppel's assistant:

> The fact is, when I put them back in their portfolio I congratulated myself upon my moderation in buying Hadens...but I presume someday the sheriff will appear and then I will send them to you for the enjoyment of some collector who cares more for Hadens than I do.[15]

As Freer's confidence grew, so did his arrogance, an arrogance in this modest man that was inherently defensive, to protect his reputation. His fussy eye was as keen to uncover fault as to find beauty. In rejecting two prints, he archly wrote Jordan: "I am much disappointed in the Le Gros [sic], and the Whistler is so uncharacteristic that I should feel quite unhappy with it in my collection." Always a demanding customer, he resented any sloppy transaction and bluntly informed even a friend of his displeasure, expecting in reply not only apology, but reform.[16]

Both a pragmatist and a perfectionist, he kept those two natures in synchronized tension. In collecting prints, he created a process for buying art that would serve him for the next thirty years. Based on his experience selling railroad cars, he analyzed the quality of the workmanship and materials, the relative value and price—all to minimize risk in his investment. He established personal relationships with artists to assure authentication and accountability, and he collaborated with other collectors to increase his leverage. A student constantly tutoring himself, he read, compared, consulted, and practiced his eye for quality. He specialized in art where his purse could compete and where he could develop an expertise. When he found one field out of his reach, he moved on to explore new fields.

Yet in his pursuit of beauty, he looked for the most sublime expression of the loftiest ideals. Buying art was as much an emotional decision as a rational one. He knew what he wanted when he saw it: a tone, a harmony, a mood, his kind of reality. He spent lavishly for a "specimen" he coveted, even as he bargained ruthlessly for others. He could be stubborn and opinionated, demanding and high handed, but when proved wrong, he usually acknowledged a lesson learned. The lessons learned in print collecting were gentle compared to the clashes he would encounter later in the Oriental art world.

The amateur, not yet a connoisseur, was content with his hobby. He had yet to meet the imperious Mr. Whistler. A grander vision was to come. As a business leader and gentleman of standing in Detroit, however, he first needed to establish a social life and create a beautiful home environment.

— 4 —

A NEW LIFESTYLE
1885–1892

In many ways Charles Freer was a maverick. He bowed to social expectations when he rented a pew at the Fort Street Presbyterian Church, but he was not a church man. Except for a passing interest in Buddhism and curiosity about Hinduism, religion and God are virtually ignored in his papers and in descriptions of him by his contemporaries. Nature filled his spiritual needs. A mountain view or a glorious sunset awakened awe in him and reverence for something beyond himself. He was not likely to call on a God for help or even pray for others; he held himself and others personally responsible for their decisions and the consequences of their actions.

Reluctant to simply enjoy the fruits of his early austerity and hard work, he lived by the moral values of usefulness and uplift. "Things worthwhile" was his motto. Fun was confined to private places where he could safely slip off "the harness" of propriety. He even vacationed with a purpose. His escape from business pressures was an annual autumn trek in the mountains near Kingston. Although he toted a gun, he seldom fired his weapon; beauty, not booty, lured him there. His jaunts were for physical exertion and spiritual renewal laced with good companionship and liquor. As meticulous in pleasure as he was in work, he covered the hills almost as a cartographer, taking care to avoid areas he had explored on previous trips, intent on making new discoveries.

His hiking companion was Frederick Stuart Church, an artist with the build and bravado of Teddy Roosevelt, whom he vaguely resembled. (He is not to be confused with the now more famous Frederic Edwin Church, who was an artistic force in the Hudson Valley when Charles was a teen.) Twelve years older than Freer, Church, the son of a Michigan lawyer and politician, had left school at thirteen to try his hand at business. It did not suit his playful artistic personality. Combining a poetic imagination with serious study of nature, he sketched animals in New York's Central Park Zoo as an illustrator for *Harper's* magazine. His fanciful vision appealed to the romantic in Freer. "I paint sentiment," Church declared. His canvases of languid ladies and docile animals bore titles that suggested grand symbolism and morality. In *Knowledge Is Power*, the first oil painting Freer owned, Church painted a young woman in academic cap and gown surrounded by tigers tamed by her powers of the mind. The title could have been Freer's mantra. Church was serious when he described to Freer another picture entitled *A Cold Wave*:

> Represents a beautiful maiden seated asleep in a vine of grapes and green foliage—dressed in pink and white. Reflection in a pond of water coming down from the sea—a lot of polar bears with fans—this is in water color—does it coincide with your subject.[1]

In 1889, Freer's answer was an enthusiastic yes, but the aesthetic appeal would not last. As Freer's critical eye matured, none of Church's paintings survived in his final collection. The man, however, was a genuine sport and a kind friend who introduced Freer to the contemporary American artists centered in New York.

They were two Victorian men on a lark as they tramped through the mountains together in the early 1890s. They were hardly serious hunters. Church's dog Jack, interested mostly in cornering chipmunks, failed to find the partridges. As for Freer, he had all he could manage just shooting the Hawkeye camera, invariably forgetting to insert the plate. On their first trek, the horses stolidly refused to leave the barn. Another time a bear made off with Church's overcoat and Freer's whiskey bottles. Church suggested that the bear might gripe that the coat was out of style, and the bottles were empty: "Of course both faults are characteristic of us and he had no business to complain."[2]

Their correspondence, embellished by Church with delightful line drawings, is full of jests. Fiendishly they played practical jokes. After returning home from one of their trips, Church wrote to Freer that a crate had just arrived anonymously at his doorstep containing a large antlered moose head, one so large that when extracted from the crate, it would not fit up the stairway. Uncertain whether this treasure was really his and preferring to confirm ownership before tearing out the front wall to install it in his rooms, he accused his friend of sending it. Regrettably, Freer failed to record what choice gift Church sent him in return. Admitting that Church was a unique man, Freer praised his friend's "manly qualities" and his freedom from "the conventionalities of artists as they go."[3]

Charles Freer lived on several levels and kept each compartmentalized in its proper time, place, and person. With Church, he hiked, played pranks, and drank heartily, but the serious, high-minded moments he saved for Hecker, his oldest friend, to whom he could write honestly as he might in a diary:

> No rain! but one day for two hours we lived amidst the clouds…The roadside and forest, the stream and the sky, have each a glory of their own, and as we have seen them thus far, they stand for the perfect ripeness of life—and tell us that life is worth living.

From Panther Mountain, he recorded that "the wonderful calm and peace of night in the mountains made irresistibly mysterious by the unfamiliar sounds of the forest, the subtle harmony of the procession of the stars." Freer never lost his belief that some encounters with nature or a work of art were rare spiritual moments, perhaps even unique to him.[4]

With the earthy Church, Freer could broach the subject of women. Coyly the two bachelors refer to "Miss C" and "Miss D" in letters exchanging news and innuendos of romance. Miss D was possibly Lora Dutcher, whom Freer called "Dainty Lora," daughter of the owner of the inn where he and Church stayed in the Catskills, or perhaps the daughter of Freer's business friend and Alfred Street neighbor, John Dyar. Freer's cryptic diaries note women only by initials and an address. His papers are so circumspect that speculating on his involvements with women is hazardous. Miss Amelia Y. Candler of Brookline, Massachusetts, possibly won his affection for a time. His business trips to Boston usually included Brookline and often were followed by a few days at Newport, Nantucket, or Old Orchard. A frequent diary entry, "EWW," probably referred to Miss Edna Webb, a lady friend he met during his visits to New York (possibly of the extended Webb-Vanderbilt family, who ran the

Wagner Palace Car Company). He squired the young woman and her mother on a fall trip through the Berkshires, this time in a buckboard without dogs or gun. He left no evidence of serious amorous attachments, and he certainly never came close to marriage.[5]

Without a wife and family, Charles depended on male friends to relax with, to confide in, and to travel with. He found good companions on his business travels, especially men in railroads or banking. Dinner and evening invitations often waited in his hotel mailboxes. In New York City, he found men who shared his enthusiasm for art; with them he visited the Washington Square and Union Square galleries. For the young pillar in Detroit's business community, the elegant Detroit Club offered a venue for entertaining and maintaining business contacts. His monthly meetings at the Witenagemote provided intellectual activity among the city's artists, writers, and architects. But they did not fulfill his need for fraternal companionship, so Freer and ten friends created the Yondotega Club, adopting the Algonquin name for Detroit meaning "great village."[6]

The "Yon," as it was affectionately known among its members, gave Freer a sense of belonging that only his ties to Kingston could rival. A few years before he died, he fondly recalled when he and a "small group of sympathetic men...wishing closer personal relations and wider social development through more intimate co-operation" organized it:

> Wishing for the club no place in the sun nor share in material activity, its founders sought a hut, a small garden and a high wall—'not wholly in nor quite beyond the busy world,'—where, without infringing on the rights of others, the savage energies of the

Yondotegans could be diverted to playful solution of the eternal verities.[7]

On April 12, 1891, the men gathered at the home of William C. McMillan. Their group included McMillan; his father, James; Truman Newberry; George Hendrie; Frederick W. Whiting; Cameron Currie; Howard Meredith; William F. Jarvis; Clarence Carpenter; Thomas Jerome; and Charles Freer. Except for Senator James McMillan, they were all younger men, many unmarried.

The club opened its doors on June 24, 1891 in a brown frame home on East Jefferson Avenue. Members elected Will McMillan president and Charles Freer vice president. They invited thirty-nine other worthy gentlemen, including Frank Hecker and Freer's doctor, Freddie Mann, to join them. Some of the chosen, like his friend Church, lived outside Detroit. The club's stated aim was to promote sociability and friendship, or as Freer put it, "Frivolity and Alcohol." The real Yondotega man "knows how to slip off his harness indoors and always wear it outdoors." The club founders maintained iron-clad control over membership. Stakes in the games were limited to $1; character, not wealth, counted in their club.[8]

Appropriately, the insignia of the club was the rose and vine: rose for purity and beauty, vine for its alcoholic product and its binding strength. The first published book of the club proclaimed, "The public has no right to know what we are doing." It could well have been their motto; the high wall around the "hut" assured they could "unharness" in complete privacy. There the buttoned-down Charles Freer and his friend Cam Currie became the "high priests of whatthehellishness." An art committee of two, Charles Freer and Tom Jerome, accepted responsibility for architecture, interior design, landscaping, and accepting gifts, such as "the very interesting elk head, the three-horned freak," which Freer gamely described as "rare and attractive."[9]

He formed his closest friendships within the walls of Yondotega. His greatest pleasure came in sharing what he called "old time entertainment...when safety signs were in the low light and the King [alcohol] reigned." Remarkably, the Yondotega Club today still reflects the influence of Freer and his friends: no women and only rare guests cross its threshold; the gentlemen members are forbidden to discuss business; a member's death is required before a new member is admitted.[10]

Freer had long outgrown his rented rooms on Alfred Street. He needed a home worthy of his rising wealth and social position. In 1887 Hecker and Freer purchased adjacent lots on Ferry and Woodward, only a mile from their new freight car plant, one more of their many joint ventures. They built their new homes far enough away from urban congestion by the river to be spared destruction for later development. Hecker's castle still towers over Woodward Avenue, while Freer's home hugs the earth on the side street, its idiosyncratic design suited to his need for beauty and modest comfort.

Unlike Hecker, whose forty-nine-room mansion is a copy of the famous Chateau de Chenanceau built by Francis I in the Loire Valley, Freer bucked the prevailing fashion for houses in elaborate European imitations. He was more comfortable with an informal American style, reminiscent of the Albany Avenue homes he had envied in Kingston. Not one to gamble on a new design, he studied houses as meticulously as he studied art and business. A perhaps apocryphal story suggests that on business trips he took horse-drawn hack cabs to examine local domestic architecture. On one such drive, the lodge at the gate of a Philadelphia Germantown estate attracted his eye. He inquired, learned the architect's name was Wilson Eyre Jr., and engaged him. Just as likely he discovered the architect in the journal *American Architect and Building News*, where Eyre homes were published.[11]

Eyre designed for him an elaborate cottage characterized by steep, gabled roofs and broad verandas, and anchored by an elegant garden. The simplicity of the Shingle-style home with spacious sunlit rooms and garden vistas responded to a contemporary lifestyle rather than to historical tradition. Its intimate scale suited a bachelor life, and its calculated asymmetries met his client's demanding taste.

With unabashed sentiment, Freer imported the narrow, dark-blue stone from quarries near Kingston to clad the exterior on the first-floor level, and he imported the masons as well, because Detroit craftsmen could not or would not cut the exceptionally hard sandstone. The second- and third-floor exterior and the roof were faced with thick slate shingles. From that solid mass, Eyre projected gables and undulated bays. Freer's living quarters filled the long rectangle of the L-shaped building along the street; the smaller part of the L toward the rear housed the service wing. The carriage house and stables connected to the service wing with a large Romanesque arch, forming a three-sided enclosure for a formal garden. Its open side looked toward the Hecker chateau. High hedges of bright green honeysuckle soon screened the house from the street. Persian and white lilac bushes brightened the dark exterior of the house and appeared to root it more firmly to the ground.

Freer's home reflected his refined and efficient personality. Each room served its purpose with style. The spacious reception hall was anchored by a free-standing, double-sided fireplace rising from the middle of the room. The small parlor and the dining room to the right created an intimate, elegant mood with coved ceilings, chair rails, corner fireplaces, and spare furnishings. In a library to the left, a generous bay projecting over the garden accommodated the round table that served as Freer's desk. His bedroom suite on the floor above included a large den, a dressing room, and a bathroom. A private porch opened to his prized garden, and a bay window filled his bedroom with light. The grand stairway in the back of the large reception hall rose to the wide-open second floor with galleries on two sides; an oriel window projected from one of the two guest bedrooms. The arresting effect was of an interior courtyard, a concept remarkably like Olana, a Persian-style castle the other Church (Frederic E. Church) erected on the Hudson River near Kingston. The teenage Charlie Freer could not have missed Olana in 1871, as it rose above the Catskills in exotic splendor.

Function was as important as style. The home was electrified and modern. Drawers, closets, armoires, bookcases, and benches were all built in to simplify lines or to camouflage heating elements. A special elevator next to the reception hall fireplace carried wood up from the basement; another elevator connected the vegetable storeroom with the kitchen. A large safe, lined with hollow bricks and faced with steel doors, hid behind the reception hall paneling.

In May 1892, Freer congratulated Eyre on completing exactly what they had planned despite builders who "don't take kindly to clients who insist upon having the specifications lived up to." Specifications were Freer's business. He supervised all details, overlooked each inch of insulation, each joint of timber, and each cut of stone. For him this home was a deeply personal expression; small details had symbolic meaning. The leaf-and-vine lighting fixtures reflected the Yondotega spirit. The elaborate front doorbell, designed by his hiking buddy Church, sported a bear reclining on laurel leaves with his head turned toward the door; his paws held the bell button.[12]

To assist with the interior decoration, Freer hired the famed

New York designer W. C. LeBrocq. Sloane's of New York shipped Oriental rugs and carpets for each room. A. B. Davenport of Boston made most of the furniture. Apparently, Detroit offered nothing of sufficient quality for Freer's exacting taste except for the local nuns who monogrammed his linens and with whom, in a rare moment of compromise, he agreed that machine embroidering would be adequate for the linens to be used by the servants.[13]

At last he could surround himself with beauty. He wanted the house and the art that graced it to grow together in harmony. To realize his dream, he engaged just the right artists to decorate its walls.

— 5 —

AMERICAN ARTISTS
1889–1895

FREER BEGAN BUYING OIL PAINTINGS for his house even before its architectural plans were drawn. The home and its artworks grew together; walls accommodated certain paintings, and paintings were created to fit certain walls. Color, tone, scale, and light harmonized until the home became a single work of art. Guided by his friend Church, he met American artists whose works expressed his idea of beauty. Rather than the realistic style of painting then in vogue, their images awakened emotion, a spirit that Freer understood as uplifting and pure.

He gravitated first to the landscape paintings of Dwight W. Tryon, an American tonalist artist who created the essence of nature rather than a specific scene. He painted the mist of sunrise, the glow of sunset, and the quiet of moonlight; the chill of winter and the fragrance of summer. His images of long, low horizons intersected by tall, narrow trees are aesthetic constructs meant to capture a mood. Experience in nature, not classical education, enhanced the pleasure of a Tryon.

In late spring of 1889, Freer paid his first visit to Tryon's studio. A large canvas of a simple haystack, *The Rising Moon: Autumn* caught his eye. He offered to buy it for what was, to him, the extravagant sum of $1,050. Tryon faced a dilemma. Mr. and Mrs. Potter Palmer of Chicago had breezed into his studio just before embarking for Europe and asked him to hold the painting for inspection on their return in the fall. The practical New Englander decided to take the bird in hand and accepted Freer's offer, warning him, "You must not look for a general appreciation of it by many—it will be a picture which the average person will see nothing in and at first sight will not reveal itself to even more cultured ones." Freer relished not being average.[1]

The two men developed a comfortable friendship. Tryon had also left school at fourteen to work in a factory. He had educated himself working in a bookshop. With little formal training, he set sail in 1876 to study art in Paris for seven years. After his return to the United States, he painted and supported himself for the next thirty years teaching art at Smith College. A "down east" practical man, he finished his commissions on time. Like his landscape paintings, similar in construction, each finished with technical accuracy, Tryon's personality was reliable, polished, and perhaps a bit monotonous. Both he and Freer were studious and frugal; they exchanged books and shared comments on print exhibitions.[2]

In the spirit of Whistler and William Morris, who insisted that artists should control interior decoration, Freer engaged Tryon as a partner responsible for the design of the reception hall, where seven of his paintings would hang. The commission would take him two to three years to complete and cost around $5,000. The paintings arrived from his studio at reliable intervals. With smug pride, Freer wrote after the arrival of *Winter*: "It will take many years for the

Philistines to understand [its financial value]." In letters addressed simply "Dear Freer," the artist conscientiously asked his friend to stop sending money until he had nearly finished the pictures, for it made him feel guilty.[3]

Eyre and Tryon debated the details as the house developed, but Freer made the decisions. Praising Eyre as "every inch an artist," Tryon wrote, "We talked over all matters which we could think of in connection with your house—even the colors of all rooms leading out of the hall so a perfect harmony may be felt." In his paintings, Tryon created horizons and offsetting verticals to match the architecture of the room. He advocated for fabric to cover the walls. Freer insisted on painted surfaces and had the walls and ceilings covered with fine, five-inch square leaves of Dutch metal, copper below and silver above. Irregular patches of color were then blended with a big brush over the metal surface. It was an expensive procedure, but Freer wanted it right. His home was his work of art.[4]

In late 1891, Church recommended the figure painter Thomas W. Dewing to Freer: "There is an air of refinement an aristocrativeness (if I may use the word) about all Dewing's late work...you ought to have a Dewing and you know what you like." Very different from Tryon, Dewing was neither businesslike nor even-tempered. In the earliest remaining letter to Freer, he frantically asked for additional time to complete a painting that was already overdue. His colorful language and gruff manner contrasted with the ethereal beauty of the women he painted.[5]

The artist had been forced into the work world before he was a teen by the death of his alcoholic father, who had squandered the family's reserves. He had studied art in France and returned to a successful but frustrating career in America. He tried teaching for a few years, but he just wanted to paint. His bravado in response to adversity masked his underlying insecurities. He bristled easily, was often sarcastic and bitter. Other times, the handsome spendthrift could be affable and charming. He liked being the center of attention, especially at his summer retreat in New Hampshire where a colony of artists and writers entertained each other with elaborate dinners and masques.[6]

On canvas, his attenuated female forms, veiled in a haze of soft color, appear rootless in an unreal world, in much the same way that Tryon's trees float unmoving on the canvas. The women are beautiful, genteel props that the artist toyed with in various arrangements. In emphasizing the two-dimensional limits of the canvas, he shadowed devices used by Whistler to give the impression of a still life, a setting, a presence conveyed without drama or anecdote. In an 1891 Dewing painting that Freer owned, entitled *The Piano*, a regal lady serenely plays the piano without a hint of emanating music.

Freer's seemingly unfettered support buoyed the two artists. Quite in awe of their talent, he stood ready to serve their cause and honor their rare gifts, declaring that his money could never make more than a partial payment for the fruits of their talent. American artists circa 1890 were more accustomed to the treatment accorded a skilled tradesman. Such a reverent attitude was refreshing and most welcome.

Dewing took over the design of the parlor where his paintings would hang. The small, formal room seemed to fit the big man's sensibilities, but frequently the artist and the owner clashed. Freer did not want "any stuff on the walls"; the rich brocades and silks hanging heavy in contemporary homes were not for him. Like Tryon, Dewing tried in vain to persuade Freer that painted plaster alone would be "austere." He recommended rich gilding around the fireplace of the parlor, pleading with Freer, "Do not be afraid that this plan of mine will be tawdry or undignified." The parlor remained austere. An arch panel over the mantle of the corner fireplace eventually framed one of his paintings: *Early Portrait of the Artist's Daughter*, a portrait of a young girl with two kittens. Predictably, his paintings arrived more slowly than paintings from the efficient Tryon. Unlike Tryon, Dewing asked for the final $500 in advance. On the day after Thanksgiving in 1892, Tryon and Dewing arrived to administer the finishing touches on the new home.[7]

Freer's friendships with Church, Tryon, and Dewing led him to a new circle of men: dealers, artists, and collectors. N. E. Montross, the owner of an art supply store whose famous clients hung pictures in his hallway, evolved into their dealer. He became Freer's favored dealer in American art.

Charles Freer was now a participant in the American contemporary art scene. Men as diverse as Abbott Thayer, Augustus Saint-Gaudens, Stanford White, Charles Platt, Horatio Walker, William Merritt Chase, Childe Hassam, and John Twachtman had entered his orbit. They congregated around summer homes away from the din and heat of New York City. Dewing, Saint-Gaudens, Platt, and Walker were part of a group that migrated to the Cornish, New Hampshire area. Freer frequently visited their colony as well as the Tryons at their cottage in South Dartmouth, Massachusetts. He joined the National Art Association and attended the annual dinner of the Academy of Design, America's premier art establishment since its founding in 1826. He associated with fellow patrons of American art, W. T. Evans, John Gellatly, Thomas B. Clarke, and W. H. Payne, men who challenged America's fixation on European art. Their vanguard spirit meshed with Freer's ambitions.[8]

Church had another artist in mind for Freer. As early as 1888, he wrote of a painting by Abbott Handerson Thayer: "I think it's fine. It's a work of art that picture and not of technique—One cannot place it to [sic] high in modern art." Thayer arrived on the scene too late to be assigned a room. Such confines in any case suited neither his personality nor his ambitions. For a single painting, Thayer commanded more money than Tryon and Dewing combined in their paintings and room designs. Freer was first captivated by the artist's genius when he saw a large Thayer painting on exhibition at the American Society of Artists in May 1892. It had already been sold to John Gellatly. Enraptured, he wrote to his friend and dealer Montross:

> I saw The Enthroned Virgin. How tender and yet how strong! How dignified and yet how kind! An emblem of purity; a protest against sin! It speaks in countless ways and sings many unsung songs... Writing under an influence so fine, I cannot express envy, neither would I suppress admiration...if I had seen that picture in time, and could have gained Mr. Thayer's assent, it would have been mine, even had I been compelled to mortgage my few earthly possessions.[9]

Montross arranged a meeting with the artist, and Freer bought another painting entitled *The Head*, a portrait of the artist's son. Thayer wrote Montross that he had found Freer to be "a fine man" and assured the dealer that he had no difficulty in parting with paintings of his children because he currently used only his family as models. The artist nonetheless played on Freer's sentiments by bringing up the subject of "endur[ing] the partings from these portraits of my children." Freer insisted on paying somewhat more as compensation for taking away a painting of his son.[10]

Thayer differed from Tryon and Dewing in his art and temperament. While their paintings reached toward modern impressionism, his turned back to a compositional technique reminiscent of Renaissance art. He filled canvases with trios of figures, their bodies swathed in drapery, their idealized faces radiant with innocence and trust. Using as his most frequent theme "spiritual motherhood ineffable in its strength and beauty," he created angels with evanescent wings, children with faces of expressive wonder, and young women of serene, sexless beauty. An optimist and a dreamer, he thought in grand schemes and conceived his art on grand themes.

Shortly before he met Freer, Thayer had moved with his second wife and extended family to a farm in Dublin, New Hampshire. Thayerland as local residents called it consisted of a "hideous farmhouse...small cottages, farm buildings, privies, and a rustic gazebo scattered about." In his messy, cluttered studio, Thayer painted from photographs more often than from models. Assistants copied his work as it progressed so that several canvases of the same painting were available for the artist to experiment on. Struggling over each work for months if not years, constantly retouching, invariably in the process of finishing. His personal affairs appeared disorderly at best. By the time he met Freer, he was verging on bankruptcy. In short, he was the sort of man whom Freer might have summarily dismissed, but he was an artist. The two men, in fact, got along very well. Thayer just assumed Freer would support him.[11]

Less than a year after they met, Freer invited Thayer to accompany him to Chicago to inspect the progress in building the 1893 World's Columbian Exposition. Both men had official connections with the fair: Freer as a member of the committee for Michigan's pavilion, and Thayer as an artist exhibiting his *The Enthroned Virgin*, which had so captivated Freer the year before. It was a heady time for Freer. In addition to works by Whistler, he had lent four Tryon paintings, three by Dewing, and one by Church to the famous exposition. He exalted in a letter to Dewing: "After careful study at the Fair I am more thoroughly impressed than ever that the art of yourself, Tryon, Thayer, and Whistler is the most refined in spirit, poetical in design and deepest in artistic truth of this century."[12]

After the exposition, Thayer and the New York collector Howard Mansfield were Freer's first guests in his newly completed home. Later, Freer wrote to Mansfield:

> It certainly was not harder for you to leave that morning than it was for Thayer and myself to see you go...Thayer is a rare genius, and I am inclined to believe that he is one of the very greatest artists of this century.

He also confided that he had just purchased Thayer's "latest master-piece," *The Virgin*. The painting (7.5 feet by 6 feet), which Thayer described as "one of the most beautiful things I may ever do," was hung on the large wall of the reception hall that faced the wide stairway. As grand as its $10,000 price, it depicts a trinity of his three children, nearly life size, draped in filmy fabric and embraced by clouds, striding confidently toward the viewer.[13]

In a final sentimental touch, Freer hung Church's painting *Flapjacks, or Bears Baking Griddle Cakes*, a typically whimsical painting of a very attractive young lady offering campfire fare to a group of seven thoroughly charmed bears, an apocryphal allusion to their hiking escapades. Freer declared, "The painting is a great success; one of your very best," and that it was "in perfect harmony with the dining room." His home was now complete. He had an ample kitchen staff, a competent butler, a coachman, a housekeeper, a maid, and a chef.[14]

Once the house was finished, however, Freer halted purchases from his artist friends. Instead he facilitated the purchase of their paintings by his business friends and surprised the Heckers, who were vacationing in the Sandwich Islands, by installing in their home a triptych by Tryon and Dewing. When Freer's funds stopped flowing, each of the three painters reacted differently.

Tryon responded with gratitude for the four years they had worked together. He asked only for Freer's advice on how to invest surplus cash. In late spring of 1893, a year of severe economic depression, Freer counseled him against investing in stocks because of "the present unsettled condition of business and the uncommon financial stringency." With Hecker, he controlled $200,000 worth of Central Car Trust Company notes at 7% interest. Freer drew up the papers for Tryon to invest $3,000 in the offer. The typically businesslike Tryon insisted that Freer should feel no responsibility for the performance of his new investment. Later that year Tryon and his wife were Freer's house guests for two weeks during the Christmas holidays. Their friendship continued unabated. In admiration, Freer wrote of his friend, "I know no one who gets more pleasure or less woe." During the next few years, Freer succumbed occasionally to a new treasure from his gracious friend:

> You are very kind to let me have that marvellous [sic] night scene in pastel. Would you consider me too selfish if I asked also, for that wonderfully fine early Spring scene—the one so pearly, I mean. It has

haunted me all day and because of it, New York has seemed less ugly than usual.[15]

Dewing, of a different character and lacking Tryon's sinecure of a teaching job, regarded the end of Freer's patronage with dismay. Through 1893 and early 1894, Freer frequently sent him checks of up to $500 as a loan. He encouraged Dewing to "jack up" his prices and referred him to Mansfield as a potential customer. However, when the lawyer called to see Dewing's work, he found the prices too high, a pettiness in Mansfield that increasingly annoyed Freer.

Dewing wanted to go to Europe to paint and hinted to Freer that $5,000 would see him through two years on the continent. Freer instead accepted in return for his loans *The Carnation*, a painting of a woman in white seated in profile and holding in her hand a single flower, a composition reminiscent of Whistler's "Mother." When Freer finally agreed to subsidize Dewing's European venture, the perpetually disgruntled artist lasted only one year abroad. He returned to New York "damned glad" to be back and vowed never to leave again. Patiently Freer continued to assist the artist over the next decade.[16]

Abbott Thayer regarded Freer as a sympathetic admirer rather than as a personal friend. Assuming that his special genius entitled him to be cared for, he wrote, "You cannot make an artist. To the artist is given the divine gift of vision—of seeing." His words echo Whistler's, but he lacked that artist's proud independence. He complained to Freer of the "pinching poverty and squalor" and lamented his physical weakness, which limited his work to only four hours a day while his friends Dewing, Tryon, and Saint-Gaudens seemed to know no limit to their physical powers.[17]

Freer helped Thayer through the depression year of 1893 with periodic loans of $500 and $1,000 as investments in some future work of art. When Thayer continued to ask for more money, Freer cautioned that he had limits and that his walls were full. In 1894, the artist escaped to Europe, where he continued to work, to sell, and to win prizes. On his return, he again proposed an annual stipend of $5,000 to guarantee Freer ownership of all his life-size works. This time Freer flatly refused, but he did so in a long letter full of reason and compassion.[18]

Rather than monopolize the talents of his friends, Freer insisted that their genius was great enough to command a broad market and promoted their careers through art exhibitions. In spite of the inconvenience and risk involved in shipping and the personal sacrifice of living with bare walls in his new home, he dispatched his prized paintings to distant cities so that the artists might expose more people to their transcendent images. In return he demanded that the exhibition committees give the works proper treatment.

Like an acolyte, he had picked up his artists' ideas and their philosophies, and he often parroted their words. His expressions mimicked words they must have used in conversation. Even the popular George Inness could not compare in his view with their genius. In 1893, he tried to dispose of the Inness painting he had bought two years earlier, declaring: "Poor Inness is sure to be forgotten while Tryon will live forever." Alas, today the reverse is true; the art public honors Inness and his works, but mostly scholars and a few admirers know Tryon's name.[19]

Inspired by the artists' summer colonies, Freer toyed with building a summer sanctuary for his own quiet communion with nature. Before the interior of his home in Detroit received its final coat of paint, he had picked out property in the Catskills. In a detailed letter to his architect, Wilson Eyre, he outlined his plan. A large living room and dining room would fill the central part of the log cabin with wings jutting diagonally on each side, "one wing being a room to be occupied by ladies and the other room by gentlemen." The gentlemen's wing he marked "Studio" and proposed to light it with a large window in case "any of my artist friends wish to do any work at the cabin." He wanted neither a large nor expensive cabin, but "I would like the proportions carefully thought out," and simple enough to be erected by local farmers and lumbermen. Eagerly he hoped to begin construction before snowfall 1892. Problems with the land title postponed the work. Then other priorities: business, travel, and an economic depression took precedence; the cabin in the Catskills was perpetually postponed.[20]

The 1890s had begun auspiciously for Freer with the creation of his home, his entry into the contemporary American art scene, and his leadership in private men's clubs. His life seemed replete. After meeting James McNeill Whistler in 1890, however, his life took on a new trajectory.

— 6 —

WHISTLER
1890–1893

ON FEBRUARY 18, 1890, FREER crossed the Atlantic for the first time aboard the SS *City of Paris*, on business. He spent eight days at sea each way to spend only five days in London. On Sunday, March 2, he noted in his diary, "Chelsea during P.M." He was scouting the home of James McNeill Whistler. On March 4 he recorded simply, "Lunch with Whistler." Of the three days he spent on freight car business, he left no notes. His visit with Whistler, however, he recounted in a lecture to the Witenagemote Club, and in a rare press interview, extolled, "It was during this conversation that I was impressed, became saturated as it were, by the man's personality and originality…his greatness." A man of immense personal magnetism, Whistler would spark in the industrialist previously undreamed-of aspirations. With hindsight, we can credit their first meeting as the beginning of the Freer Gallery of Art.[1]

The notorious Whistler was only 5'4" tall, an alert little man whose delicate gestures and light footsteps gave no warning of his lethal energy. He strode the streets of London, his lithe body clothed in a black suit topped by a flowing black cape. A ribbon of color that Keppel called his "aggressive cravat" darted from his black attire. The broad-brimmed hat crowning his mass of black curls slanted at just the right angle to show the white curl he cultivated at the center of his forehead. He walked as if on stage, imperiously preceding each step with the tall, slim rod of Japanese bamboo he affected as a prop. In obvious contrast to the unpretentious Freer, Whistler's presence cried out for attention. A less bold man might have been cowed, but for Freer any encounter with the formidable artist promised to be an adventure.[2]

Stealing a break from his sales calls, Freer rode the underground to Sloane Square. At Whistler's home, the thirty-six-year-old railroad car builder greeted the feisty artist, twenty years his senior, by stating firmly that he had come all the way from Detroit, and "being like himself, an American, I expected to see him." He could not have chosen a better tactic for ingratiating himself. Whistler often talked of returning to his native land, yet feared America was not yet ready for him or for his art. In 1881, he had sent two important paintings to America for sale—to no avail. Very few Americans owned Whistler's etchings, and none had bought his oils. Although neither man knew it then, Freer would become the artist's most important patron.[3]

An inveterate collector of news clippings, mostly about himself, Whistler awed Freer with his command of art and literature. Equally impressed by the dignified American who seemed to know something about his art, Whistler introduced Freer to his new wife, Beatrix, or Trixie as she was known to her family. Plump and slightly taller than her husband, she had an elegant style born of education and exposure to the arts through her first husband, the famous architect Edward Godwin.

Overwhelmed, Freer declared his new artist friend a "cordial, big-hearted, jolly man with a keen sense of humor," a far cry from the public image of the contentious artist, well known as a butterfly with a sting. He later claimed Whistler's "versatility…his attention to all details…his peculiarly distinct individuality" distinguished him as "the greatest since the days of Rembrandt." An affinity for art united them: a reverence for beauty, a belief in art for art's sake, an interest in the Orient, and a veneration of the artist. As Oscar Wilde quipped, "Whistler spelled art with a Capital I."[4]

In their pleasant conversation that first afternoon, they discovered other sympathetic connections. Whistler's father was a consultant for the Moscow-Petersburg railroad from 1842 until his death in 1849 when James was fifteen. After shuttling from America to Russia to England during his childhood, he returned to America and followed his father's footsteps to West Point Academy. Its romantic traditions appealed to him but the uncompromising regimen did not. In 1855, he sailed to Paris and joined the bohemian life of impecunious artists like Henri Fantin-Latour and Alphonse Legros. He painted with Gustave Courbet, who said of him: "Il a du talent, le petit Whistler." He knew Monet, Manet, and Degas; the latter lamented, "He behaves as if he had no talent."[5]

After several years struggling in France, he settled in London to etch and to paint. He considered the English people aesthetic dullards, but he had family in London. At first he lived with his older stepsister Deborah, wife of Dr. Francis Seymour Haden, who had lectured in Detroit in 1882 and was then considered the greatest painter-etcher in England. Whistler fumed with artistic jealousy over his host's numerous artistic awards, including a knighthood, and the pompous Englishman disapproved of Whistler's libertine lifestyle. A few years after he moved to London, Whistler quarreled violently with Haden, and the two men never spoke cordially again.

Haden was only the first of many supporters the quixotic artist attempted to impale with the barb of his wit and the thrust of his animosity. Whistler described his early patron Frederick Leyland, who had commissioned him to decorate his dining room (the Peacock Room), as the "quintessence of plutocratic putrefaction." Whistler was, in the words of his erstwhile friend Oscar Wilde, "a miniature Mephistopheles mocking the majority." In his most famous public foray, after John Ruskin, the art critic and doyen of artistic England, attacked him as "a coxcomb ask[ing] two hundred guineas for flinging a pot of paint in the public's face," Whistler parried him to court. The libel trial made front-page news in 1878, but the judge awarded the artist only a farthing.[6]

The butterfly with a sting—creative, capricious, and prickly—encountered in Freer a man of hummingbird-like persistence, patience, and chary presence. Both men, however, benefited from their connection. Whistler, eager for recognition in his native country, could sell his artworks to an appreciative, rich American; and Freer, by going to the source, could eliminate the cost and interference of a dealer. Over the next thirteen years, without ever having a falling-out, they found common cause in a business arrangement and in their aesthetic values.

During the 1880s, as Freer made his fortune with the Peninsular Car Company, Whistler's paintings gained acceptance at the Paris Salon. By 1890, the artist was enjoying the happiest years of his life, with a devoted young wife whom he adored and awards and medals from every country—except England. No English museum or academy purchased a painting during his lifetime, a nettling slap. Two of his major paintings would soon enter important public collections: The City of Glasgow bought *Arrangement in Grey and Black,*

No. 2: Portrait of Thomas Carlyle in 1891; a year later, the French government bought *Arrangement in Grey and Black. No.1: Portrait of The Artist's Mother*. The latter was the first American artwork acquired by the French state. Whistler could hardly contain his joy at receiving the French Legion of Honor. The arc of success for the two men coincided nicely.

On that first visit, Freer scored an exciting coup for a print collector: he was among the first to see Whistler's newly pulled and now rare Amsterdam prints. He bought a complete set of those "last great etchings of the artist's career, which Whistler autographed for him with the butterfly." He also treated himself to a "charming" pastel. For his fellow collector Mansfield, he brought back a selection of etchings, including some from the Amsterdam plates. After proclaiming "My visit with yourself and Mrs. Whistler was the event of my trip," Freer left a standing order with the artist to send "anything that he might do." Thus began a steady stream of prints for Hecker as well as for himself. He gave prints to his artist friends and then requested that Whistler replace them.[7]

His collection of prints grew steadily under Whistler's guidance. Each letter from London, many written by Beatrix Whistler, assured him that his interests were being looked after with comments like: "Mr. Whistler will select the Venice etchings for you," and "Mr. Whistler has sent you all the lithographs which are in existence so far." Freer's American dealers alerted him to their finds, but they seldom matched the quality he secured from the artist himself. Assuring Whistler, "You can depend upon my taking at least one impression of each of your etchings, dry points and lithographs," he asked, "Will it trouble you too much to select and forward to me accordingly?"[8]

In 1892 Mansfield saw the oil painting *Variations in Flesh Colour and Green - The Balcony* by Whistler in Paris and encouraged Freer to buy it. It was painted in 1868 when Whistler was experimenting with Japanese effects. Freer asked Mansfield to "take another look at the painting at Durand-Ruel's and advise." He knew he could afford to buy only one oil by Whistler and wanted to be sure that it was a good one. When the painting arrived at the Wunderlich Galleries in New York, Freer saw it and purchased it for 1,000 guineas, about $5,000. The sale marked a milestone for Whistler as well as an important step for Freer. *The Balcony* was the first important Whistler oil bought in America.[9]

American collectors had long ignored Whistler's paintings. When the painting of his mother was exhibited in Philadelphia and New York City in the 1880s, it was offered for sale at $1,000, and rumor spread that even an offer of $500 might be accepted. No offer was made. The few who seriously valued Whistler's art invested in his etchings. After Glasgow and France purchased his paintings and Frederick Leyland's collection of his paintings was sold at auction, Whistler's art rose in prestige, and prices escalated closer to his high expectations. Goupil Gallery in London added luster with a large retrospective exhibition of Whistler's nocturnes, and marines.

The new values placed on his paintings created a conflict for the sensitive artist. To Alexander Reid, an art dealer in Scotland, he wrote that since the Goupil exhibition, "already eight or nine of my pictures have changed hands, at least, an average of ten times what I got for them" He fumed at his early patrons, the "sneaking amateur tradesmen" who were profiting from "my labour—my brain—my name!" He contemptuously called them "art patron picture dealers."[10]

Confidently taking the next step in his relationship with Whistler,

Freer commissioned a painting for his new home, requesting that the artist create a watercolor. He specified a landscape "showing the first flush and delicate tones of early spring...or perhaps this idea might be beautifully translated in a single figure in pastel." When the artist failed to respond, the patient Freer let two years pass before pursuing the subject again. This time he granted the artist more leeway: "I hope you will do that figure about which I wrote you—to in a way, hint at Spring. Let the medium suit your own taste and mood. It will of course be charming." He did specify the dimensions: 8" by 12" if pastel and 16" by 20" if executed in oil. Whistler, it seemed, had joined Freer's personal stable of artists.[11]

His purchases from Whistler met the same businesslike firmness he used with his other artist friends. He bought only what he needed. He refused to join "the Jimmy syndicate." Possibly he declined on principle, but the timing was also wrong. By 1893 the two men faced devastating challenges: Freer, a business collapse, and Whistler, his wife's fatal illness.[12]

— 7 —

BOOM AND BUST
1892–1894

THE BUSINESS TAILWINDS IN 1892 promised prosperity. The Peninsular Car Company had succeeded handsomely since 1885, when production in the modern Ferry Avenue plant reached capacity. In next six years, the number of cars manufactured annually tripled, from 2,445 to 7,779 cars. The future looked bright, fed by a robust demand by the railroad industry. The competitive climate, however, was changing. Five major consortiums had wrested control of the railroad industry through agreements, mergers, and acquisitions. Larger railroads needed larger suppliers. The Detroit partners smoothly adapted. In 1892 Hecker, Freer, and the McMillans decided to merge the Peninsular and Michigan Car Companies with Senator James McMillan as titular chairman, Hecker as president, and Freer and McMillan's son Will as managing directors.[1]

In July 1892, a tombstone ad in the *New York Times* for the Michigan-Peninsular Car Company announced the offer of cumulative preferred stock (50,000 shares) paying a dividend of 8% interest and common stock (30 ,000 shares) with a 12% dividend, a capitalization of $8 million at $100 per share. The dividends would be paid in gold. Their finances were solid and their competitive reach broad. The two companies, "the largest manufacturers of freight cars in the world," together owned 78 buildings on 83 acres of property "touched" by seven railroads. The vertically integrated companies had wheel, forge, and foundry units; their 5,000 employees could produce 100 cars per day. Boasting a backlog of 9,000 cars sold in advance, "It is believed that the business will continue to increase in the future as it has in the past." The directors included three McMillans, Hecker, Charles and Watson Freer, Russell Alger, and two bankers. (Newberry had died in 1887.) The principals firmly controlled their enterprise. As proof of their glowing confidence in the new company, they all agreed "to remain in its service for five years."[2]

The stock in the new company was soon oversubscribed. Hecker and Freer held a joint account of 1,995 shares of preferred stock and 5,000 shares of common stock in addition to separate accounts in their own names. Confident of their prospects for healthy profits, they took care of their friends. As Freer wrote Dwight Tryon, "[F]eeling some of our friends might be late in making their own subscriptions, Mr. Hecker and I subscribed for a certain sum, which we are holding for our friends." The dividend alone promised to be lucrative.[3]

Freer still directed the sales effort, but the new company now operated with a large staff. While he continued to negotiate the contracts, others like R. E. Plumb, the general manager of the Contract Department, followed up on the details. From a tightly knit partnership working with relatively few supervisors, their company mushroomed into a corporation with semiautonomous divisions and thousands of employees. The change was jarring. Freer, always happiest in a small world he knew intimately, where he felt personal responsibility and control, felt out of touch in the more impersonal world.

He became restless. He was just about to move into his new home. His world had expanded beyond his business life. Despairing that he could only spare a few days for his summer visit to New England, he wrote Dewing that "after a year or two, I hope for greater freedom." He longed to go to Europe but complained, "The mills are still grinding, and unless the speed slackens or stops entirely, there will not be much left of me." By late 1892, he admitted, "After my charming outing in the mountains…I felt capable to undertake almost any sort of work, but to-day I feel like the small boy, much in need of a vacation."[4]

In early 1893, rumors circulated that the new Michigan-Peninsular Car Company planned to become "the largest institution of its kind." The press tried to interview Freer, but "that gentleman declined to talk about the matter, saying the scheme was not yet ripe enough for publication," thereby admitting it wasn't "mere rumor." With their original plants scattered across Detroit, they hoped to acquire five hundred acres and consolidate into a new plant "surpassing anything now in existence." Monroe, Michigan, offered them land and to pay all moving costs. Chicago was also in the mix, but Senator McMillan was running for reelection and could not risk a move that would alienate his Michigan constituents. His fellow directors debated. Before any decision could be made, a financial panic blew through the United States economy. By the end of 1893, it hit like a tornado.[5]

The Depression of 1893, second in severity only to that of 1929, destroyed businesses and the lives of millions of people throughout the country. Major railroads including the Union Pacific declared bankruptcy; hundreds of smaller railroads went bust. At the Michigan-Peninsular Car Company, sales dried up, production slowed, workers were laid off, and profits disappeared. Their plants shut down for five months. Faced with fixed costs and no orders, the officers sold unissued common stock from the treasury, stock they had set aside to fund future expansion. Still they could not pay the promised dividends. Earnings in 1896 did not cover costs, let alone pay the $100,000 due on the bonds. The stock value collapsed from $8 million to $2 million, and the plant value sank to $3 million. Senator McMillan and his associates reacted with alarm; their preferred stock had no voting rights. Hecker and Freer owned controlling interest in the common stock and the 5% bonds. They remained outwardly cool.[6]

Detroit citizens were devastated by the economic collapse. It lasted well into 1897, exacerbating a discontent that had been smoldering beneath the upper-crust leadership of Detroit. In 1891, the Hendrie Brothers' streetcar workers, who were required to work eighteen hours a day, went on strike demanding a ten-hour day. A riot followed. As laborers flexed their new power, management drew their lines tight.[7]

The *Detroit Tribune*, a morning paper owned by Freer's nemesis James Scripps, castigated the "pigheadedness of Detroit aristocracy." Desperate to forestall any change and hoping to cement their power, McMillan's coterie in 1889 had engineered the election of Republican Mayor Hazen S. Pingree, to wrest city control from the Democrats. The maverick Pingree, once in office, attacked the McMillan establishment. He challenged the city tax structure, which sheltered their businesses and protected their privately owned electric and gas monopolies and the city trolley. He initiated home rule for Detroit to free the city from the state and federal power exercised by politicians like McMillan and Alger. Hecker, who had been appointed Detroit police commissioner, was replaced by a Pingree appointment. With the help of Scripps, Pingreeism rather than Republicanism ruled Detroit.[8]

The powerful Michigan-Peninsular Car Company suffered the brunt of his stinging attack. The city's "largest industrial consortium" paid its workers only 90 cents a day. The mayor charged that even before the Depression, the car company employed men "at barely enough to keep body and soul together," giving their employees no opportunity for saving. Then, in 1893 when the company closed its plants for months, it dumped 5,000 destitute men on community charity. Pingree proposed to increase the company's taxes. Hugh McMillan, James's brother, threatened to uproot the company and deprive the city of one of its biggest employers. Pingree backed down and modified the tax. After the dust had settled, Hecker claimed the rumor of the company's moving from Detroit was "veriest rot."[9]

Shocked by the scathing rebuke and sobered by the economic collapse, the M-P car company executives waited out the storm. Detroit's elite suffered disruptions but minimal pain. Hecker took his family to Hawaii for a lengthy stay and left again in January 1894 for a six-month trip to Europe and Egypt. Will McMillan sailed the same month on his own Atlantic cruise. The collapse staggered Freer. Neither shrewd management nor attention to detail nor cooperation among powerful colleagues had spared them the impact of market forces. He couldn't control the fortunes of the car business any more than he could fight the takeover of the Eel Railroad in Logansport, Indiana. This time, however, he had sufficient wealth. When Hecker and McMillan returned to take over the business responsibilities, he departed for his first long vacation in over ten years. Making up for lost time, he did not return to Detroit for twelve months.

By the fall of 1894, Freer was drained physically by the pressure of the business crisis and emotionally by concern over his brother Watson. The tall, handsome baby of the family, now part of the beleaguered company's management team, had fallen in love with Hecker's eldest daughter, Anna. They had married in November 1891, happily forming yet another bond between the two partners. The young couple built a fine home next to Freer's on Ferry Avenue. Suddenly in 1893, Watson became ill with symptoms of paralysis alarmingly reminiscent of the illness that had plagued his father and grandfather. Given his new family and business responsibilities, the stress of the economic collapse might have sapped the young man's health, destroyed his equilibrium, and "shattered his nerves."

Watson's chronic illness remains a mystery. The Gilded Age "epidemic" of neurasthenia, sometimes called Americanitis, was a possibility. The malady, associated with class and refinement, most often struck women stifled in domestic life or men of particularly sensitive natures, the "brain workers" as opposed to manual workers. With his wife and child, Watson retreated to the calm security of rural Kingston. Concluding that the attack had been caused by heat and over exercise, Charles advised his brothers Will and George in Kingston to help the young father to get back to his old self, to avoid overheating, sudden scares, and fast driving: "Don't let him drive alone."[10]

The young man's partial paralysis and nervous instability stunned both families, but not enough to postpone his brother's travels. Charles was by nature a mentor who provided opportunity and financial assistance for his family; he was not the nurturer. He could express genuine concern and offer heartfelt, optimistic condolences, but he usually kept his distance. Just before his ship sailed on its twelve-day journey to Italy, a relieved Freer noted he had received from Watson a clear and hopeful letter, "the best letter from Watson's pen since he was first taken ill."[11]

When the SS *Kaiser Wilhelm II* pulled away from New York harbor at noon on September 22, 1894, Freer was feeling a bit shaky himself. Deeply touched by the grand sendoff his friends had given him both in Detroit and in New York, he admitted to Hecker:

> The affection bestowed by my friends together with the regard lavished by the King [liquor] resulted in a smash up of my nerves. But I have pinned (excuse spelling) my faith to the former and have forsaken the latter and soon I hope to be myself again.

His voyage was pleasant, "and her commander, dear old Capt. Stoermer is one of the jolliest old sea dogs my mind can fancy. Of the passengers enough are worth knowing." He had time to "read Trilby carefully—to the very end." (Written by George du Maurier, a former friend of Whistler's, the character Joe Silby was supposedly a parody of Whistler.) The sea journey proved to be a tonic. He confided to Hecker that he planned to return with his philosophy broadened, his intelligence increased, his heart softened, and his life richer. "If I enjoy it not the fault will be mine."[12]

The steamer landed in Italy, where his pace was fast: two days in Genoa, one in Milan and one in Verona, and on through the rest of the country. The indefatigable sightseer, accompanied by "an unusually intelligent and capable guide," was prepared for each city and country he planned to visit. Dewing's friend Charles Platt had given him an itinerary of the best gardens to study. He found

Milan's famous cathedral, the Duomo, "simply imposing and overgrown, overdone." Verona and the Guisti garden pleased him more: "For me rather one Verona than a thousand Milans."[13]

The preservation of Italian art made a powerful impression on him. Thayer once slyly compared his patron to the Medici, patrons of Italian Renaissance art. Freer now understood the Medici legacy: "Yes, surely they knew or they would not have encouraged those great artists who did so much to make Medici remembered today." Had Thayer planted a seed? Could Charles Freer be remembered for a similar contribution to the world of art? Whistler nourished the seed planted in Freer's fertile mind, asserting that, with or without patronage, the artist bore a gift from the gods, "which they left him to carry out." The patron's responsibility was the preservation of a masterpiece for posterity.[14]

Before Freer left for Europe, Whistler had taken over their correspondence from his wife, who was ill. Now convinced that Freer was not one of those "artist patron picture dealers" out to make a profit, he engaged with his wealthy American client in his own way. He remained dependably undependable in filling requests. Without mentioning the pastel Freer had requested with a spring theme, Whistler offered another painting, *Nocturne: Black and Gold—The Fire Wheel.* Freer declined, still hoping for the spring picture. Periodically, the artist supplied Freer with his latest prints, each time carefully sending duplicates so Hecker "can have his lot too." He insisted that when Freer finally came to Europe, "of course we shall expect to see you here." He and his wife had moved to Paris and established themselves in a "palatial" residence with a large garden in the Latin Quarter. They were struggling to find some relief from her illness, eventually diagnosed as cancer.[15]

After a month in Italy including a day on the Isle of Capri,

Freer arrived in Paris on November 10 for his second encounter with Whistler. Captivated, he reported to Hecker:

> Whistler has been perfectly charming. He called upon me at my hotel during the terrible wind storm of last Monday evening—since when I have lunched twice at his beautiful little home.

For the next two weeks, they wined and dined together in private or in company with other artists; they toured museums and art shops together. The businessman pressed the issue of his springtime picture for which he had paid Whistler 1,300 guineas in advance. The artist had at least begun a painting, "Little Blue Girl," of a delicate young girl standing nude beside a vase of flowers, her raised arms holding a film of drapery over her head and shoulders. To the extent that the girl is maidenly and emerging, the picture vaguely "hints at spring." Freer left France without seeing his prize but blithely suggested that Whistler send the picture to Detroit. The watercolors, pastels, and lithographs that he had purchased in Paris reached Detroit, but not his "Little Blue Girl."[16]

It was not all business for artist and patron. Thomas Dewing, still in Europe on the sabbatical he had inveigled Freer to support, arrived from London. Freer exalted, "Well, it's been one continued whirl...Dewing and I are having the treat of our lives." Frederick MacMonnies, the American sculptor living in Paris and a friend of Dewing's, introduced him to fellow artists. At the Musée du Luxembourg and the Louvre, he was seeing old "friends": artworks he knew well from photographs. He liked especially the famous *Winged Victory of Samothrace* and *Venus de Milo*, declaring, "I would wager anything that both are by the same artist." His eye for art was still a little raw. He praised *The Portrait of the Infanta Margarite* by Velázquez, a taste for that artist possibly inspired by Whistler. Curiously, he failed to mention Whistler's painting of his mother, which was owned by the Luxembourg.[17]

The highlight of his stay in Paris was a sumptuous dinner lubricated by Walker Club whiskey. Freer hosted it for American art students, the selected ones culled from the numerous aspiring artists in Paris. MacMonnies recounted the affair:

> [Freer], a friend of Whistler's and mine, spoke to me of giving a dinner to the American artists. I dissuaded him, by saying they all hated one another... Better to invite all the young fry—the American students. He gladly went into it. You can imagine the wild joy of the small fry, who had, of course, never met Whistler. Some got foolishly drunk, others got bloated with freshness, but they all had a rare time, and Whistler, who sat at the head, more than any, and he was delightfully funny. [Freer] was enchanted, and also a distinguished American painter, [Dewing] who sat opposite to Whistler, and who was much respected by the youth.

Freer reported, "The affair opened at eight o'clock in an old, curious, tumbledown restaurant in the Latin Quarter and lasted until practically dawn."[18]

His stay in Paris including visits with the painter Mary Cassatt and the sculptor Auguste Rodin: "I have lots of pleasant little attentions from various artistic circles and find the days flying like wind." Eager to head eastward, he skipped England in order to catch the one ship with a vacancy leaving Marseilles for Ceylon (now Sri Lanka) and India. With a new relaxed attitude in his foreign environment, he exalted: "I have gained about 10 pounds and feel years younger." Whistler sent him off with a touching farewell message: "I do not pretend to tell you how delightful your visit has been to me, and how really sorry I am to say Good bye—yesterday afternoon is not readily forgotten in the studio!"[19]

Their relationship would grow more symbiotic over the next nine years, but in 1894, they still had disparate goals. Whistler's most immediate concern was his wife's health. He also had masterpieces to create and coffers to fill with portrait commissions. Freer's immediate mission was to enrich his life by traveling to Asia.

— 8 —

ESCAPE TO ASIA

1894–1895

An intrepid Charles Freer set off to discover the eastern half of the world. He left Marseilles on November 25, steamed by Alexandria, Egypt, and arrived three weeks later in Colombo, Ceylon (Sri Lanka). His first goal there was to climb Adam's Peak, "the 'holy of holies' to the Buddhists, the Mohammadans [sic], and to many Roman Catholics." For most travelers it was a pilgrimage to witness the footprint of Buddha, Adam, or Shiva, depending on their belief; for Freer it was a climbing challenge. And should he fail the climb, he proposed to have no one at home the wiser.

> Well, I did not fail. I reached the very top, and saw the apparition, and witnessed the most magnificent panorama of my life—perhaps as fine as the world has—also most interesting religious observances of a band of pilgrims.

He spent Christmas at Anuradhapura, a buried city that nineteen centuries earlier claimed a population of over six million. In 1895, it held only a dozen white government officials and fewer than 2,000 inhabitants. Freer was the only visitor. Gently he established a rapport with the "natives" and paid homage at their Sacred Bo Tree. In return:

> [A] large number of the natives from children two years old to men nearly one hundred, all in various stages of nakedness, many very beautiful and intelligent, came bringing me flowers and danced and sang and played upon their weird musical instruments.[1]

Through his letters, we watch Freer's horizons expand as he sailed on to India and settled there for two months. In Tamil Nadu, he gained admittance to the fifth inner wall of the great Vishnu Temple at Srirangam, where he witnessed a religious festival attended by 20,000 Hindus and personally observed "the taking of the most sacred idol from its throne." During the New Year holidays, gaily dressed East Indians sang, marched, and danced, presenting flowers to bystanders as they carried great bejeweled idols through the streets. A high priest sent a "splendid big elephant with a crowd of servants to walk beside me so that I should have plenty of room (in the crowd)…It was great fun." Very often he was the only white person in a group, a fact in which he took growing pride. He confided to Hecker, "Alone is the way to do the thing that I am up to…this will, I fear, sound to you cold and distant but it's neither and it's right as well."[2]

His empathy for the Indian people increased as he witnessed their treatment by the government. He even went so far as to write,

"Give me Pingree [the reform mayor] any day rather, than some others I know of here," rebel words from one of Detroit's finest. On board his ship from Colombo, a "terrible north east monsoon struck...I was the only white passenger, but the two or three hundred natives on deck suffered fearfully without one single word of complaint." Freer had a cabin; they had none. "It's the most brutal plan of carrying passengers imaginable—and I think that nowhere in the world but here would the powers that be permit it. The English are devilish rulers." In America he callously criticized the poorer classes; in India he studied the poor with sympathy.[3]

In Peshawar (now in Pakistan), a place rarely visited by Europeans, he described the population as "a splendid aggregation of outcasts, horse thieves, adventurers, fakirs, traders and highwaymen from all over Central Asia" and mused, "If I could spend one week here and devote the whole time to the bazaars I could make money enough off my purchases to pay all of my personal expenses in India. But then one hates to become a dealer in stolen property." He admitted that "Oriental art and architecture is [sic] 'crawling through my innards' so to speak, and whether it will prove a tonic or tape worm is still an enigma." In Rajasthan he saw a copy of the *Gulistan*, a Persian prose classic circa 1258 AD, and discovered some "splendidly illuminated Persian Manuscripts." In fact, after two months, Freer was "daft" over all of India.

> I am very well, and over my head in love with India. The discomforts, of which I have not told you, are many, but they are like the one raveled fringe of a Rajah's cashmere shawl—a sort of hall mark of experience.

He welcomed India's pervasive atmosphere of tranquility and calm, noting with approval that "there's no hurry in this blessed land and tomorrow is always better than to-day." If a ship had enough people and if the Indian in charge was ready, the ship would sail; if not, everyone waited. Freer now signed his letters with the greeting "Tranquility to one and all."[4]

Before leaving Paris, he had promised to look for a Thama Merle, an unusual singing bird coveted by Mrs. Whistler. Whistler had cautioned in his farewell letter: "My wife…bids me say that you are not to trouble yourself terribly with the bird if he turns out to be bigger than we fancied!" During his travel through India, Freer searched for the bird, but he found only stuffed ones. At last on the outskirts of Calcutta, he found two alive. Captain Doheen of the steamer *Baroda* was already dickering for them; Freer won them from him, undoubtedly at a generous price. The captain offered to deliver them personally to the Whistlers in Paris.[5]

Freer's personal tranquility was taxed by a physical debility. During the two weeks he spent in Delhi, Benares, and Calcutta, he had been troubled by a "game right leg." A doctor suggested the numbness and weak muscles had been brought on by too much walking and recommended rest. Five days later he boarded a ship headed for China. The pain settled in the groin, and he could not walk. Optimistically he remarked on his good timing; confinement on shipboard promised a propitious cure.[6]

Two weeks after sailing from India, he docked for a day in Singapore, for two days in Hong Kong, and finally traveled up "the treacherous coast…of China" to Shanghai, where he had to wait six days for a ship to Japan. The businessman reported that "the commercial importance of Singapore, Hong Kong, and Shanghai impresses one deeply." He had not intended to spend any time in

China and therefore had made no preparation for even short call at its ports. He bought "a piece or two of old pottery made by the Chinese centuries before they became enemies [of the Japanese]." He then sailed on the SS *Natal* for Nagasaki, Japan, arriving on April 23, 1895.[7]

Struck by the contrast between immense India and the island of Japan, he assumed that his impressions of India would emerge as the most profound and the most lasting from his yearlong grand tour. With an ever-curious mind, he set off to explore the exotic kingdom for the next four months. In Nagasaki he was entertained "Japanese fashion by several good families—not the highest, but very interesting people." At first, he felt especially awkward with the Japanese women. Their politeness, their names, their subtle beauty and gentle manners, all so different from Western women, left him unsure how to respond.[8]

He praised the Japanese businessmen who, unfettered by pressure and haste, found plenty of time for leisure. These "reasonable" men fully enjoyed their prosperity. That prosperity, however, had come to the Japanese at headlong speed in the company of a Westernization that threatened native Japanese culture. Eager to experience the authentic culture of old Japan, Freer decried the modern Japanese rush to copy the West: "The half-Europeanized Japs sicken me." He preferred men who wanted to "arrest the degradation of their people," men who wore Japanese clothes and revered the ancient culture; they alone [he singled out a few by name] possessed "the old time refinements of Japan of our dreams."[9]

As he had done since the beginning of his trip, Freer moved rapidly from place to place with a full schedule of sights to see and miles to cover. In Kyoto he hired as his guide Yozo Nomura, a young man of twenty-six who had attended school in America and who consequently spoke and wrote English fluently. With Nomura and a bevy of servants at his command, Freer mapped out his survey of Japan. After three weeks combing the sights of Kyoto, they took a three-day trip to Yamada. They then moved on to Nagoya, where his principal object was to see the old palace and castle of Hideyoshi, the great 16th century daimyo. Although armed with permission provided by the United States minister, he could gain entry only to the castle. The Japanese officials were evidently a little wary of the tall American who marched with such alacrity and determination through their country. A "diligent officer" trailed behind Freer's party along the route and through each town. Freer was both annoyed and flattered by the attention.[10]

Nomura arranged trips reaching out in all directions from Kyoto. With eight men they set out on a ten-day journey into the mountains along the Nakasendo Trail, picking up additional men along the way to run the rickshaws when necessary. After his strenuous assault on Adam's Peak, Freer declined to do any mountaineering in Japan. When his guide had to return to his home because of a supposed illness, Freer ventured into the hinterlands for a month with just his rickshaw men. The long trip took them along the northern sea coast, then little known to foreigners, through the mountains and the old daimyo towns with ruined castles, and along the giant trees lining the roads to Nikko. For his rickshaw men, he reserved his highest praise:

> Think of a human horse who will haul you one mile or fifty per day—whom you never overdrive and seldom tire, with whom you can eat, drink, smoke, sleep and <u>live with pleasure</u>. I have six such chaps with me now—all fine fellows—one cooks

> excellently—another speaks a little English and teaches me Japanese—Another does the hard drinking for the crowd, a fourth flirts with the country girls—the other two see to it that I interfere not with the prerogatives of the fourth—They all have surprisingly good judgment in matters artistic, especially my two Kioto men—when we go shopping they put on good clothes, and ride in jinrickisha, and look wise and handsome enough. The Curio dealers are fearful liars and swindlers, as a class, but my gang generally equals the worst. It's great fun and I really am having a good time, and am securing a few mementoes worthy of a more intelligent, appreciative owner.[11]

Like a sponge, Freer absorbed the Japanese values that meshed with his own, but he remained confounded. He had grown to love the Japanese people as "simple, light-hearted and tremendously artistic," yet he described them as "odd, fantastic, curious." Their customs challenged him: "Customs such as modest bachelors are unfamiliar with but not unwilling to study—shall I say practice?" That allusion is as explicit as Freer ever gets about sexual activities.[12]

The country inns offered no table or chairs for writing; yet following the Japanese customs in modes of travel, kinds of food, and places of interest gave him the greatest pleasure. Still distinguishing between "a real Jap" and the "half Europeanized cuss," he began to feel at home in his new country. He admired the architectural simplicity of the Shinto shrines and the Japanese commitment to gardens and forestry, an attitude he described as "intelligent, discriminating, reverential." Flirting with their religious ideas, he mused: "If the Buddhistic idea is correct and I am inclined to believe it is, not one earthly existence alone is sufficient but several are required to develop an imaginative mind. Does this then mean experience—and does not intelligent travel bring experience?"[13]

When Freer returned to Yokohama, he found his guide in prison, charged with misdemeanors committed in Paris two years earlier and sentenced to three months of hard labor. The woman who the suspicious Freer wrote "purported to be Nomura's wife" tried to cover for him by describing his continued serious illness; but with his new "Oriental" patience he allowed her to think he believed her story. She had, after all, rescued Freer's things from Nomura's confiscated possessions. The woman fascinated him; she was "a curious mixture of Oriental morals in which the devil and the butterfly seem ever present." She was indeed Nomura's wife, and a decade later, the intrepid woman visited Freer in Detroit.[14]

In four months little had escaped his appreciative and inquiring eye. He had explored Uji and Nara, Lake Biwa and Chuzenji, Hakone and Kobe, Ama-no-Hashidate and Atami. He traveled by rail, steamer, rickshaw, and occasionally by chair. He braved harrowing terrain to get as close as possible to Mt. Fuji, and he survived an earthquake:

> In Tokio recently I was dining in the upper (better) story of a swell tea house and as usual upon such occasions dancing and music was being performed for our amusement when suddenly the building tried to turn itself inside out, the geishas and samisen [sic] players bowed their heads to the floor and I experienced an earthquake felt all over the Tokio district.

> I hope there are no more to come during my stay—I like them not.

Always acutely conscious of social classes and eager to associate with people on the highest level, Freer found entrée into Japanese society difficult. In India he had been received by maharajas; in Japan he met good people but not those in the top echelons of society. Freer had come to Japan as a sensitive, curious tourist. He left with ambivalent feelings but with a sharpened understanding of the Japanese culture and its aesthetic.[15]

Not yet a collector, he kept a keen eye out for the best shops and dealers who might support his growing interest in Oriental art. He bought little, a few hanging scrolls, some folding screens, and a few pieces of bronze and silver. Just before departing for the United States, he took a final tiffin, a traditional Japanese afternoon tea ritual, with Mr. Toranosuke Kita, a curio merchant with the large firm of Yamanaka and Company. Kita and Yozo Nomura would later serve as important agents for his collection of Asian art.

On August 23 Freer bid a sentimental "last 'Sayonara' to those who taught me the word which I so deeply regret to use in its final sense." The steamer *Empress of China* carried him from Yokohama to Vancouver, where he boarded the Canadian Pacific Railway to Fort William on Lake Superior, then traveled by boat to Sault Ste. Marie. He stopped for a brief visit with Mrs. Hecker on Mackinac Island. Finally, he arrived in Detroit by train on September 12, 1895. His travels had opened his mind to an exotic world beyond Detroit and kindled a new fascination with Japanese art. At home, the Depression of 1893 had abated but left turmoil in its wake. Charles Freer returned a changed man to a rapidly changing America.[16]

— 9 —

EXIT FROM BUSINESS
1896–1899

Settling back into his routine, Freer was relieved to find some progress in his absence. His brother Watson had recovered enough to resume his position at the car company. With his young wife and baby, he had returned to their new home less than a block from the Hecker and Freer homes. The smallpox hysteria that had gripped the large ethnic population during the winter of 1894 and 1895 so devastated Detroit that it briefly halted the mayor's reform program. The city's capitalist leaders could breathe a little more easily. The consequences of the economic depression, however, persisted. Glumly, Freer predicted "extraordinary business depression now existing in our line and dullness ahead." In fact, the Depression of 1893 had changed the business environment irrevocably, striking blows to both capital and labor. Mayor Pingree's reforms were slowed, not defeated. America was transforming.[1]

The Gilded Age, a moniker given to the glittering post–Civil War economy by Mark Twain, was tarnished by corrosive greed and social disruption. Rural village life, where laborer and employer worked side by side, had morphed into an industrialized urban life, where workers were relegated to commodities to be hired and fired, based on market conditions. Factories were clustered in cities near transportation and financial centers. New immigrants crowded into city tenements where they competed for jobs and drove wages down. Open sewage and an appalling lack of clean water were common; the mud and horses didn't help. Financial panics wracked America. Busts followed unsustainable booms: money tightened, banks closed, business orders dried up, and workers lost their jobs. Labor reacted desperately to each panic with railroad strikes in 1877, the Haymarket riots in 1886, and the Homestead and Pullman strikes in the mid-1890s. Demands for reform escalated into a war between capital and labor.

Charles Freer's rational capitalist order had collapsed in the wake of the depression. Capacity surpassed demand as railroads consolidated. Buffeted by competitive pricing, profits in the freight car industry plummeted. Pressure continued to mount within the Michigan-Peninsular Car Company. Six months after his return from Asia, Freer launched a new strategy to protect their company. With the support of William K. Bixby, president of the Missouri Car and Foundry Company, an operation started in 1876 by the McMillans, he sounded out other builders regarding "concerted actions, etc.," to wit, price controls. A year later he attempted to consolidate several companies into a proposed United States Car Company. As usual dodging the limelight, he suggested that Bixby lead the initiative: "I deeming it better to play in the background with U. S. car company's matters."[2]

Manipulating furiously behind the scenes, Freer warned ominously of "close combat" with the enemies. As a temporary measure, he and his associates organized a "Committee of Seven for the purpose of maintaining an offensive and defensive position in the trade." Freer was in his element—staying in the background, plotting strategy, keeping his ear to the ground. "Rumors rife," he declared. He excelled amid intrigue. The more political Hecker stayed above the fray and left the tactics to his partner. With a perspective broadened by his recent world travel, Freer next proposed a joint venture with Bixby and the passenger car builder Barney & Smith to build railroad cars for Russia and possibly Japan as well.

> The scheme was to do the iron work in Chicago, the woodwork at Tacoma, and ship all knocked down to Vladivostok, at which place temporary erecting sheds would be built and the cars put together there.

He saw a lucrative opportunity in Russia's emergent Trans-Siberian Railway. He also considered expanding to South Africa and South America "to keep our three companies more regularly employed... and put us at the front of all American builders and far in advance of foreign competition." Hecker solicited Russell Alger, who had just been appointed secretary of war, to take the matter up "direct with President McKinley." Freer awaited an invitation to come to Washington.[3]

Unfortunately in 1898 the United States entered the Spanish-American War. McKinley and Alger had their hands full. Hecker, instead of lobbying for the car companies, was pressed into war service. He took charge of the Division of Transportation with the rank of colonel and orchestrated the logistics of sending ships and supplies to and from Cuba. From June to December, he was in Washington, D.C., or Cuba, returning to Detroit only for the Christmas wedding of his daughter Louise. When the war ended in a quick American victory, Hecker resigned his position in April 1899.

Meanwhile, the market chaos continued. Worried that railroad deals were "of the sort that suggests blood," Freer pivoted to another tactic: the consolidation of four or five car builders that used the traditional wood material with two steel companies: Schoen Pressed Steel, a steel car builder, and Fox Pressed Steel, a steel car supplier. Steel was the future of the car business. Billy Wilson, the president of Fox, was a good friend, and Freer served on the company's board of directors. Unfortunately, Wilson died suddenly in November 1898; shortly thereafter, the two steel companies merged on their own. It was a crushing disappointment for Freer, who represented the interests of the Wilson estate as well as the holdings in Fox Steel of "Col. Hecker, myself and a few other friends for whom I am trustee."[4]

Freer was spent. The work, the travel, and the failures wore him down. He became ill during the fall of 1898 and retreated to Hot Springs, West Virginia, for a cure. Between January and March of 1899, he was again too exhausted to work. During his second illness, Bixby took the reins and merged thirteen car companies into the American Car and Foundry Company, a monopoly of the nation's railroad car building industry. The Scripps *News-Tribune* credited (or blamed) the merger as an accomplishment of Charles Freer "more than any other one man" as it chided Hecker and Freer for unloading their increasingly obsolescent wooden car business. The headquarters of the new company, which controlled 70 percent of the nation's rolling stock production, was in St. Louis under the direction of William K. Bixby and Will McMillan. Sales offices in New York and Chicago coordinated the nationwide enterprise, but Detroit, where railroad car building constituted the number-one industry until 1906, was still its hub.[5]

Charles Freer immediately retired. With understated pride, he acknowledged that the Michigan-Peninsular Car Company had "turned out to be a fine investment for a great many people." In his personal portfolio, worth nearly $2 million in stocks and bonds, he retained only $75,000 worth of American Car and Foundry stock. That minimal investment marked his clear break with the car industry that had created his fortune. He had no stomach for modern business practices and had no regrets in abandoning the car business now so rife with jealousy and "blood." The cooperative competition he had enjoyed among gentlemen of the right sort had vanished. Even when the stock plummeted during the first few months, he admitted to Hecker, who had also retired, "Personally I would prefer to see 50% lower than to have continued the old M. P. Co." Like a man paroled from prison, Charles Freer slipped away from the business world that had nurtured him for twenty years.[6]

During his three-year struggle to bring order to the freight car world, he found relief in art. His trip to Asia had stimulated him to explore Asian art, a new field he could probe as he had the print market a decade earlier. As for Whistler, Freer resigned himself to the fact that the artist wrote only "whenever he happened to be in the mood." When his car-business associate R. E. Plumb, on a trip to London, tried to retrieve the "Spring" painting, Whistler received Plumb but instead sent him away with a nocturne painting along with a pastel and watercolor. Pacified, Freer penned Whistler gratefully, "And now comes the long wished for Nocturne—and of exactly the kind I most admire—real night—actual nature—unceasing mystery." Actual nature was an important criterion; he wanted recognizable subject matter, misty and mysterious, but a real essence. The "Spring" painting, for which he had already paid, did not arrive. Freer waited.[7]

Dewing wrote from Paris that Whistler's dear wife Trixie had died on May 10, 1896, and expressed the fear that Whistler himself, so torn with grief, would soon follow her. Freer sadly agreed, keenly aware that such vulnerability jeopardized his investments. Deeply involved with his company's negotiations, he had little energy to nurture his friend. Nearly a year went by. On March 31, 1897 he cabled Whistler, "Can you forward 'Blue Girl' and pastel to reach me before April fifteenth and save me twenty five percent duty?"[8]

Whistler's first response in over two years arrived on April 6. The long epistle, effusive and rambling, began without salutation:

> Shall I begin by saying to you, my dear Mr. Freer, that your Little "Blue and Gold Girl" is doing her very best to look lovely for you?—Perhaps it were well—and so you shall be assured that though steamer after steamer leave [sic] me in apparently ungracious silence, it is that only of the pen!
>
> I write to you many letters on your canvas!—and one of these days, you will, by degrees, read them all, as you sit before your picture—
>
> And in the work, perhaps will you, of your refined sympathy and perception discover the pleasure and interest taken in the perfecting of it by the other one who, with me liked you—and delighted in the kind and courteous attention paid on your travels to her pretty fancy and expressed wish—

> She loved the wonderful bird you sent with such happy care from the distant land!
>
> And when she went—alone, because I was unfit to go too—the strange wild dainty creature stood uplifted on the topmost perch, and sang and sang—as it had never sung before!—A song...of my despair!—
>
> And suddenly it was made known to me that...the spirit of my beautiful Lady had lingered on its way—and the song was her song of love, and courage, and command that the work in which she had taken her part, should be complete—and so was her farewell!"

Freer cabled immediately, "Regret last week's cable," and responded by letter to his grieving friend:

> Your letter with its exquisite memories, tenderness and friendship came this morning, and as I read of <u>her</u> sympathetic interest in the "Little Blue and Gold Girl"
>
> Forgive, I pray, those cold words of last week—colder to you I fear, than the icy waves of the Atlantic through which they were flashed. And be assured, my dear Mr. Whistler, that whenever in your own good time and way, you are quite ready to complete, and transfer to my keeping, that which she loved, and which all who have seen loves, [sic] I shall be rejoiced to receive and care for as you would have

> me. And when I am gone, the picture shall rest with its own beautiful kind, so, that in after years, others shall pass that way, and understand.[9]

Although chastened and touched, Freer was wary of further investment with the artist. The 65-year-old Whistler survived his grief, but his work at the easel was fitful, as was his correspondence with Freer. The elderly artist tried Freer's best intentions; his procrastination in finishing work and his indifference toward settling accounts left Freer sputtering. The businessman could only bide his time, confident that someday the pieces would all fall into order and hope it would happen before Whistler's death. He mollified the artist with comments like "How deeply grateful I am to you for entrusting to my care," and that the sum he paid was only "partial payment," for the paintings were priceless. Whistler had longed for years for such unreserved appreciation of his work.

As a print collector, Freer's goal was to own one impression of every Whistler etching and lithograph. The value of a print collection lies not only in the quality of each item but in the comprehensive holdings of a single subject or artist. With Whistler's assistance, he had made impressive progress over an eleven-year period, from his first purchase in 1887 to 1898. In 1898 he nearly realized his ambition in one stroke when he captured the Haden collection of Whistler etchings and dry points assembled over a period of forty years by Whistler's brother-in-law and fellow etcher. Braced by new confidence, Freer declined to share his bounty with his fellow collector Howard Mansfield. The ensuing years had altered their relationship.[10]

Newly liberated from business responsibilities and uncertain of what life he wanted to create with his new freedom and wealth,

Freer harkened back to his days roaming the Catskill Mountains. He bought another farm, this time in Sheffield, Massachusetts, near the Berkshire Mountains and again dreamed of a second home near his artist friends. In February 1900, he corresponded with his friend, the architect Stanford White of the prominent McKim, Mead & White firm, about the design, suggesting galleries over the living room and cautioning him to keep it compact. He envisioned retreating there occasionally and perhaps tilling the land before he realized that the site was, in his words, "pretty tough." With heavy snow in the winter and ninety-degree heat in the summer, plus a settlement of hunters and trappers nearby, he realized he could never take pictures to the farm and feel secure about their safety. Although White had already drawn a final sketch for a new farmhouse, Freer abruptly abandoned the property for his own personal use. Until he sold the land in 1910, he maintained the farm, raised livestock, grew feed, and kept a man to run it, but he seldom stayed there.[11]

Freer instead turned to the more sophisticated charms of Europe. Less than two months after his escape from the car business, he crossed the Atlantic for a third time. In the company of his good friend Tom Jerome, he steamed out of New York in early May 1899; they traveled without plans or itinerary. In Jerome, a fellow bachelor, a founding member of the Yondotega and a cultivated gentleman, he had an ideal companion. Tom's father, David Jerome, had served as governor of Michigan, but his only son, who had trained for the law, preferred books and leisure to either work or politics. When his father died in 1896, Tom inherited a small fortune as well as release from parental pressure. Freer, accustomed to traveling alone, wrote Hecker enthusiastically: "Tom is a genuine tar and the same dear fellow at sea as we have always found him on land."[12]

After "hopelessly indolent" days on the beautiful Isle of Capri, they visited Rome and Florence. The rest of the month they toured throughout Italy. Jerome responded to the ancient Roman civilization with such alacrity, his friend feared he would soon be wearing a toga. Freer responded to the famous artworks in museums: "I have renewed my acquaintance with some earlier friends at the Uffizi and Bargello in Florence." From Venice they moved on to Geneva, Paris, and London. As Charles sailed for the United States, he paid his companion a rare compliment in a letter to Hecker: "I shall feel lost without him." Tom returned to Capri to find a home the two bachelors could share. In short order he purchased the Villa Castello in the names of Charles Freer and Thomas Jerome. The 200-year-old villa had been part of a convent; its garden was one of the oldest on the island. Jerome remained on Capri and made it his permanent residence.[13]

Freer was back in Europe in September 1900 to inspect his new villa. The Atlantic passage was by now a familiar ritual for him. He found this voyage both "comfortable and entertaining. Ship clean, service good, eats excellent, company all solid—a host of New England girls bound for Florence to complete their musical studies." After a year abroad, Tom was as handy as a native. He met Charles on his landing in Naples, whisked him through customs "like a whirlwind," and then ferried him to Capri on the thirty-foot cutter he had leased for the season: "an ideal way to approach Capri!"[14]

After making some side trips to his favorite spots in Italy and joining his lady friends, the Misses Webb, briefly in Florence, he settled in Capri to work on the house and the "largest little garden I know." He and Tom bought furniture in Naples, "a few very appropriate things…including…the entire woodwork of a large room in a splendid old Convent…now being torn down." Although he thrived on the creative work involved in finishing their villa and enjoyed the camaraderie of his friend, the island's exotic Moorish influences, and the beauty of his surroundings, Freer chafed under the weight of a desultory life. He soon found Capri fascinating for only short periods. Its residents, a colony of intellectuals and gadflies, spent their time in the coffee house, walking the seashore, or holed up in their studios. Their languorous, seemingly unproductive lifestyle nettled Freer. Before the season and the tourists arrived on the island in October, he moved on to Paris for a few days and then to London to visit Whistler. He had been away less than two months, and already he longed to get back to his home in Detroit. To Tryon, he wrote, "I find after all, however, that there is just one house in which I feel most content."[15]

The erudite Jerome settled comfortably into island life and devoted his hours to writing the history of Rome. Through their friends in Washington, Charles secured a sinecure for him as vice consul of Capri. Scripps' *Evening News* took a dim view of the affair and publicly accused Senator McMillan of merely making things pleasant for his friends. The paper listed "three citizens whom Michigan can spare": Jerome, Freer, and William G. Thompson (newly appointed to the Paris Exposition Commission and the mayor of Detroit whom Pingree had defeated in 1891), describing them as members of the "genial social arty crowd in sunny Italy." The *Detroit Tribune*, also under Scripps's control, joined the diatribe, calling Jerome "Our Literary Wonder…a good fellow…whose social graces made him a popular, gay, young club man" and questioned how much work was possible to a man so devoted to "sunny leisure."[16]

Back in Detroit, city politics snared the newly retired Freer and caught him unaware. For the first time, he threw his energy into a major civic project. The bluebloods of Detroit proposed a grand gift to their city, a magnificent Bicentenary memorial in tribute to Antoine Cadillac, the French explorer whose fort marked the beginnings of Detroit in 1701. They envisioned an elaborate structure on Belle Isle in the Detroit River to add glory to their fair city. An executive committee appointed to oversee the project included Senator James McMillan, Mayor William C. Maybury, the banker Frank H. Walker, Charles L. Freer, and, ominously, James E. Scripps. The committee selected several artists to draw up plans for the memorial: Stanford White, Augustus Saint-Gaudens, Frederick MacMonnies, Dwight W. Tryon, and Thomas W. Dewing, all Freer's friends. Each of the artists graciously proposed to charge only actual costs, refusing additional fees. Their plan called for a white marble Doric column rising 220 feet at the base of Belle Isle and encircled by groups of statuary with an immense rectangular lagoon surrounded by colonnades and leaping flames fed by jets of natural gas.[17]

To raise the projected $2 million cost, the mayor appointed Frank Hecker to lead a committee of 100. A stereopticon display of the plan, lauded as Stanford White's "chef d'oeuvre," was displayed at city hall. Letters flew weekly between Freer and White in 1900. To a suggestion that European architects be included, White recorded, "Our friend Freer got up on his hind legs and said that we had architects, sculptures and painters equal to any in the world." The conservative *Detroit Free Press* gave the memorial enthusiastic support and asked for popular donations. Scripps' *Tribune*, predictably, satirized the memorial as a thing of beauty without utility, a colonnade without shelter, and questioned the artists' motives in not charging a fee. The project died ignominiously for lack of funds. Freer later wrote that one man was responsible for the failure, without naming the obvious culprit. Offended and embarrassed by Detroit's failure to rise to an opportunity in which he found such noble and artistic purpose, he avoided further civic responsibility.[18]

Freer kept himself busy. He had remained engaged with the art world, experimenting in Asian art and collecting Whistler's prints. He supported the careers of his New York artist friends, occasionally participating in their less conventional lives, like playing the go-between for Dewing and his current mistress. He attended to Yondotega business and supervised development of its Italian garden, even permitting *House & Garden* to publish an article on it, a "privilege which we have heretofore never given to any other publication" He traveled in Europe and cavorted on Capri. When attending to business affairs in Detroit, he shared a downtown office with Colonel Hecker, whom President Theodore Roosevelt had appointed to the Panama Commission to supervise the construction of the new canal. In his partner's absence, Freer looked after their interests, kept up with correspondence, and monitored investments.[19]

With one fortuitous investment, he caught another gold ring. Parke-Davis, a Detroit pharmaceutical company producing treatments for diphtheria and tetanus, had reorganized in 1899 after the forced retirement of George Davis in 1896 and the death of Hervey Parke in 1898. Theodore Buhl, a major stock holder, became the company's president. Freer participated in the new syndicate of his friends, little knowing the investment would provide his second fortune and fund his serious collection of ancient Asian art.

PART TWO: PURSUIT OF PURPOSE

— 10 —

DISCOVERING ASIAN ART
1887–1900

THE FIRST EVIDENCE OF CHARLES Freer's attraction to Oriental art was in 1887 when he bought a Japanese paper fan decorated with a simple painting of a crane, the earliest object of Asian art retained in his permanent collection. The purported artist was Ogata Kōrin. Was it a whimsical purchase, an appealing scene from nature, a potential gift for a lady friend? Or had he already read praise of Kōrin by the leading American scholar of Japanese art, Ernest Fenollosa, in his 1883 *Review* of Louis Gonse's *L'Art Japonais*? In any case, Freer, deeply involved in his print collection, was only dabbling in Asian art. The fan's subtle suggestive image and simple brushwork mirrored the contemplative mood of his first purchase of pottery, a delicately decorated Satsuma bottle. They expressed his kind of beauty and piqued his thirst for new knowledge.[1]

On his trip to London in 1890, he had observed the spare purity of Whistler's home, accented by blue-and-white Chinese vases. In his art, Whistler blended the flattened two-dimensional designs of Japanese prints in the profile painting of his mother and mimicked their shallow perspective in his nocturnes. He often included Japanese prints, Chinese vases, and models in kimonos in his paintings. Although he had neither visited the Far East nor seriously studied its art history, Whistler must have expounded on his belief that the Orient harbored a profound ancient art.

In Freer's Gilded Age, Asia and America were separated by vast ignorance as well as vast distances. Scholars and tourists with firsthand experience of the East were rare; the Eastern people and their art were mysterious to Westerners. Americans first distilled their understanding of the Orient in the eighteenth century through European imports of chinoiserie: imitations of Chinese motifs in dainty wallpaper scenes, in paintings on porcelain jars, or on lacquer screens. Fanciful and idealized patterns of arched bridges and pig-tailed gentlemen represented what they knew of the remote East.

After the first American merchant ship sailed to China in 1784, New England sailors regularly edged along the coast of China, returning with the ivories, lacquers, and silks prized by their townspeople. Missionaries, hoping to harvest souls, followed. Their direct contact changed the American image of the Orient: richly dressed mandarins leisurely philosophizing amid fragrant blossoms did not exist for the merchant or missionary. Laboring coolies, rude officials, and craggy cliffs more often greeted them. The xenophobic Chinese had little interest in the Western industrialized world. A people ripe for Christian salvation stubbornly refused to abandon their Confucian and Buddhist faiths. American visitors were restricted to port cities and given summary treatment. Suspicion grew on both sides.

After 1850, Americans, especially those living along the California coast, began to feel invaded and threatened. Chinese immigrants arrived in alarming numbers, mostly laborers imported to work on the railroads and in the mines. They took jobs away from American workers, and they proved frighteningly resistant to assimilation. When the railroad building slowed and hordes of workers were no longer needed, the United States Congress passed the Chinese Exclusion Act in 1882, banning Chinese immigrants.

Japan was different. Isolated from the West for over two centuries, the island country opened to the West only after Commodore Perry with his formidable American ships arrived in 1854. In 1868, the feudal Tokugawa shogun was overthrown in the Meiji Restoration by young samurai bent on modernizing Japan. They welcomed expertise from the West; they emulated Western political systems, education, and technology. Unlike the Chinese, who demanded that foreigners, even conquerors, adopt their customs, the Japanese imitated their foreign intruders. Encouraged by such an enlightened attitude, American artists, scholars, and scientists went to Japan to study and teach. Some arrived in Japan as early as the 1870s and stayed for years. Men like Edward S. Morse, William Sturgis Bigelow, and Ernest Fenollosa gave America her first authentic introduction to Asia, its culture, and its people. They collected Japanese art and eventually presented it to the Museum of Fine Arts, Boston, the only significant collection in America that predated Freer's. While China turned inward, Japan looked outward.

The first Bostonian scholar to arrive in Japan knew nothing of Japanese art and in fact stumbled on it by accident. Edward Sylvester Morse, a Harvard professor, went to Japan in 1877 to study brachiopods. In excavating for shells at the Omori mounds, he uncovered pottery shards and utensils from early Japanese civilizations. By 1880, with a bounty of ancient pottery in hand, he returned to the United States to direct the Peabody Museum in Salem, Massachusetts. Twelve years later he sold his collection to the Boston Museum and accepted its keepership of Japanese pottery.

When Morse returned to Japan briefly in 1882, Dr. William Sturgis Bigelow, a young Harvard man from an old Boston family, accompanied him. Although a medical doctor, Bigelow had little interest in becoming a practicing physician. He stayed in Japan for seven years, absorbed Japanese culture, converted to Zen Buddhism, and accumulated Japanese art. At the death of his father in 1890, he inherited a trusteeship in the Boston Museum. Asserting his new influence, he brought in as curators two art scholars he had known in Japan, Ernest F. Fenollosa and Kakuzo Okakura. In 1911, he gave the museum his collection of 26,000 art objects from the Far East.[2]

Fenollosa, who later became Freer's mentor, was a dynamic, self-promoting scholar with an arrogance perhaps born of financial insecurity. Four years after graduating first in the Harvard class of 1874, he had found neither a suitable occupation nor social acceptance. The old-line Bostonian parents of the young woman whom he had courted for years refused to allow their daughter to marry the son of an immigrant Spanish musician, wary of his heritage and skeptical of his prospects. On Morse's recommendation, the Imperial University in Tokyo, striving to equip its students with the tools of Western progress, offered Fenollosa a position teaching political economy and philosophy. The honored position in Japan appealed to his flair for drama and enhanced his prospects as a husband. In 1878 Fenollosa and his bride left Boston to sail east.[3]

In accord with its ancient feudal tradition, Japanese artworks had been hidden from public view. For centuries they were privately passed down through generations of *daimyo* families and temple monks. Late in the Edo period of Tokugawa rule (1615–1868), social and economic upheaval in Japan cracked open the art world. New ukiyo-e paintings and prints of courtesans and actors were distributed on a mass scale. The Japanese elite, however, scorned those cheap, gaudy creations depicting the coarse subjects of low-class life; they clung to the classic Chinese-inspired paintings of bamboo, rocks, and mountains. With the advent of the Meiji regime in 1868, new cultural leaders encouraged artists to imitate art from the West, especially the art of Botticelli and the Italian Renaissance. Young painters learned Western ideas of perspective in drawing classes; art schools exchanged brush and ink for the modern pencil. Twelve centuries of Japanese art were forgotten in the rush to absorb a new vision. This was the volatile environment that welcomed Fenollosa to Japan in 1876.

The American professor capitalized on his opportunity and devoted more time and energy to exploring his new country than to imparting Western knowledge to his students. He learned the Japanese language and studied Japanese literature, cultural traditions, and art. To his dismay, he discovered that Western techniques had subverted the practice of native fine arts in Japan. As he systematically uncovered ancient Japanese art, he was overwhelmed by the beauty he discovered and began to purchase old paintings. During his summer vacations, he traveled through remote provinces, previously forbidden territory for Westerners. He saw Tofuku-ji, the ancient Kyoto temple, before the fire of 1882 destroyed many of its treasures. In 1884 with his student Kakuzo Okakura, he toured temples and go-downs (private art storehouses) in Kyoto and Osaka and compiled the first modern inventory of their artworks. He boldly claimed, "I have recovered the history of Japanese art from the 6th to the 9th centuries A. D. which has been completely lost…" and bragged, "I have bought a number of the very greatest treasures secretly. The Japanese as yet don't know that I have them." While publicly advocating protection of Japan's national treasures, he profited. In 1886 Fenollosa sold his large collection of Japanese art to a fellow Bostonian, Dr. Charles Goddard Weld.[4]

When the Museum of Fine Arts, Boston opened the first Oriental department in the West in 1890, Fenollosa returned in triumph as its curator. More an entrepreneur and crusader than a scholar or administrator, he hustled into a whirlwind of activity. He unpacked hundreds of boxes languishing in storage, hired assistants, wrote catalogues, arranged his own lecture engagements, and installed a first-class display of the museum's Oriental treasures. He organized ambitious exhibitions to engage Americans in the art of the Orient. His inaugural exhibition was of Hokusai's works, shrewdly capitalizing on the popularity of the ukiyo-e artist. His final exhibition of 100 extraordinary Chinese Buddhist paintings of the eleventh and twelfth centuries on loan from the famed Japanese temple Daitoku-ji closed in March 1895.

Japan had treated Fenollosa as a dignitary. Boston, however, had certain standards, and Fenollosa was caught off guard when he offended them. He had divorced his wife, whose socially prominent Boston family had so reluctantly accepted him eighteen years earlier, and almost immediately he married one of his assistants. Boston society could not forgive his abandoning one of their own. To his dismay, in 1896 the museum dismissed him, and lecture engagements dried up. He and his new wife returned to Japan.[5]

While Fenollosa was making waves in Boston in the early 1890s, Charles Freer was running his business, building his home, cultivating American artists, refining his collection of prints, and exploring Japanese art. With Howard Mansfield, who was already a collector of Japanese prints, he attended a Grolier Club Exhibition in early 1892 and purchased his first prints by Hokusai, the ukiyo-e artist then popular among Westerners. Freer continued to buy ukiyo-e woodblock prints over the next ten years. His first purchase of an oil painting from Whistler, *Variations in Flesh Colour and Green - The Balcony*, was indebted to ukiyo-e style, its composition reflecting the influence of Japanese woodblock prints. It hung on the wall of his new home along with the paintings of his other American artist friends, a first stone in his bridge linking West and East.[6]

Through Mansfield, he discovered Tozo Takayanagi, owner of Sanshodo, a Japanese curio shop on lower Fifth Avenue in New York City. At first, Freer shopped for trays, ash receivers, match safes, and paper holders for his new home. As Mansfield canvassed the shops to add to his own collection, he chose painted scrolls or pottery for dealers to ship to Freer in Detroit. The collector/dealer Rufus E. Moore, at Mansfield's direction, sent Freer fourteen kakemonos (hanging scrolls), "the cream" of a collection gathered fifteen years earlier and painted by the "best old masters of Japan." Their average cost was twenty-nine dollars. The two friends often worked in tandem, sharing the purchase of a pair of folding screens or portioning out a portfolio of prints, just as they did with Whistler prints. The Chinese porcelains of the Ming and Qing dynasties that appealed to most wealthy Westerners and decorated Whistler's studio were antithetical to Freer's taste and perhaps to his budget. He avoided them.[7]

With only his inexperienced eye and no adviser to guide him, Freer relied on the scant written information available in the West. When Louis Gonse, a French art connoisseur and editor, wrote the first comprehensive history of Japanese art published in the West, *L'Art Japonais*, he was limited to the artworks available in Paris or copies for his analysis of the ancient art of Japan. Ernest Fenollosa, who had used Japanese documents, examined original artwork, and consulted many Japanese scholars, critiqued Gonse in a fifty-four page *Review* written in 1884. It was later acclaimed the "first adequate survey of the development of Japanese art, in its true perspective and proportions, ever published in a European tongue." By summarizing Gonse's ideas and correcting them, he gave contemporary English readers the benefit of both viewpoints and their first history of Japanese art.[8]

Freer owned Fenollosa's short *Review* critiquing Gonse's history and in his own way joined their debate regarding the artists Ogata Kōrin and Hon'ami Kōetsu. In the early seventeenth century, Kōetsu and Tawaraya Sōtasu had founded the Rinpa School to capture the ancient indigenous traditions of Japan in images of nature and the seasons. Gonse claimed that "collectors and critics of true refinement worship Korin [a follower of Kōetsu] as a demigod." Fenollosa agreed, but he dismissed Kōetsu: "The lacquerer, ought not to have been placed among the great painters of Japan...he was only the merest amateur." Fenollosa also scorned the popular ukiyo-e paintings and prints, insisting they should be "despised, not because the subjects are vulgar, but because their form of painting is vulgar...without refinement or depth." Following his own instincts, Freer collected ukiyo-e prints and paintings and more importantly, he became an early collector of Kōetsu's art.[9]

From 1892 to 1894, Freer's relationship with his first dealer, Takayanagi, resembled his earlier association with Keppel in collecting European prints. Boxes of goods from New York arrived regularly in Detroit, and occasionally Takayanagi himself came. Freer seldom passed through New York without stopping at his shop. In frequent letters, he pressed his new expert for information. "Does the word 'Kiri' refer to a family, a location, or a period?" he asked and at the same time requested a biographical sketch of Kanō Tan'yū. As Takayanagi grew bolder and shipped greater quantities of his goods to Detroit, Freer grew more selective and frequently rejected items. Less than six months after he first entered Takayanagi's shop, he wrote with undisguised confidence explaining why he found it necessary to return much of the recent shipment.

> Far be it from me to criticize the art of as great a man as Ogata Korin, but this particular piece has too many details and is not fine enough in color to thoroughly satisfy my preferences; hence I return it.

Still, his first Japanese masterpiece, an ink kakemono by Kaihō Yūshō, came from Takayanagi.[10]

No complete record remains of what Freer bought and later discarded or gave away. He generously shared his passions. In the 1880s, friends, relatives, and business associates all received etchings as presents; a decade later they found pottery, kakemonos, or prints in their gift boxes. Each year, increasingly finer specimens arrived from Detroit, until they "ascended to T'ang and Sung pottery." Whether limited by the inferior supply of goods or his inexperienced eye, few of his early purchases survived his later, more critical judgment. Of the items he acquired on his visit to Japan in 1895, only a piece of silverwork, two paintings by Ganku, a Rinpa painting, a makemono (horizontal hand scroll painting), and two pieces of bronze entered his final collection.[11]

After his extraordinary four months in Japan, Freer embraced the study of Japanese prints, paintings, and pottery. Yamanaka & Co. in New York and Bunkio Matsuki in Boston became his primary sources for Japanese art. He had known the Yamanaka firm through Mr. Kita in Japan, and it was, according to Freer, the "largest concern in existence dealing in Japanese Fine Art goods, and nearly all the other dealers in New York buy from them."

Operated by an extended family, it offered an abundant selection and the lowest prices, Freer proudly confided to a business friend that they granted him wholesale prices. Sadajiro Yamanaka, an amusing little man whom friends affectionately called "Monkey," was not over five feet tall and thin as a crane. He directed an international empire with meticulous care, shipping objects from the old warehouse in Osaka where hovering clerks tended a chaos of treasures hidden under cloth wrappers, in wooden boxes, or tucked away in closets. Freer made his first purchase from Yamanaka in 1895 in Japan and his last just before his death in 1919. No other dealer served him so long.[12]

Bunkio Matsuki had been a Buddhist monk in his teens and lived in China before he arrived in Boston in 1888. Edward Morse, the Japanese pottery expert, took him under his wing. The twenty-nine-year-old responded with diligence; he learned English, earned a high school degree, joined Almy's department store, and returned to Japan in 1891 to import items for sale at the store. The next year Matsuki opened his own shop on Boylston Street, where Freer first called on him in July 1896. As the two men examined artworks together, they exchanged "lovely reminiscences about Japan." Freer bought a kakemono and some pottery. Even through the formality of his correspondence, Freer sounded genuinely grateful for the comfortable acquaintance of this new friend and expert. He commissioned Matsuki or his associate H. Shugio to buy paintings for him in Japan. Similar to the requests he had made of Keppel in the 1880s to find etchings of Dutch scenes by certain artists, he specified a marine, a landscape or river scene, and artists of the Ganku school. He wanted "something sketchily done and not too high in color," paintings like those by Bunrin he had seen in Japan, which "came so near in spirit to the work of Whistler." Whistler's art was his touchstone for beauty. By it, Freer first measured the merit of both American and Asian art.[13]

The Japanese art business in the 1890s was risky and expensive for dealers. An inventory had to be purchased and shipped from Japan with no assurance that sales would be profitable or immediate. Yet without an impressive inventory, sales were even less likely. Freer loaned money to trusted dealers enabling them to import quality goods. Private loans from him were customary; in a practice common among his wealthy peers, he provided an informal banking service. In the fall of 1898, Matsuki went to Japan armed with a $1,500 loan from Freer and returned with treasures, among them the second great masterpiece to enter the Freer collection, a large, four-fold screen by one of the most famous of Japanese painters, Maruyama Ōkyo, *Geese Over a Beach.* Selling it for $700, Matsuki boasted gleefully to Freer that "you can beat any Okio under the Sun in the land of rising Sun." He and Freer pooled their ideas, shared new information, and argued attributions for thirteen fruitful years.[14]

With growing confidence, Freer bought paintings by Kōrin, Kōetsu, and Sōtasu, artists not widely appreciated in Japan until after 1905. His early purchases of the works of the Rinpa School predated those of any other American collector. Some of the paintings were subtle and soft in tone; but often their bold decorative designs and vivid masses of color were the antithesis of his preference for "something sketchily done" and a far cry from his dictum "not too high in color." His purchases, stimulated by the writings of Gonse and Fenollosa and nurtured by Matsuki and Yamanaka, marked Freer's new sophistication in Japanese art. In his appreciation of the ancient Japanese spirit, he refuted Fenollosa's argument that "the pure Japanese element, if it exists, is a latter product…after the vitalizing contact with China." Freer was expanding his horizons beyond the influence of Whistler aesthetics. The Rinpa masterpieces remain a major asset to the Freer Gallery collection today, a prescient contribution by the confident pioneering collector.[15]

By the time Freer retired from business in 1899, Japanese art was more than a hobby for him; it was a collection. And he was doing it on his own. Fenollosa's writings on Asian art totaled barely 200 pages, yet they were the most comprehensive published in English. Freer tapped Edward Morse for validation on pottery by inviting the crusty Bostonian to spend a week in Detroit to examine his purchases of the last eight years. Morse, who was in the process of writing his compendium on Japanese pottery, declared the collection so valuable he promised to include Freer's name in his book. Three months later Freer inspected the Morse collection at the Museum of Fine Arts, Boston.[16]

Freer sought companions in art collecting who were not dealers nor associated with an institution, fellow travelers with whom he compared purchases and attributions as he had with Howard Mansfield in collecting prints. Charles J. Morse (not related to Edward), an enterprising bridge builder in Chicago and a sensible, discerning student of Japanese and Chinese art, became a trusted comrade. In 1897 they exchanged visits to examine each other's collections. Morse asked Freer's advice for his planned yearlong excursion to Japan. Freer supplied him with letters of introduction to his associates in Japan: his guide Nomura, Kita the dealer, and his servants Tora and Ko.[17]

The Chicagoan returned from Japan bursting with fresh impressions and information for Freer. With an engineer's thoroughness, he typed a detailed list of nearly 100 dealers, shopkeepers, and booksellers in Japan with comments on their services, their merchandise, and their reputations for rascality. He prepared an outline on the sculpture and painting of the Nara period, Japan's oldest period of Buddhist art, including the location and evaluation of many works of art and an index of the deities frequently represented in the works of that period. This was an invaluable source of information to collectors so bereft of written material. The two friends continued to share their ideas, reviewing publications and analyzing purchases, until Morse's death in 1911. Morse was one of the first to suggest that Freer establish a permanent home for his collection and advised him on what conditions to impose with his gift.

He also introduced Freer to the Chicago banker, scholar, artist, and art collector Frederick W. Gookin, who had accompanied him on his trip to Japan. At the Chicago Institute of Art, Gookin served as a special adviser to Clarence Buckingham, one of the earliest collectors of fine Japanese prints. Until Gookin arrived in Detroit with Morse in 1901, Freer's letters to him were formal and even cool. After examining artworks together with one day devoted entirely to screens, another to kakemonos, and a third to pottery, Freer assured him that "the latch string is always open," an invitation he reserved for special friends. Warmed by Gookin's informed appreciation of his most treasured objects and especially by his response to the Rinpa artists, Freer declared him one of "so few who really care for the art of Sōtasu and his followers." He called on Gookin's expertise on Asian art periodically over the next eighteen years, a sometimes-rocky association that lasted longer than any other scholar he engaged.[18]

Freer was at a personal crossroads. He had retired from business and had yet to establish a new direction for his life. A perpetual life of leisure at his villa on the Isle of Capri was not the answer. He had ceased buying European prints; two to three dozen paintings by American artists filled the walls of his home. His life had changed.

He now was a collector of Japanese and some Chinese art, but to what purpose? James McNeill Whistler had the solution.

Charles L. Freer

Capri, ca. 1901

2

Twilight: Early Spring

Dwight W. Tryon

3

The Piano

Thomas W. Dewing

James McNeill Whistler

ca. 1886

5

The Two Doorways

Etching. James McNeill Whistler

6

Harmony in Blue and Gold: The Little Blue Girl

James McNeill Whistler

Variations in Flesh Colour and Green - The Balcony

James McNeill Whistler

8

Raqqa ware jar

Syria, 11th – 12th century

9

Raku ware tea bowl

Style of Hon'ami Kōetsu. Japan, Edo period

Freer and his two rickshaw men

Japan, 1895

Fans and clouds over rocks and water (detail)

Screen. Hon'ami Kōetsu. Japan, Edo period

Mimosa tree, poppies and other summer flowers (detail)

Screen. Tawaraya Sōsetsu. Japan, Edo period

13

Landscape: mountains, stream and houses

Kakemono. Japan, Muromachi period

14

Bodhisattva

Wood lacquer sculpture. Japan, Kamakura period

Nymph of the Luo River (detail)

Handscroll. China, Southern Song dynasty

Crabapple and Gardenia (detail)

Handscroll. China, Yuan dynasty

Guan ware vase

China, Southern Song dynasty

18

Bodhisattva

Stone sculpture.

China, Tang dynasty

19

Ritual wine container

Bronze.

China, Zhou dynasty

Charles L. Freer

Photograph by Edward Steichen, ca. 1915

Courtesy of the George Eastman Museum

21

Charles L. Freer memorial

Kōetsu Temple. Japan, 1930

22

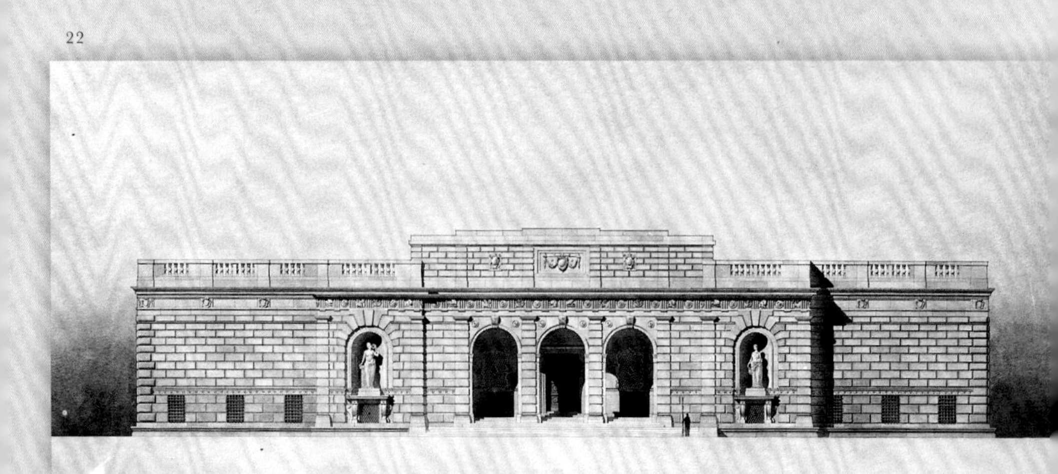

"Building for the Freer Collection"

Sketch by Charles A. Platt, ca. 1915

— 11 —

THE COLLECTION

1899–1904

ON HIS TRIP TO LONDON with Tom Jerome just months after he retired in 1899, Freer saw two oils recently painted by Whistler: *Rose and Brown: La Cigale* and *Rose and Gold: The Little Lady Sophie of Soho*. He asked to buy them. Whistler, ill with influenza, had retired to a spa near Dieppe, France. Surprisingly, he replied promptly, "They are yours of course—and I will tell you when we meet how glad I am that they go to the group you have of my distinguished work in your Gallery." Then he slyly suggested his new agenda:

> And now you must yield a point in proof of friendship and sympathy already proven!...I think I may tell you without the least chance of being misunderstood, this: I wish you to have a fine collection of Whistlers!!—perhaps The collection.[1]

"The collection" of Whistler art was an intriguing idea for the newly retired businessman as well as for the aging artist. Money, energy, and time, all now available to Freer, could be devoted to the master's art. Did the specter of the Medici hover in his mind? Might he too serve art as a patron of the gifted? As always, he moved cautiously. Wary of risk, he needed assurance that "in the event of Whistler's unlooked for death, nothing would occur to the paintings contrary to my interests." Whistler prodded him to buy *Nocturne Blue and Silver—Bognor* before returning to the States and whined, "You see the Englishmen have all sold...whatever paintings of mine they possessed!—turning over, under my very eyes, literally for thousands what they had gotten for odd pound!" The Bognor nocturne's modest size could find a place on Freer's walls, but he declined.[2]

In June 1900, still in the mode of a businessman relishing retirement, he wrote Whistler: "I am thinking of visiting Capri next September and of returning via Paris and London. Are you likely to be in either of those cities during the latter part of September or early October?" and added plaintively, "Shall the 'Little Blue Girl' be ready for her trip to this side by that time?" Freer devoted three days in Paris to visit its great Exposition Universelle and then met Whistler, for only the third time, in London. They spent five days together.[3]

The idea of becoming a patron by gathering *the* collection of Whistler art had been planted. He felt a sense of responsibility to protect the masterpieces of the man he acclaimed a genius and was competitive enough to realize he might leave an important legacy attached to his own modest name. Whatever the motivation, the seed germinated into a strategy for his "little group" that would encompass all aspects of the master's art.

Prices were rising for works by Whistler; owners were reluctant to part too early with their gems. Freer declined to buy a pair of marine paintings because he already had enough works of that size, but he offered them to Hecker and Bixby, warning that prices of Whistler's works had doubled in the last two years and were "likely to go much higher in the future." He enlisted Whistler's respected London dealer, William G. Marchant of Goupil Gallery, to take responsibility for packing and shipping and paperwork on purchases Freer made in England. When W. J. Rawlinson had demanded 2,000 pounds for a nocturne he owned, Marchant advised that the price was "above the market value if such a term may be applied to a picture by Mr. Whistler." Freer tightened his reins. He bought the Bognor nocturne he had refused a year earlier, but he did not raise his offer for the Rawlinson painting.[4]

The unpredictable Whistler postponed a dinner and canceled meetings, but he wrote pleading to paint Freer's portrait: "And do manage to stay that together we may manage something in the studio." Freer declined, complaining, "The weather here is hell." He returned home without delay. Instead, he wrote glowingly from Detroit that his new purchase, *Little Lady Sophie of Soho*, now hung in "supreme triumph" on his walls along with *The Balcony* and *La Cigale* oils, the Bognor and Portsmouth Harbour nocturnes, and a group of watercolors and pastels. "I am positive that I have never thanked you sufficiently for having placed her [*La Cigale*] in my care and I fear that I never can."[5]

Before sailing for home in 1900, he compiled a list of the owners of Whistler paintings, making notes on their personal backgrounds and interests as well as their artworks. Knowing the client and product had served him well selling freight cars. George McCullough was a Scotch-Australian who owned the Valparaiso nocturne. Mr. Douglas Freshfield, a mountain climber, owned *The Artist in His Studio*. Mr. G. P. Jacomb-Hood, an artist, owned *The Gold Scab*, the burlesque of the maligned patron Leyland as a grotesque peacock. Freer made briefer notes on Whistler's paintings already familiar to him: the Rawlinson's nocturne, W. C. Alexander's portraits of his daughters, Graham Robertson's *Portrait of Rosa Corder*, and Arthur H. Studd's *Little White Girl*.[6]

In 1901, Whistler again journeyed south in search of strength and health. Impishly he wrote Freer from the Corsican town of Ajaccio, "Happily you know, that it is not my way to seek my effects in the glories of others!—Still 'Napoleon and I'...enfin!" He complained of his inability to work, found the south freezing, and wished he had gone to Detroit with Freer. The real purpose of his letter, however, was to entreat Freer to participate in his newest project:

> And now it is time to think about the exhibition in Paris we talked over together. I should like then the pastel and the water colour figures—The Bognor—& The Lady Sophie—& La Cigale...Now I want much to make a beautiful show of the etchings—& if you can send me a choice set of your proofs of course it will be perfect...I shall write to Mrs. Gardner for some of her pictures—& pastels—and also to Mansfield.

Freer responded graciously to Whistler's suggestions, but the hard-headed Dutchman would not be harnessed to his cart. Firmly he stated that the Sophie and Cigale paintings could go to Paris in the spring, but the Bognor he would send to New York and then to Buffalo for the Pan-American Exhibition. The relationship between artist and collector remained guarded.[7]

Freer's assertiveness stemmed from conflicting interests. While he carried the banner for Whistler's art, in 1901 he had engaged Ernest Fenollosa, and his involvement in Asian art expanded. His new mentor matched Whistler in his aspirations. The failing artist, hoping to absorb all Freer's effort and money, pressed him for more time and insisted that on his next trip he spend three weeks in his London and Paris studios. Not ready to adhere to the artist's dogged demands, Freer responded politely, "It would give me much pleasure indeed to see you again, even if for an hour only."[8]

Onboard his steamer to Naples that summer, he discovered his favorite cousin, Jeanne DuBois, daughter of his mother's sister, en route to Paris to prepare lectures. Still rebounding from the failure of his efforts to create Detroit's Bicentennial memorial with his artist friends, he planned to relax at the Villa Castello on Capri and take a drive along the Amalfi coast before traveling in Europe. Bad news from home suddenly unsettled his plans: his sister Emma was seriously ill and partially paralyzed. Alarmed, Freer mused, "The disease seems to run most persistently in our family on my father's side." Without naming it, he noted that his "father and grandfather had died of it plus one or 2 others lives much affected." Two weeks later, he reported "good prospects of gaining use of her injured side." In another letter, he described "the disease" as a stroke. Stoically, he kept his plan to travel on to Germany.[9]

In Munich, he declared an international exhibition of modern art saved from "complete rottenness by Whistler, [John S.] Sargent and [Gari] Melchers," but valuable in showing us "to what depths of imbecility the great hord [sic] of modern painters have fallen." At the Royal Museum in Dresden, he was pleased to discover that their Japanese pottery was "away behind my little group" and was only partially identified.[10]

With neither the time nor the will for a long encounter with

Whistler, Freer agreed to meet him in Paris for a few days before he sailed home from Cherbourg, to which Whistler responded blithely:

> And you will put off your return...until we two shall have talked together at our ease, &, to our exceeding satisfaction, as becomes those of our distinction, for whom breathless words of greeting & parting should scarcely be mingled over the same shaking of hands!

Not to be bullied, Freer countered that even "breathless words... [are] still better than nothing." Whistler arrived in Paris in time for dinner late on July 28, and Freer's ship sailed home on July 31. The two men had known each other for slightly over ten years, but they had spent very little time together. Since their first afternoon in London in 1890, they had met in Paris for two weeks in 1894, for five days in London in 1900; now they had two days in Paris.[11]

Acknowledging and perhaps monitoring the collector's new interest in Asian art, Whistler accompanied him to the shops of his friends Siegfried Bing and Tadamasa Hayashi, the best dealers in Oriental art in Paris, whom Freer knew of from books and from Fenollosa, as well as from their impressive exhibits at the 1900 Paris Exposition Universelle. Freer also spent hours at Whistler's Paris studio. Scattered over the studio were paintings, some finished, some unfinished, many of them ten or twelve years in the making. Some of them he might have bought, but the temperamental Whistler would part with none of them, hinting maybe the following year he could have them. Freer's "Little Blue Girl" remained hidden. Whistler claimed that many of his smaller paintings had been "stolen from his studio" and had appeared for sale in Paris shops. He asked for Freer's help. The daunting task of locating Whistler's missing artworks formed another bond between artist and patron.[12]

Although reluctant to sell his studio paintings, Whistler prodded Freer to buy his artworks held by private owners. Writing after Freer had returned home, he insisted that John J. Cowan of Edinburgh was willing to sell and that he had pictures "you really ought to have." Recommending *The Thames in Ice* and a watercolor of Mrs. Whibley (Trixie's sister), he wrote, "They will cost money but I should be sorry to know they went anywhere else." In a rare tribute to Whistler's advice, Freer bought them both "sight unseen." Frankly, he found buying from private owners less trying than buying from Whistler. The Cowan pieces arrived in Detroit less than two months after purchase.[13]

The year 1901 was pivotal for Freer. He was on the cusp of a new purpose in his life. He ended his annual retreats to Capri. His health had strengthened considerably. His visits to German collections of Asian art had boosted his confidence in his Asian purchases. With a quickened competitive spirit, he was keen to work again, and he now had money. "Local financial conditions brighter," he wrote in typical understatement in April 1902. Indeed, his own financial condition brightened considerably thanks to the investment he had made in 1901. Freer's investment of $360,000 in the Parke-Davis pharmaceutical company would fund his activities and ambitions for the rest of his life. By 1914 it was valued at $3.2 million, almost 88% of his net assets, and paid $160,600 in annual dividends. With the means, the dealers, and two formidable mentors, he could reach for a new set of gold rings.[14]

He set his purpose and checked his caution. In 1902, he traveled directly to London on what he described as a "fishing expedition." With a new boldness, he netted Whistler artworks quickly and spent money with near abandon. He paid Mr. Rawlinson the 2,000 pounds he had demanded three years earlier for the *Nocturne: Blue and Silver, Battersea Reach.* At Agnew's Gallery he acquired another painting, *Blue and Silver: Trouville*, explaining to Hecker, "The picture is one of the most subtle I have ever seen, but while the price is outrageous I could not resist its purchase." He spent two months in England making an exhaustive survey of Whistler's art scattered among private collections.[15]

Whistler sensed the imminence of his own death. In 1900 after rejecting two other candidates, he made the painter-etcher Joseph Pennell and his wife Elizabeth custodians of his life's story by assisting them in gathering material for his biography. To protect his artistic legacy, he made Charles Freer his confidant on art matters. As his fame reached its apogee, fewer of his peers remained to see his glory and admit his triumph; many were dead, most he had estranged along the bitter road of his insults. Severed from his own family, he claimed the Birnie-Philip family and adopted Trixie's much younger sister, Miss Rosalind Birnie-Philip, as his ward, his legal heir, and executor. Another sister, Mrs. Charles Whibley, and their mother were his frequent companions. These were "the ladies" of whom Whistler was so protective and solicitous. They surrounded him and doted on him. Freer won their affection just as he had charmed Trixie.

By 1902, Freer had become part of Whistler's family. With a hint of pride, he confided to Hecker, "He is in great feather and insists upon painting my head before I leave. I have declined, but he says he must have his way this time." A month later he wrote that the portrait made him look "like a pope…but then that is all right for there will of course, be little of Freer in it. It will surely be all Whistler!!" With a touch of pride, Freer wrote in his usually cryptic diary that he stayed at Whistler's home "until 7:30 p.m. when Miss

Birnie-Philip sent me away."[16]

Traveling through England and Scotland, he examined important Whistler paintings and engaged with their owners, hoping to facilitate future negotiations. Lady Meux invited him to Waltham Cross. Mr. Edmund Davis invited him to see *At the Piano* and *Symphony in White #3*. Mr. Watney, current owner of the Leyland house, invited him to see the famous Peacock Room. He called on Mr. W. C. Alexander; the portrait of his daughter Cecily Freer declared one of "the three great portraits—His Mother, Miss Alexander and Carlyle." In Glasgow he contacted Mr. W. Burrell, "the former ship owner and old-time collector" and the current owner of *Princess of Porcelain*, the painting that had presided over the Peacock Room. Counting his tour a great success, he wrote, "No one ever had finer opportunities to study Mr. Whistler's work—and I shall have seen every important painting done by him."[17]

Between scouting trips Freer bought art. Soon after his arrival in London, he wired his partner to sell more Pressed Steel stock and send him 2,000 pounds, explaining, "I have neither lost my head, had my pocket picked, nor spent more than 450 pounds yet. I have kept sober too or perhaps I should say decently sober. But I have lost my heart…to some paintings by Whistler." He captured the H. S. Theobald collection of thirty-one works, ranging in size from 3" x 5" to 8" x 10," for the substantial price of 3,000 pounds and crowed, "undoubtedly the finest group of Whistler's small things in existence." He even pried a painting from Whistler's hands. The artist agreed to sell him *Purple and Gold: Phryne the Superb! Builder of Temples*, one of his recent treasured works exhibited at the International Society in 1901 and currently hanging at the Salon in Paris. Perhaps it was to serve temporarily as a surrogate for the "Little Blue Girl," for it is a painting of a nude figure similar in mood to the painting Freer had commissioned in 1892. Whistler was particularly protective of his *Phyrne* because critics sniped at its insignificant size (8" x 10"). To them Whistler retorted:

> Would she be more superb—more truly the Builder of Temples—had I painted her what is called lifesize [sic] by the foolish critics who always bring out their foot-rule? Is it a question of feet and inches when you look at her? [18]

By the end of his visit, Freer's drafts from home had run to 7,000 pounds ($34,000). Hecker continued to sell stock to cover him. Poetically Freer replied, "What I am picking up here is worth much more to me than Pressed Steel—a good name for my new findings would be pressed or compressed joy." He insisted that the purchases remain private to avoid "embarrassing questions…and then too, the assessors must be remembered."[19]

Whistler and Freer were frequent companions in 1902 on the streets of London, in the artist's home, and at Freer's hotel. They visited museums and galleries together. On the night that peace with the Boers in South Africa was announced, Freer's Carlton Hotel was the center of much English jubilation. "Whistler invited himself to dine with me…He cracked anti-English jokes, mixed up with good Burgundy and Gin slings till the lights went out." To escape the mobs of people and the "wilderness of senseless decorations and illuminations costing millions of pounds," rolled out for the coronation of Edward VII, they skipped out of London to tour Holland and then planned to leisurely make their way to Paris.[20]

Their plans, however, changed suddenly as Freer reported to Hecker from The Hague:

> Enroute Mr. Whistler was taken with a rather severe attack of heart weakness...The physician is the celebrated Dr. Coert who attended the Queen during her recent illness...Of course, I must stand by during the illness regardless of earlier plans, so in the future my movements will depend entirely upon his condition.

Nine days after the attack, Freer despaired. "His case has I fear become hopeless." Freer and the two sisters, Miss Birnie-Philip and Mrs. Whibley, nursed the artist, one of them with the patient at all times. Freer was soon worn and tired. His euphoric mood of the first two months ended with a depressing vigil.

> [T]he days...drag wearily onward...Mr. W. is brave as a lion and true to West Point principles:—he dreads not the gaunt figure with crossbones and skull lurking in the great trees of the Plein fronting our hotel.[21]

Witnessing Whistler's fine spirit during this illness, Freer railed at the public image of Whistler's character, calling it "a fabric of complete ignorance or misunderstanding. A gentler, nobler, purer soul never entered heaven if such a place exists." He justified Whistler's stinging satire as the weapon of a great man who "lacked not the power of self-defense when fighting barbarians." As Whistler awaited the "call of the Supreme Painter...He bears no ill will, he wants no praise, no crown!" The Whistler Freer described is hardly recognizable to the less devoted. Where is the butterfly who stung the baronet, the artist whose art included that of making enemies, the dandy who dared to "fling a pot of paint" at the London art world? Whistler had given his last commands and simple messages to "a very, very few people who still understand." Death hung close, but it did not come. Twenty-one days of "gloom and misery" were suddenly followed by a bright recovery.[22]

Freer prepared to leave. He had planned to meet the Capri artist Charles Coleman in Paris and travel with him through Moorish Spain for four weeks, then sail home after a few days on Capri. No longer in the mood for such adventure, he departed abruptly from Antwerp, Belgium. The traumatic month with a dying Whistler and his family had left him spent and wistful. He groped for words to express his experience: "The world is a curious shell, and I wonder of what is the real kernel?" Ever optimistic, he encouraged Whistler and "the ladies" to visit him in America as soon as Whistler was well enough. He suggested October as a pleasant month in Detroit.[23]

More tragedy awaited him at home. His sister Emma had suffered a setback, an aftermath of the stroke that had incapacitated her the previous year. His older brother George was seriously ill and died six months later. Freer's family was disintegrating. Richard had died of pneumonia shortly after opening his shoe store; and Watson, long since retired from business, now lived with his family in Kingston, constantly attended by nurses. Freer had given Watson and Anna the Maple Lane farm originally purchased for his brother Will, whose irresponsible lifestyle and attempts at horse breeding had lost thousands of Freer's dollars. He now dispensed financial assistance only surreptitiously through Will's daughter Ethel. Disappointed by the misfortunes of his siblings, he turned to the next generation and offered to put Richard's son through dental school, but the young man failed chemistry and dropped out of school. As his family shrank, Freer turned more insistently to art. His art collections became his progeny.

From America he monitored Whistler's recovery through an exchange of letters, many of them with Miss Birnie-Philip. He wrote enthusiastically of a fellow American whom he had first met at Whistler's studio the previous May:

> I met Mr. Canfield accidentally while in New York recently. He seemed happy to see me and is coming here as my guest—to spend a few days soon. He has bought Mr. Whistler's portrait called "Count Robert!"!! Good! I wish I could be equally lucky.

For the first time since the cooling of his friendship with Howard Mansfield, Freer had found a companion who shared his appreciation of Whistler's art. He had little connection with notable fellow collectors like George Vanderbilt, Mrs. Gardner, or Mrs. Palmer. Richard Canfield, however, became a friend, another maverick to whom Freer was attracted.[24]

The cultured and refined Canfield appreciated pottery and paintings; his business, however, was disreputable and illegal. Touted as "the greatest gambler in the world," he once served six months in a common jail. His well-known Club, a four-story brownstone at 4 East 44th Street in New York City, only a few doors from New York's famed Delmonico's restaurant, was "a combination of art gallery and temple of chance for authentic men-about-town and Pittsburgh millionaires." He also opened "palatial houses" in Newport, Rhode Island, and Saratoga, New York, during their seasons. A commanding figure, though quiet and reserved in public, Richard Canfield walked with authority, head back and chest forward; his 5' 8" frame carried 200 pounds. He acted decisively, judged people on the spot, and saw life in black and white.[25]

By 1902, his illegal gambling operation had become a public scandal. William Travers Jerome (no relation to Tom) launched a political campaign for district attorney in New York, promising to see "Dick Canfield behind bars." Canfield hated the limelight; he found the public furor distasteful as well as inconvenient. He escaped for a few months to Europe. In London he sat for a portrait by Whistler. Jerome won the election, and on December 1, 1902, with a squad of policemen, he smashed into the Club with axes. Canfield returned to New York to plead guilty and pay the $1,000 fine. Two weeks later he arrived in Detroit for a visit with Freer, and then retreated to Europe until the publicity died down. He was a frequent visitor in Whistler's home as well as at his studio, despite scandalized reactions from the artist's friends.[26]

Freer and Canfield shared a sporting spirit in collecting art and often pooled their efforts and their information. Each cheered the success of other. When he bid Canfield bon voyage after hosting him in late 1902, Freer encouraged his new friend to bring back more "treasures." They agreed the two great masterpieces still in private hands were the *Rosa Corder* and *Miss Cicely Alexander* paintings. Canfield wrote from England that buying the Alexander portrait seemed impossible; Freer urged him to try for the *Rosa*. Canfield acted quickly to snag it. When the owner, Graham Robertson, refused his offer of 1,000 pounds, he raised it to 2,000. Young Robertson accepted. "Damn fool!" Canfield commented later. "I would have offered five thousand and jumped at the chance of getting it for that." Freer sent enthusiastic congratulations, admitting without rancor that earlier he had offered $10,000, the equivalent of 2,000 pounds, for that same *Rosa* and had been rejected.[27]

Infected by Canfield's bold spirit, Freer authorized him to

negotiate a joint purchase: "If you think that the Piano, Symphony in White-Number three and Nocturne—Battersea Bridge could be obtained in one fell swoop, I am perfectly willing to join you in the effort." He had been negotiating for the first two paintings, with Marchant of Goupil and Thompson of Agnew's Gallery as his agents. He encouraged Canfield to work whatever channels he could, offering to pay as much as 3,000 pounds for *At the Piano* alone. When Canfield's efforts failed, he ceased his negotiations to give Freer free rein to bargain on his own.[28]

Freer returned to London in late June 1903 after spending time in Spain, Italy, and Paris. Whistler cabled Freer's hotel in London impatiently: "Are you there—expected your appearance by now." Now nearly sixty-nine years old, the artist's health was failing fast. His patron went directly to him and remained on call. Occasionally Whistler joined him for a carriage ride, but most of their time was confined to quiet hours at Whistler's home. Freer reported to Hecker:

> Poor old man!...confined to his home and sees only family and doctors...if I fail to appear he wires me come, and I go...It is pathetic to witness his illness, but ennobling to see his affection for his own beautiful art, in the midst of which he sits in an invalid chair and communes...he has made his own little world in which to die.[29]

On July 16, Freer took his friend for a drive through Hyde Park. They enjoyed an hour and a half together; the old man seemed remarkably stronger. The next morning Charles visited at the home of Mr. Alexander and joined Tom Way, Whistler's lithograph printer, for lunch before returning to Whistler's house. As he noted in his diary, "Whistler died at 3:35. I arrived at 3:40." He described the details to Hecker, stipulating "for your personal information," and concluding, "Need I say that in all things of perfect refinement of beauty the greatest masters are now all gone—at least all known masters."[30]

Charles served as one of the six pallbearers. "The ladies" honored him with responsibilities of the gravest importance, as he modestly confessed, "I have done what was required in my feeble way." The night of Whistler's death, he stayed at the Whistler home. "General Utility" (as he was dubbed by Whistler and the sisters) stood by Miss Rosalind Birnie-Philip, often keeping other intimates of the dead artist at arm's length. The Pennells described Freer as "wearing a rather professional air of grief," a jealous, unkind remark but probably accurate. He arranged for the funeral and for settling the estate, informing the Pennells and others only at the last minute. His butler-like efficiency and discretion dovetailed with his reading of Whistler's wishes and Miss Philip's own inclinations. He advised her but always deferred to her final decision.[31]

Charles Freer subsequently assumed the role of Miss Birnie-Philip's lieutenant in preserving and protecting Whistler's name in the world he had left behind. In America, and occasionally in Europe, he worked to enhance Whistler's reputation both as a man and as an artist. He influenced exhibitions of Whistler's art by granting or withholding his support. He encouraged the purchase of Whistler's works by American museums and assisted private citizens in adding Whistler's art to their collections. While preventing reproductions of the Whistler masterpieces he owned, he generously shared the originals wherever the audience might appreciate them. He cooperated with biographers who promised honor to the master; to other writers he turned a stony facade. And he completed his collection of Whistler's works.

The Freer collection of Whistler's art eventually became the largest repository of the artist's work in the world: *the* collection the artist had hoped for. Less than a month after Whistler's death, Freer captured the artist's prized *Rose and Silver: The Princess from the Land of Porcelain*. But when Obach & Co. offered to sell him the Peacock Room in which the "Princess" had hung, Freer responded by offering to buy only the shutters and the panel with two peacocks, admitting "the architectural design of the shelving and ceiling I have never liked." He asked for Miss Birnie-Philip's opinion. She replied immediately, "Will you please use those railroad bonds that you transferred to me and just buy the whole of the room… You must not refuse this, please, as I have too much at heart and am sure Mr. Whistler would have liked it too." Freer examined the dismantled room in London and purchased it in secret in May 1904. Avoiding the press, he allowed the *New York World* to speculate that it had been purchased by J. P. Morgan.[32]

His spending spree included *The Golden Caprice in Purple and Gold: The Golden Screen*, *Arrangement in Black: Portrait of F. R. Leyland*, *Nocturne in Blue and Gold—Valparaiso*, and *Nocturne: Cremorne Gardens*. In all he bought 61 oil paintings plus many pastels and watercolors. He failed to capture *At the Piano* but helped Frank Hecker secure the other early Whistler oil, *Harmony in Green and Rose: The Music Room*, which his partner eventually gave to the Freer collection. Some great paintings like *The Fur Jacket* and the portrait of Henry Irving he declined and instead encouraged other American buyers to take them. Freer had limits. He bought with an eye to protect his purse as much as to compose his collection. He selected fine representative specimens that together spanned Whistler's entire career.

He refused to monopolize the market, for he believed in giving the largest possible audience exposure to that artist's genius.

Just as important, in 1901 he had begun to work with Ernest Fenollosa, America's foremost expert in Asian art.

— 12 —

ART CONNOISSEUR
1901–1904

As Whistler had catalyzed Freer's energies toward a premier collection of his art, Ernest Fenollosa propelled Freer to a serious collection of ancient Far Eastern art, Chinese as well as Japanese. Spurred by those two mentors, Freer's purpose evolved beyond a collection of Whistler's art to a national art museum that connected Eastern and Western art.

Once again Charles Freer was attracted to a defiant, self-isolating man. Like Whistler, Fenollosa was a talented egoist caught between two cultures, an iconoclast who saw himself as better than most people around him. And like Whistler, he often left people in his wake amazed and offended. Much to his dismay, he commanded few disciples. In 1901, he was living in Japan in self-exile after his dismissal from the Boston museum, and he needed money. He sailed back to America to arrange a series of lecture tours.

In late February 1901, Fenollosa spent a week in Detroit as Freer's guest. The man was charming and modest one minute, presumptuous and overbearing the next, but Freer had long accommodated to the artistic temperament. After his visit the expert wrote Freer with opportunistic praise, "In your house one takes a perpetual bath in the True and Beautiful. Koyetsu [sic] and Whistler and Thayer and Rossetti are spiritual brothers," and pressed his new friend to arrange lucrative lecture engagements. Back in America in October, he wrote Freer rudely expressing his disappointment that his course on the history of Japanese art had not yet been scheduled in Detroit or Ann Arbor and reminding him, "I stand as the greatest discoverer and authority…I can assure to my audiences a unique treat." Patiently, Freer arranged three lectures. A mollified Fenollosa announced that Detroit had become his "second American home thanks to you and your friends."[1]

Fenollosa's knowledge of Japanese art, his command of the Japanese language, and his familiarity with Japan's private collections and temple storehouses were invaluable to the ambitious collector. In turn, the frenetic scholar/dealer realized that Freer was the most discerning and committed customer he was likely to find in America. The two forged a profitable association.

The scholar periodically appeared in Detroit to offer advice, to appraise shipments from other dealers, to pass judgment on the merits of an attribution, and to calculate an object's value to the collection. His visits ranged from a night or two to one or two weeks. Although granting Fenollosa the rare freedom to borrow objects from his collection and to photograph them as he chose, Freer set boundaries for his new adviser as he had with Whistler:

> It is extremely good of you to continue your intelligent interest in my group of Oriental paintings, and I trust you understand what great assistance you have rendered me in the work. I feel there is a

> fair hope of eventually making it fully equal, in an artistic way, to the Boston Museum's collection, but I do not care to have it so bulky. I am confident that quality should be the standard, and I know you agree with me in this.

On the matter of prices, Freer treated Fenollosa with the same delicacy he showed to Whistler. He didn't quibble over the amount asked; in his mind, his purchases compensated the dealer for his services as well as for the objects. Fenollosa once asked if he was "presuming too much in suggesting to send things of mine for sale." Then barely waiting for an answer, he shipped off another large crate of paintings and accompanied it with an eight-page typewritten letter describing the history and value of each in full. Freer bought the entire lot for $5,000.[2]

That shipment included a painting of remarkable value, the famous *Lohan Laundering*, one of the earliest dated scroll paintings now in the Freer Gallery of Art. Fenollosa claimed it was Chinese:

> The old Sung painting is one of the best of a set of Rakan [Lohan], which were brought to Japan by the Ashikaga Shogun early in the Fifteenth Century as genuine works of Ririomin [Li Lung-mien], the greatest Buddhist artist of the Dynasty.

In 1894, the indebted Daitoku-ji temple had sent 80 paintings for exhibition and possible sale in America and Europe. Fenollosa, who had exhibited half of them during his reign at the Boston Museum, was allowed to keep one for himself, the one he now offered to Freer. Assuring his client that it was "among the greatest treasures of old

Chinese painting that had come down to our time," he then elaborated on the characteristic Chinese technique "quite different from the Japanese, of putting a white body color under the silk...a practice that leaves figure portions so treated relatively unaffected by the slow darkening of the silk with age." Such instant education was hard to come by in books or even from other dealers. As it turned out, these paintings were later determined to be Japanese—but this only emphasizes how rudimentary was the information on Asian art available to Fenollosa and Freer.[3]

Fenollosa advised Freer on the New York auction sales and inspected new inventories for sale at the import shops. Although he was charged with the delicate responsibility of confirming whether a work was genuinely the work of the master to whom the dealer attributed it, he remained a welcome visitor in all the shops. A positive comment from him, after all, could raise the value of a single work and enhance the shop's reputation. Each work of art he judged by two criteria: its importance within the entire known body of the artist's work and its potential for making Freer's collection comprehensive. He assigned to each piece a number between one and 100 based on its relative merit. For these services Freer paid his travel expenses and usually "some other recognition as well."[4]

Sometimes the two men inspected important shipments in New York together, with Fenollosa rambling at length as if he were on the lecture platform; at other times he wrote lengthy reports. In March 1903, for instance, arriving in New York just after Freer had departed, Fenollosa went directly to Yamanaka's, where the postman had delivered Freer's "long clear letter" of instructions written from the train on his way back to Detroit. Fenollosa replied with his critique. A two-panel screen he rated not great but a "fine specimen" by an artist Freer already owned in such strength he should aim "at completeness in it." Of the ukiyo-e kakemonos (hanging scrolls) that Freer had liked and set aside, the expert stated flatly there were "several, which were either false, or by worthless pupils. Few of their attributions of name are correct." On the other hand, among those that Freer had not reserved, Fenollosa "found some very fine pieces, which, in your hasty examination, you had not time fully to criticize."[5]

Freer resisted Fenollosa's rivalry with his longtime dealers. Yamanaka's worldwide operation had access to objects from auction sales in both Europe and Japan, and Freer guarded his good relationship with the firm. When Matsuki arrived in 1903 with his shipment of "remarkable Chinese and Japanese paintings," Fenollosa provided "criticism and advice." Balancing Matsuki's abundance of fine things against Fenollosa's appraisal, Freer made his own decisions. One lovely Sōtasu screen of painted fans he declined because he had so many screens of that subject. He harbored his cash, especially after hearing the rumor that the Daitoku-ji might sell some of its treasures in 1904.[6]

Matsuki provided a significant number of genuine and accurately attributed articles. By 1904, Freer was spending $10,000 to $15,000 on each shipment from him. When sixteen paintings attributed to "Ririomin," (Li Lung-mien) arrived, Freer exclaimed that they "rank with the greatest masterpieces of all time" and hailed them as the "most important examples of Chinese paintings owned outside of the Orient." Although, like Fenollosa's Chinese "old Sung" painting from Daitoku-ji, the "Ririomins" today are attributed to the Japanese fifteenth-century artist Ryōzen, they are still a rare treasure.[7]

In the absence of scholarly literature or training, Freer had two assets: his own eye for quality and Fenollosa's commanding opinions. Conflicting opinions were increasingly common as more information on Oriental art came to light. Especially in Japan, young students of Japanese art challenged the conclusions drawn by older scholars. Fenollosa countered, staking his authority with a flair worthy of Whistler. He claimed insight that stretched back to the greatest age of Chinese art and ran in a continuous line from Song to Ming dynasties directly to him. He challenged his critics:

> A certain school of young Japanese of to-day however, who came too late to be trained by an unbroken line of feeling from the past...seem disposed to throwaway all keys of tradition...they assert that no T'ang masterpieces whatever exist.[8]

While Freer called him "the greatest living expert" on Oriental art (and Fenollosa quite agreed), the collector followed his own instincts. He purchased ukiyo-e paintings and asserted his own authority on works by Kōetsu. Debating with Matsuki whether the artist of a pair of screens was Kōetsu or Sōtasu, Freer argued that the date alone offered no proof and that

> young Sotasu was just clever enough to have worked upon screens far enough to excite admiration of Koyetsu, and then after filling the old man thoroughly full of sake, so as to get him at his strongest point of finish, he induced him to pronounce his benediction by powdering the clouds and contributing the superbly decorated sheets.

In the face of strong, conflicting opinions, Freer also declared that the two-fold screen *Coxcombs, Maize and Morning Glories* attributed to Sōtasu was in fact by Kōetsu. (Today the screen is attributed to the Rinpa School, artist unknown.) When Yamanaka announced they had secured a remarkable Kenzan screen for the Havemeyer collection, Freer confided to Fenollosa his view that the master was Kōetsu, not Kenzan. Freer, it seemed, had become the authority on Kōetsu paintings. In his compendium, *Epochs of Japanese and Chinese Art* (posthumously published in 1910), Fenollosa admitted:

> To rehabilitate the fame of Koetsu, as the founder of the school, and by far the greatest artist of Tokugawa days—in fact one of the greatest artists of any race—is one of my satisfactions in writing this book.

Typically, he credited Freer only obliquely with opening his own eyes to the painter's merit.[9]

They made a formidable team. The scholar gave his critical advice; the increasingly independent collector clarified his own opinions. Fenollosa tutored Freer in Chinese art, especially the art of the Song Dynasty, which he considered the high point in Chinese art history. He favored the Buddhist and Chinese traditions emulated by Japanese painters; Freer focused on the native folk traditions in ancient Japanese art. Freer's experience and knowledge now marked him as a connoisseur of Oriental art. His penchant for pottery, ukiyo-e paintings rather than prints, and the art of Kōetsu and Sōtasu set him apart from his contemporaries like Howard Mansfield, Charles Morse, Clarence Buckingham, Horace O. Havemeyer, Benjamin Altman, and J. P. Morgan.

Freer's purpose in life and his art collection were gelling. Impelled by Whistler's death in 1903, he was gathering *the* collection of the

American artist's works and contemplating a permanent museum to care for it. He was strengthening his collection of Asian art under the tutelage of Fenollosa, who wisely acknowledged that "[Whistler] stands forever at the meeting point of the two great continental streams: he is the nodule, the universalizer, the interpreter of East to West and West to East." His new focus was reinforced on his annual trips to Europe. In the shops and salons of Paris, Freer found a compatible group of connoisseurs who matched his curious mind and his passion.[10]

— 13 —

THE FRENCH CIRCLE

1900–1905

THE RARE BIRDS WHO APPRECIATED Asian antiquities flocked together, and eventually they all courted Charles Freer. His understanding of Asian art was first acknowledged by French amateurs in Paris, later by Japanese tea masters in Tokyo, and finally by Chinese mandarins in Shanghai and Peking. No other American collector received such international attention.

Paris was the art center of Europe and a gateway to Asian art. After Admiral Perry opened Japan to the West in 1864, European bazaars offered trinkets and pottery manufactured by the Japanese expressly to cater to Western taste. The cheap woodblock prints stuffed as filler in the packing crates enthralled French artists and dealers with their striking design. Early collectors like Edmond de Goncourt took a lively interest in the Japanese aesthetic and bought what a later generation described as "Goncourt's dainty toys." As they clamored for the contemporary ukiyo-e prints, those *japonists*, including Whistler, barely scratched the surface of Japanese art. Few understood what the Japanese considered fine art. Scarcity allowed little comparison, and paucity of knowledge hampered discrimination: "What Goncourt liked best the Japanese themselves regard as works of the decadence." By 1900, however, a small group of sophisticated dealers and collectors had moved beyond import ware and awakened to the hidden art of ancient Japan. These men welcomed Freer into their circle.[1]

Charles Gillot, a fiercely independent collector searched Japanese art for its "character, its dignity, nobleness and medieval power," and uncovered art the Japanese had created over a period of ten centuries. He collected some paintings, but he focused on sculpture, netsuke, and lacquer, including the boldly designed lacquer ware of the Rinpa School. "Every Japanese connoisseur in Paris is his disciple," claimed one of his peers.[2]

Without the services of two very keen dealers, however, Gillot would not have discovered ancient Japanese art, nor would Louis Gonse have written his seminal *L'Art Japonais.* Tadamasa Hayashi, an immigrant from Japan, and Siegfried Bing, an immigrant from Germany, guided an entire generation of French and a few Western collectors, including Charles Freer. From 1870 to 1900, the two men opened windows to the broad vista of Asian art.

Hayashi first came to Paris for its World's Fair in 1878. He dressed impeccably from spats to bowler, his round face expressionless and his round glasses covering discreet eyes; or when it suited the occasion, he dressed equally impeccably in layers of kimono with flowing sleeves, a pair of *geta* (wooden sandals) on his small feet, and a straw hat perched on his head. He installed partitions in his apartment so that buyers would neither meet nor would they see the objects offered to their fellows. To some he showed only Utamaro, to others he showed Toyokuni, but to all he offered primarily ukiyo-e prints. The serious amateurs who entered his apartment learned to distinguish works by master artists from copies by craftsmen. Gradually he gathered a small coterie of perceptive followers including Louis Gonse, Henri Vever, and Charles Gillot.[3]

Bing rivaled and aided Hayashi's ambitions. Unlike the gentle Hayashi, he was an engaging character. The courteous, charming man, "with inquiring eye, the shrewd smile, the fascinating ways," was the essence of an elegant, erudite Parisian. He spoke in classical French and typically held a pince-nez solemnly in one hand. His fascinating ways covered a need for caution, for he was a German Jew living in Paris during a period of anti-Semitism culminating in the Dreyfus Affair. When he hosted exquisite informal dinners in his home, he too might dress in a fine kimono.[4]

Bing opened his shop in 1871, and unlike the privacy offered by Hayashi, he encouraged open competition among his clients. Collectors and passersby flung open armoires, thumbed through portfolios, and reached for pieces of ceramic. A garret held the print collection where men elbowed each other as they sorted through the colorful sheets. After scouting for months in China and Japan in 1880, he expanded his shop and, like Hayashi, he built storage space for the antiquities while he educated his clientele to their value.[5]

Two influential collectors, Gaston Migeon and Raymond Koechlin, became Freer's close friends. They persuaded French museums to display Japanese art, and the French government to purchase Japanese art. Migeon, a handsome, ambitious librarian/curator at the Louvre, first discovered the beautiful potteries of Syria and Persia on a trip to Algeria. As he haunted the boutiques of Paris importers looking for Near Eastern faience, he uncovered the ceramic ware of China and Japan. Frustrated by the proliferation of bazaar wares, "ces pauvretes," as he called them, he turned to Bing and Hayashi, attended Bing's monthly dinners, and eagerly awaited their shipments from Japan.[6]

Raymond Koechlin, a tall, lean aristocrat with deep-set, kindly eyes and a shy, gentle manner, had a small but choice art collection typical of his peers: French impressionist paintings, French Gothic ivories, Persian miniatures, and Damascus plates. After attending an exhibition organized by Bing, he declared, "Ce fut le coup de foudre"—like a bolt of lightning; the beauty of Japanese prints had struck him. He went immediately to see the Gonse collection, bought his first prints from Hayashi, and prowled in the attic at Bing's shop. In writings and lectures, he spoke with passion and erudition of the significance of Oriental art. A legacy inherited at the death of his father in 1895 enabled the Frenchman, a widower since the death of his wife soon after their marriage, to retire as a journalist and devote himself to art and to museums.[7]

Men like Hayashi and Bing, Gillot and Gonse, Migeon and Koechlin blazed the trail in Europe to the appreciation of ancient Japanese art. A dramatic breakthrough for the French collectors and for Freer came with the Paris Exposition Universelle of 1900. In a large pavilion shaped like a Buddhist temple, Hayashi, commissioner general of the Japanese exhibits, installed artworks created over a period of fifteen centuries, masterpieces drawn from the collections of the imperial family, from daimyos, and from temples. Many of the objects had not been seen even by the Japanese people for centuries. Hayashi gave Europeans their first public glimpse of Japan's true artistic heritage. The display at the Trocadero awakened newcomer and connoisseur alike to the surprising range and beauty of Japanese art. After the 1900 Exposition, Paris exploded with dealers, collectors, artists, and critics devoted to Japanese art. Still, two years later, Koechlin decried the shallow understanding of Japanese art, claiming that no art was so little known or so much belittled by the general public.[8]

Freer had known of Bing by reputation at least as early as 1896, for he had accepted without reservation Mansfield's claim regarding three kakemonos: "All have been pronounced genuine by Fenollosa, I believe; at least the two Tanyus were by Fenollosa and Bing." In 1897, Freer bid on the Goncourt auction through Bing's agent in Chicago for his first piece of Korean pottery. In Paris in 1895 on his way to Asia, his attention had been absorbed by Whistler and other American artists; but in 1900, he devoted three of his five days in Paris to the "rush and roar" of the Exposition Universelle. Carried away by its array of Japanese art, he glimpsed new possibilities.[9]

The following year his focus on Asian art sharpened as he engaged with Fenollosa. During his sojourn to Europe that year, he made a study tour of the museums of Germany. German diplomats and merchants, from their bases and trading centers in North China, had long probed the art markets in both China and Japan. In the name of their emperor and with funds from their government, they had filled their public museums with Oriental treasures. After eighteen days in Germany, Freer was bursting with new confidence that his collection of pottery was superior to theirs.

In Paris in 1901, he and Whistler visited the shops of Bing and Hayashi. The venerable Hayashi had retired after the exposition, but Freer dined at Bing's home, saw the dealer twice more, and purchased from him kakemonos by Rinpa artists: Kenzan, Kōrin, and Sōtasu. In 1902, he bypassed Paris. Exhausted after nursing Whistler in Holland, he went directly home.[10]

By the spring of 1903, he was back in Paris. This time accompanied by his Capri artist friend Charles Coleman, he first spent a month in Spain. They studied the cultural remnants of Muslim rule and searched for pottery left centuries ago by Muslim artists. In Paris, to their surprise, they found on exhibition at the Louvre:

> [A] special collection of Spanish-Moresque, Persian, Arabic and Babylonian art—the great forerunners… It is said that every one of the finest specimens of the early pottery owned in Paris are shown in the exhibition.

Gaston Migeon had organized the exhibition of Near Eastern ceramics, the newest French fad. Freer knew of the collectors who had loaned to the exhibit: Baron de Rothschild, Gillot, Vever, Koechlin. The exhibition, he wrote, "offered us a great opportunity to continue our study and compare the various periods, mediums and wares." Prior to their arrival in Paris, he and Coleman had wired dealers to hold objects for their appraisal and purchase. The pottery of the Near East formed a new bond with the French connoisseurs and another link in the aesthetic chain connecting East and West.[11]

Pottery had long been Freer's favorite art form. He could caress its contours and relate its lustrous glazes to Whistler's subtle tones. Like prints, pottery was practical: portable and easily stored. He had befriended the local Detroit potter Mary Sutton Perry and incorporated her renowned Pewabic pottery tiles in his home. He studied her experiments with clay, firing, and glazes. Recently attracted to Islamic pottery because of its simple beauty, he was increasingly drawn to its technical and historic importance. Gradually, history and geography were claiming a priority along with beauty in his collecting.[12]

As late as 1900 only a smattering of pottery wares—Rhages from Persia, Raqqa (Racca in Freer's day, later Rakka) from Syria, and Fostat from Egypt—could be found hidden away in the Oriental curio shops of Paris. Freer engaged Dikran Kelekian, a crusty

Armenian dealer with shops in Paris and New York City. Although outwardly a grim-faced character, Kelekian was a benevolent man of simple manners and quiet serenity. His astute aesthetic judgment attracted a faithful following of collectors and contemporary artists who appreciated the beauty in the pottery that had served the daily use of wealthy Persians and Syrians eight to nine centuries earlier.[13]

Kelekian began shipping Persian pottery to Detroit in January 1903. A single bowl or plate of the caliber Freer demanded often cost as much as $1,000, an important commitment for the careful collector. Most of the finest pieces of ancient faience of Asia Minor still lay buried in the provinces closed off from the rest of the world. Raqqa pottery, characterized by a turquoise blue coloring and an iridescent glaze, and Rhages pottery, with human forms in a polychrome design, rarely came to market. When the area opened to European travel in 1904, Kelekian dispatched a man to buy more. He came back empty handed. A second agent finally discovered pieces for sale at a local fair and traced their source in the Circassian hills. Kelekian cooperated with Bing: "I let him buy the goods from the Turks and any piece I like I buy with reasonable profit."[14]

Freer's arrival in Paris in the spring of 1903 was fortuitous for buying Far Eastern art as well. Major collections were on the auction block. Hayashi offered his private collection, so large and so important that two auctions were held, in 1902 and 1903. Through Bing, Freer had successfully bid on kakemonos in the first sale and bought a six-fold screen by Sesson sight unseen. Gillot died in 1903 and within weeks, dealers and collectors came from all over the world for the sale of his collection. Freer joined the throng and spent 20,000 francs ($4,000). Bing accompanied him to Koechlin's charming 18th century home on Ile Saint-Louis. In another of the superlatives that pepper Freer's letters, he described Koechlin's collection as "the finest collection of Oriental art in Paris."[15]

Freer was in his element: acquiring beautiful things in the company of knowledgeable comrades. Acknowledging the value of the car business he had so eagerly escaped, he declared, "The intellectual life is, after all, the only one worthwhile, except that of an opposite nature which makes the real one possible—the means to the end."[16]

Back in Paris for a week in 1904, he again reported to Hecker in high spirits. He had been included in a dinner given by "The Friends of the Art of the Extreme Orient."

> The society includes Vever, Manzie, Bing, Koechlin, Migeon and all of the collectors of Oriental art residing in France…Before their deaths Whistler, Gillot and DeGoncourt [sic] were of their circle… The affair was most interesting and steps were then taken for the holding of an International Exhibition of Japanese Art to be held in Paris either next year or the year following. The idea is a pretty one—the collectors of Japanese art residing anywhere outside of Japan are to be invited to loan masterpieces. And eventually similar exhibitions will be held in England, Germany and America.[17]

At home Freer maintained his typical scrutiny on items sent by his French dealers. He canceled his bid on a Sōtasu painting when he "found the subject rather unpleasant." He questioned the authenticity of a painting attributed to Eitoku and shipped it back across the Atlantic. The Frenchmen acknowledged the expertise of their American peer. Even Bing, whose specialty was Japanese prints and pottery (he had written the chapter on pottery for the Gonse book), asked for Freer's analysis on pottery pieces from the Gillot collection. Freer replied with scholarly seriousness, referring in great detail to glaze, weight, and color, suggesting its source and promising to submit the specimens to the expert eye of E. S. Morse in Boston for confirmation.[18]

Shortly after Freer's visit in Paris the summer of 1904, the elderly Bing closed his shop. He dispatched his young assistant Marie Nordlinger to set up a shop in New York City and act as his sales agent in America. Before settling in New York, she called on Freer in Detroit and on his friend Charles Morse in Illinois. When Freer learned that her goal in Chicago was to sell Bing's superb collection of ukiyo-e prints, he wrote Morse, "I, too, am astonished at Mr. Bing's action in sending you his own private collection of prints." Equally astonished at the high prices, he surmised that the dealer, pressed for money, sold out of necessity. The young lady arrived in Detroit with three cases of Egyptian antiquities and potteries Bing had shipped. Freer admitted that he knew too little about Egyptian art and preferred to concentrate on Japanese, Chinese, and Central Asian art; he bought two pieces of Raqqa pottery. Bing responded, "I feel unable to express in proper terms how very grateful I am for the very cordial reception which Miss Nordlinger has enjoyed in your hands."[19]

Over the period of the next two years, twenty-eight-year-old Marie Nordlinger spent almost as much time working with Freer on cataloguing his collection as she did in New York. An aspiring painter/sculptor born in Manchester, England, she had trained as an artist in Paris and worked as an enamellist in Bing's L'art Nouveau shop. She had helped John Ruskin translate his work into French and helped Marcel Proust translate his writing into English.

An intriguing love triangle ensued: she fell in love with her cousin with whom she was boarding in Paris but discovered he was in love with Proust. Freer found her enchanting as well as competent and soon affectionately dubbed her "Miss N."

His summer shopping trips to Paris had become annual affairs. On the 1905 Atlantic crossing, Miss N. accompanied him. They stopped first in England to visit her family. In Paris, she served as his "interpreter, counselor and friend." Charles Morse came from Chicago and Charles Coleman arrived from Capri to meet them. Sadly, they found Bing in the hospital, where he died a short time later. Freer bought art with near abandon: "I hate to start in buying so extravagantly but the only thing to do is to buy when the very thing you are looking for turns up." He spent nearly $13,000 on pottery recently excavated in Central Asia, treasures he found "in hunting the several trails in Paris." He and Coleman searched in the shops of Dikran Kelekian and M. Kalebdjian, another specialist in Near Eastern wares. As usual, his Parisian friends welcomed him with open arms eager to discuss Islamic pottery and Persian miniatures as well as Chinese sculpture and Japanese paintings:

> Museum cases and private collections are everywhere thrown open to Mr. Morse and myself—seeing practically everything Oriental in this great center of Japanese, Chinese, and Central Asian appreciation. Migeon of Louvre, and Koechlin and Isaac of the Arts Decoratif are particularly kind.[20]

His French comrades had strength in numbers and the advantage of a national interest in Japanese art spanning over half a century. Yet their dependence on only the art imported to France and their competing interest in medieval and modern European art left dramatic voids in their collections of Asian art. Freer cherished the company of his extraordinary friends, but he sensed that he had nearly mined the field in Paris. For all their devotion to Asian art, Gonse, Gillot, Vever, Manzi, Comondo, and Koechlin had each gathered impressive collections without ever seeing Asia firsthand. None even ventured to America, except for Migeon.[21]

Migeon published *Chefs d'oeuvre d'Art Japonais* in 1905, the first major treatise on Japanese art, in which the ukiyo-e school played only a minor role. The art in his illustrations belonged to the most sophisticated French collections and to the collection of one American, Charles L. Freer. Finally in 1906, the Louvre Museum dispatched Gaston Migeon to Japan for three months of study and armed him with a modest purse to buy for them. He sailed to America first, where Freer planned the cities he should visit, provided him with letters of introduction to the most important American collectors, met him at portside on his arrival in New York, escorted him to Boston, and then hastened home to prepare for his friend's visit there. In Detroit Fenollosa joined them as they, with great ceremony, examined the Freer collection. Migeon recalled his stay in Freer's home as "une semaine inoubliable de longue causeries."[22]

Among his French peers, Freer stood alone in the scope and the strength of his Asian art collection. He was also unique in the legacy he envisioned. While they scattered their Oriental collections to auctions or into various museums, he had already secured institutional protection to keep his collection intact. Just after Whistler's death in 1903, he confided to William Burrell, who had sold him the *Rose and Silver: The Princess from the Land of Porcelain*. "I must tell you confidentially, that eventually it will go to the American National

Museum." He was increasing his spending on art with a purpose. Charles Freer had accepted from Whistler not only the challenge of forming *the* collection, but in the spirit of the Medici, he had also accepted the challenge of preserving it for posterity.[23]

— 14 —

GIFT TO THE NATION

1902–1906

FOR CENTURIES, EUROPEAN COUNTRIES HAD created national art museums as a matter of cultural heritage, but the young United States owned little art. Its government avoided an institutional responsibility for areas involving private judgment and taste. Not only art but also science, history, and technology relied on the private, not the public, sector for support. It took a visionary British scientist to create America's first national museum.

In 1829, the Englishman James Smithson bequeathed to the United States government $500,000 to found in Washington, D.C., "an establishment for the increase and diffusion of knowledge among men." Congress debated for seventeen years before finally accepting Smithson's gift. The nation's only so-called art collection, the National Cabinet of Curiosities, was housed in the Patent Office until 1846, when it was transferred to the custody of the new Smithsonian Institution. George P. Marsh donated his collection of etchings, engravings, and art books to the Smithsonian; but after a fire in 1865, artworks in the national collection were scattered and not brought together again until 1896, when talk of establishing a national art museum surfaced. It was all talk and no action. The Smithsonian Institution concentrated on science and natural history until Charles Freer made a singular proposal. He would donate to the Smithsonian the artworks "entrusted" to his care and create a museum to house them. In his mind, only the nation's capital and the aegis of the United States government would adequately honor and preserve the artwork of Whistler and the rare antiquities of Asia.[1]

His demand for a national arena was unique. His contemporaries passed their collections on to their heirs, exchanged their treasured objects for cash at the auction block, added to local museums, or built their own private museums. J.P. Morgan did all of the above when he died in 1913. The flamboyant Isabella Stewart Gardner opened her newly constructed home-museum in 1903 with elaborate fanfare to a select list of society guests. Built on the Fenway in Boston, it was as much a memorial to the owner as to the artists; her omnipresent personality and the décor competed with the remarkable works hanging on her walls. The coal industrialist Henry Clay Frick's home in New York City was not opened to the public as a museum until 1935, after his widow's death. William T. Walters, William W. Corcoran, and John Albright built public museums in their hometowns. Others like Benjamin Altman, H. O. Havemeyer, and Mrs. Potter Palmer strengthened their local public museums with munificent gifts.

Even in Europe, where cavernous state museums stood ready to accept gifts, the French intellectual Edmond de Goncourt spoke for many in the 19th century when he wrote:

> My wish is that my drawings, my prints, my curios, my books—in a word those things of art which have been the joy of my life—shall not be consigned to the cold tomb of a museum, and subjected to the stupid glance of the careless passer-by; but I require that they shall all be dispersed under the hammer of the auctioneer, so that the pleasure which the acquiring of each one of them has given me shall be given again, in each case, to some inheritor of my own taste.[2]

Freer had no family to entrust with the responsibility of his artworks. He had distanced himself from the Detroit Museum of Art, and since the debacle of the Bicentennial memorial, he was skeptical that the city would respond properly to his gift. Unlike Goncourt, Freer saw a purpose in his collection beyond the pleasure of acquiring. He had faith that the "careless passer-by" could be educated and uplifted by such beauty. His plan was bold, and typically he implemented it with deliberate control.

In mid-August 1902, after a month in Holland nursing the gravely ill Whistler, Freer returned to the United States energized by a new vision. He had spent hours at the bedside of the man he reverently called the Master. As they talked of *the* collection of Whistler's art and of a suitable permanent home for so great a treasure, Whistler likely suggested that a national rather than a local museum would be appropriate. Back in Detroit, relieved by the artist's recovery, Freer set to work. In September, he met President Theodore Roosevelt casually at the Detroit home of Senator Russell Alger, who had just replaced the late James McMillan. The following month Charles Moore, McMillan's administrative assistant, lectured at the Detroit Art Museum. He and Freer talked. Moore, a fellow Yondotegan, saw the potential for a Freer museum to add luster to McMillan's plan for the Mall in Washington, D.C.

Moore's agenda was to complete McMillan's beautification plan for the nation's capital, which included building the Federal Triangle, widening the major avenues, and constructing the Memorial Bridge to Arlington. The late senator had spearheaded the tunnel to Union Station that erased the train tracks cluttering the area of the future National Mall. After mailing Freer a book on the history of the Smithsonian Institution, Moore proposed a meeting in Washington to "discuss the matter." Freer declined to meet with Smithsonian Secretary Samuel P. Langley, cautiously deferring any commitment to a later date when his ideas were firmly developed. He was breaking new ground in seeking to establish a separate museum for his art collection under the umbrella of the Smithsonian.[3]

For the entrepreneurial maverick, a national art museum made sense. No other art gift of such scope had ever been offered to the American government, yet Freer had reason to be optimistic. Through Detroit friends, he had political connections in Washington, enough to give him confidence that his project might receive sympathetic attention. For nearly a year while Whistler was still alive, he made no overtures to the government or to the Smithsonian Institution. With Frank Hecker, he cemented his ties in Washington.[4]

Five days after his return from Whistler's funeral in July 1903, he requested a meeting with Charles Moore to discuss "the matter under consideration…you will be pleased to know that some progress is being made therein." Months later, he assured the owner of the *Princess of Porcelain* that it would go to the "American National Museum," yet the next day he wrote Richard Canfield that his collection might go to the Providence School of Design. Perhaps he toyed with a backup plan for Whistler's legacy, a joint effort with the gambler and fellow Whistlerite whose family home was in Providence.[5]

By March 1904, Freer felt sufficiently sure of his project to discuss it with Secretary Langley of the Smithsonian and its keeper of prints, A. J. Parsons. Senator Alger entertained Freer and Langley at his home to add the weight of his influence. Frank Hecker had the president's ear; he was recently appointed by Roosevelt to the Panama Canal Commission. In addition, for months Freer consulted his friends Charles Morse, Canfield, Dewing, Tryon, and Fenollosa.[6]

On January 3, 1905, Freer submitted his offer to the Smithsonian in writing and took the train to Washington the following week to discuss the details. He proposed to present to the United States after his death a collection of artworks that would "unite modern work with masterpieces of certain periods of high civilization, harmonious in spiritual and physical suggestion, having the power to broaden aesthetic culture and the grace to elevate the human mind." He would provide funds to construct a suitable building for the collection with the understanding that the government would maintain it in perpetuity. He outlined strict provisions to guarantee the integrity of his final collection, stipulating that no other artworks could be added to, exhibited with, or deleted from his collection after his death. He saw the collection he was creating as a unified whole, a work of art to be protected from tampering by others.[7]

Smithsonian officials received his proposal with courteous reservations. Secretary Langley objected to the exclusion of other artworks in the new building. Convinced that his restrictive condition was proper, Freer prepared for failure rather than compromise: "[T]he whole matter may hinge on it." Typically his positions were firm, taken after careful consideration. By threatening an immediate end to negotiations whether for railroad cars or art, Freer had often secured the deal. If he failed, so be it; he moved on.

Freer's offer was made public along with the Smithsonian's criticism of its terms. To Freer's surprise, the newspapers sided with him. *The New York Times* and the *New York Evening Post*, as well as papers in Boston, Washington, and Philadelphia, all ran articles in praise of his gift and in support of his restrictions. In fact, such restrictions were common among his contemporaries. Similar demands were made in the bequests of Gardner and Frick, and later Albert Barnes set even more onerous injunctions for his art collection.[8]

Before negotiations could be carried any further, a committee representing the United States government, the beneficiary of the gift, needed to examine the collection. Hoping that at least one member of the committee would be familiar with Asian art, Freer proposed two experts who happened to be his close associates: Charles Morse of Chicago and Ernest Fenollosa. He hoped in vain. The proposed committee consisted of Dr. James Angell, president of the University of Michigan; Senator John B. Henderson; Secretary Langley; Alexander Graham Bell; and Bell's daughter Marian. After postponing their visit once, the committee assembled in Detroit in late February 1905.

We can imagine the care with which Charles Freer set the scene. With over 2,000 objects of art, including painting, pottery, and sculpture to examine, he provided sufficient time and space to properly appreciate the beauty of each item. For some of the committee it was a painfully long four days. Henderson summed up his reaction: "[T]he things were all very well of their kind but damn their kind!" Prepared for such philistinism, Freer remained optimistic. He had reported to Hecker even before the committee's arrival:

> The leading newspapers of the country have treated the matter with unexpected liberality and breadth of vision…while of course the Committee are [sic] entirely incompetent to judge of the art value of the collection.

He surmised that the board of regents would be swayed in their final decision by the praise of the press. But he must have winced at the scrutiny; for him, just being in the public eye was distasteful.[9]

The committee recommended several changes to the terms of the gift, none of which Freer could accept. The regents postponed a decision, and Freer concluded simply, "I doubt very much if we can find a way to harmonize our different views; still a way out of it may occur." As long as they differed so completely on the conditions of the gift, Freer was in no rush for its approval. Some regents, he reported to Tom Jerome, "feel it wiser not to admit the fine arts into the Smithsonian collections; but, instead, to keep the Institution nailed firmly to matters of purely scientific interest." Others were concerned about assuming the cost of maintaining the museum in perpetuity, and some questioned the long delay in delivery—after the death of Freer, who was only fifty-one years old. All additions or deletions to his collection during his lifetime would remain at his discretion.[10]

Meanwhile, the patient donor expanded his home to accommodate his growing collections, adding a special building to house the Peacock Room as well as updated heating and fireproofing. Over the now-obsolete stables, his architect, Eyre, created a new gallery "like an informal living room" with skylights. In late April 1905, Freer closed his house for construction and left with Marie Nordlinger for an extended stay in Europe.[11]

As the summer of 1905 wore on and government officials procrastinated, Senator Alger approached President Roosevelt. Freer waited while months passed. Then politics conveniently played a role in promoting the value of the Asian connection. In August 1905, Roosevelt led negotiations to end the Russo-Japanese War, for which he was awarded the Nobel Peace Prize in 1906. By December, Freer boasted, "President Roosevelt has also taken a hand in the matter of securing my collection...has written me a personal invitation to visit him at the White House." To help matters along, Freer considered holding an exhibition from his collection in Washington, D.C., and asked Fenollosa to prepare a catalogue.[12]

On December 13, 1905, Roosevelt met with Freer in the White House and the following day arranged for him to meet with Chief Justice Melville Fuller, the chancellor of the Smithsonian Institution. After two days of discussions with the ranking Smithsonian officials, Freer composed a second letter revising his offer. Omitting all references to harmony, spirituality, and elevation of the human mind, he detailed the proposition in practical terms, itemizing the seven specific conditions he demanded in exchange for the gift of his collection and of $500,000 to construct a "suitable building." Money would be paid by his executors immediately after his death, and the new building would be connected to the National Museum (the original Smithsonian building) or "reasonably near thereto." He would have a voice in designing the interior of the building, which would provide space for the reconstruction of the Peacock Room and a place for students to engage in "uninterrupted study."

The collections, including additions Freer made during his lifetime, would be delivered after his death; and they, with the building, would be maintained in perpetuity by the Smithsonian at its own expense. He still insisted that no additions or deletions would be made after his death, that no other objects would be exhibited in the building, and that none of his works would be loaned for exhibition elsewhere. He stipulated that no fee would ever be charged for admission to the gallery and finally that the gallery would "always bear my name in some modest and appropriate form."[13]

Two weeks later, Roosevelt, perhaps with Asian politics in mind, published a letter to the trustees urging their acceptance of the Freer gift in the strongest terms. In it he noted that the collection, "said to be priceless," contained "hundreds of the most remarkable pictures by the best known old masters of China and Japan," many of which were of "greater worth and consequence" than the American art in the collection. Obviously, the "strange" Oriental art, unfamiliar to most of the examining committee, had been a stumbling block. With a subtle slap, the president suggested that perhaps experts in Asian art like Sturgis Bigelow or John La Farge should have been sent to Detroit, but assumed, a bit tongue in cheek, that at least the regents were familiar with the worth of Asian art. The conditions of the gift, he declared, "in my judgement are proper and reasonable." Leaving no doubt as to the firmness of his conviction, the president said it was "impossible to speak in too high terms of the munificence shown by Mr. Freer" and concluded with a threat that if the regents demurred on the issue:

> I shall then be obliged to take some other method of endeavoring to prevent the loss to the United States Government of one of the most valuable collections which any private individual has ever given to any people.

Freer considered Roosevelt thoroughly "bully" thereafter and praised the "broad and uplifting ideals of Lincoln and Roosevelt—two of the great businessmen the world has ever known." Less than a month later, the regents convened and accepted the gift on Freer's terms. Freer promptly commissioned the Detroit artist Gari Melchers to paint a portrait of Theodore Roosevelt, to hang in the future museum in honor of the man who had forced its acceptance.[14]

On May 5, 1906 Freer officially signed a deed of gift. He had succeeded not only in establishing a permanent home for his own collection; he had also committed the American government to support the arts. Although Freer protected the independence of his building and its collections, his gift pushed the government a step closer to accepting the idea of a National Gallery of Art.

His gift drew others in its wake. Two months after the formal acceptance of Freer's gift, the Supreme Court decreed that a national art gallery existed within the original Smithsonian Institution building, and a year later William T. Evans donated his collection of fifty American paintings. Freer commended his friend's action to "put his plans with the Smithsonian so quickly in definite form," and admitted, "Yes I had a talk with Mr. Evans before he made his splendid offering…keep the good movement marching strongly on." In 1910 the Smithsonian formally opened one of the large rooms in its building as an art gallery, but a National Gallery of Art in its own building waited until 1937 when the banker and industrialist Andrew Mellon made it a reality.[15]

Freer's future museum was now defined, but its contents were very much a work in progress. President Roosevelt had requested a formal list of the items he wished to present to the Smithsonian before the deed of gift was executed. Completing in three months what he had planned to play with for the rest of his life, he only half complained, "This shows what the man with the big club can do when he wields it." During the nearly four years of planning and negotiating for his museum, Freer had not only spent with near abandon adding to his Whistler collection, he had also strengthened his collection of other contemporary American painters and his Asian collection. His inventory of over 2,250 works listed 60 paintings by his American artist friends and nearly 1,000 works by Whistler; the remaining 1,200 were from the Near East, China, and Japan.[16]

With a future museum in mind, Freer scrutinized and reevaluated his Asian art collection. Working with Fenollosa, he ruthlessly eliminated works, most because of inferior quality or uncertain authenticity, but others to maintain a balance among the collections. The rejected pottery and paintings he returned to the original dealers for reimbursement at the original price. Others he saved for study and comparison, and still others he used for gifts. He returned paintings he had earlier attributed to his favorite Rinpa artists, Kōetsu and Sōtasu, as well as to the earlier fifteenth-century artists Sōami and Sesshū. He eliminated the ukiyo-e prints from his final inventory, admitting that he did not have preeminent strength in that field and sold them "not because they impressed me unfavorably, but solely for the reason that I deemed it wiser to replace them with specimens of ancient paintings." But he kept his superb collection of ukiyo-e paintings. The perfectionist planned to present to the nation the most perfect gift possible before he died.[17]

He also eliminated his modern European print collection from his future museum. When his old print dealers declined to acquire such a large number of prints, Freer kept the collection and willed many to the Library of Congress, excluding only the prints by Whistler and van's Gravesande.[18]

The Whistler prints would go to his future museum. He donated his 600 van's Gravesande prints, representing a nearly complete survey of that artist's work, to the Detroit Museum of Art, his gift to his adopted city. Detroit responded with respectful overtures to its newly famous citizen. The museum named Freer chairman of a purchasing committee in 1906, and he saw to it that the museum invested its money in works by Tryon and Dewing. Freer too mellowed in his attitude. "Detroit," he wrote, "is moving quite successfully along the right lines and promises some day to be a great city." When the museum decided to expand, however, Freer minced no words: "Our present Museum is notoriously false to its colors—shockingly disloyal as an Art Institution." He insisted they abandon the emphasis on what he called an "ethnological" institution and build a proper institution for art, including separate facilities for an art collection, for an arts-and-crafts school, and for exhibition of students' work. The city should pay for the land, the buildings, and the school's expenses. He consented to work on the building committee in hopes of implementing his ideas.[19]

During the years Freer was negotiating with the Smithsonian Institution, he bought thirty paintings by Dewing, Tryon, and Thayer, almost double the number of paintings he had so painstakingly commissioned from those artists the previous decade. He promised a place of honor for them in his permanent collection. With Whistler, they expressed the Western aesthetic to harmonize with his Eastern art.[20]

In the same effusive mood of earlier years, Freer wrote Tryon, "[your letter] brings, as usual, the spirit of beauty and charm which seem always so much a part of yourself and your surroundings at Dartmouth." He gave the artist's newest marine painting the usual glorious praise:

> Marvelously convincing, tremendously powerful, and extremely dignified. Nothing could be more truthful, and at the same time, so subtle...recalls the work of the great Masters of the early Kano school—Sesshu, Sesson and Masanobu.

Some of the paintings by Dewing and Thayer came to him in cancellation of debts. He had no trouble gathering over a dozen Dewing paintings to add to his collection, but as usual Thayer responded in his own time. He had already been working for several months on another monumental angel, a portrait of his youngest daughter. Freer waited patiently until he learned with alarm that Thayer had four canvases of the same angel painting. Worried that even when he secured his painting there would be three other angels floating around, he asked "Are they all of the same composition and size?" And, of course, they were. Thayer promised to consult with Freer on the disposal of the three practice canvases. *A Winged Figure* was not dated or signed until 1911.[21]

To strengthen his Western collections, he gradually added works by other American artists, a John Twachtman in 1903 and a Winslow Homer in 1908. A small painting by Albert Pinkham Ryder entitled *Evening Glow, The Old Red Cow* was shipped to him from New York along with a piece of Persian pottery for his inspection. Freer debated, as he wrote the dealer:

> You see, my experience with Persian pottery is much greater than that with the work of Rider [sic], hence my quick adoption of the bowl and my procrastination concerning the Rider [sic].

He eventually bought the painting, as well as three oil paintings by Whistler's famous rival, John Singer Sargent. All other additions to his American collection were painted by artists in the Dewing crowd, with one or two canvases each from George de Forest Brush, Childe Hassam, Gari Melchers, Willard Metcalf, John Francis Murphy, Charles Platt, and Joseph Lindon Smith. One glaring exclusion from his gift to the nation was the work of his hiking friend, F. S. Church. Although he continued to see his old bear-dodging companion occasionally and praised his work obliquely, describing his *The Mist of Stonehenge* as "filled with that misterious [sic] weirdness which you express so perfectly," he consigned his Church paintings to the reserve list. *Knowledge is Power* was given to the library in Grand Rapids, Michigan, Church's hometown.[22]

Perfecting his collection of Asian art had become more complicated. Fenollosa, for all his critical value to Freer, was a constant challenge, at one moment praising and the next criticizing the dealers Freer depended on. Boston still ostracized its former curator, and Freer's Chicago friend Charles Morse refused to deal with him. Freer and Morse carried on a quiet battle with Mansfield and Gookin, their erstwhile friends.

After the chaos of the Russo-Japanese War, Freer's dealers scoured Japan to pry loose treasures from distressed native collectors and often vied for the same item. Each attempted to secure Freer's commitment for himself by requesting large sums of money in advance to finance their efforts. Ushikubo of the Yamanaka firm wrote Freer about one of the famous portraits of *16 Arhats* (Buddha disciples who achieve nirvana), but Matsuki had already bought them for Freer. The Yamanaka firm lost again when another dealer purchased the famous *Waves at Matsushima* screens by Sōtasu from under its nose and sold them to Freer. But they secured the "marvelous painting of Monju on a Green Elephant," from a temple at Koyasan that Freer praised as "unquestionably the finest Buddhist painting I have ever seen outside of Japan. Nothing in Boston or Europe touches it."[23]

Freer questioned his old dealer Bunkio Matsuki's attributions and his fanciful tales of how and where he secured the works, but the astute Matsuki provided him with remarkable acquisitions during this period. Stopping in Detroit after a long sojourn in Japan, he created "in great mystery" a performance of unpacking seven cases of art objects. Freer waited for the dealer's effusions to subside before making his own assessment. First his eye caught three "extraordinary specimens of ancient pottery," and then a Shūbun painting, "finest ever seen" and better than the one owned by the Boston Museum, and finally two Song Dynasty kakemonos. He knew that Matsuki could stand "lots of 'clubbing'" on prices, but the dealer sold him a large Chinese lacquered screen, similar to ones he had seen in Europe, for half the European prices. Admitting that "the firmness with which he grasps the sides of his trousers and the swaggering manner in which he struts before his treasures scares me," the former accountant kept a ledger. When the dealer retired from the art business in 1908, Freer collected the $11,990.91 debt accrued over the past two years.[24]

In Paris with Bing and Hayashi gone, the supply of fine Asian art could not meet the increasing demand. Freer constantly feared his bids at auctions would prove ridiculously low. As a young man, he had refused to face off against the Vanderbilts and Goulds in railroading and sidestepped into building railroad cars. His solution to conflict and competition in the art market was the same: change course and seek new sources. To complete the grand collection he envisioned for his museum, he decided to seek antiquities for himself, to go to the countries where they originated and where, in many cases, they still lay buried or hidden.

Six months after signing the deed in Washington, he began four years of travel to the other half of the world in pursuit of ancient Asian art. He resigned from his remaining responsibilities in Detroit. He stepped down as president of the Detroit Archeological Society and from his only remaining directorship, the State Savings Bank. Now that his initial collection was owned by the United States government (he had "sold" it for $1), he capitalized on his affiliation with the Smithsonian Institution. He could route new shipments of art through Washington and the Smithsonian to avoid duty payment. (Not until the tariff law of 1909 were art objects more than 100 years old allowed to enter the United States duty free.) As long as Roosevelt was still president, Freer had letters of introduction to foreign representatives.[25]

The American capitalist returned to Asia, this time as an acknowledged connoisseur. With an institutional home secured for his collections, Freer sets his course to seek art in the remote lands of Asia. The study, the chase, and the negotiation it required were in his blood; great adventures lay ahead. In the Near and Far East, unknown art awaited his discovery.

PART THREE: ADVENTURES IN ART

— 15 —

PROBING THE NEAR EAST
1906–1909

FROM LATE 1906 TO EARLY 1911, Freer undertook long voyages to Egypt, Syria, Indonesia, Japan, or China. He explored city alleyways and remote caves; he visited ancient temples and elegant villas; he engaged servants and charmed connoisseurs. His mission was to learn, to discover, and to buy.

His affection for pottery took him first to the Near East, to which he returned three times during this period. Convinced by Fenollosa that the pottery of the ancient Persian empire had influenced Spanish and Italian ceramics and had possibly derived from Chinese pottery, he saw the Near East as a key link in the East/West aesthetic chain. Although the English Arts and Crafts movement had prompted a general interest in Near Eastern art, the field was untapped. Gaston Migeon's *Manuel d'art Musulman*, published in 1907, was the "first comprehensive handbook of Islamic art." In America, only the Boston and one or two other art museums owned objects from ancient Persia. Few besides Freer saw value in Near Eastern pottery.[1]

Setting off from Detroit in November 1906 on a six-month expedition that would take him around the world, he picked up his Yondotega comrade and Capri neighbor, Dr. Freddie Mann, in Naples and sailed beyond Europe for the first time since his grand tour in 1895. They landed in Alexandria, Egypt, and went directly to Cairo. He toured the most famous spots in order to observe the people and understand their culture. By boat, he plied the Nile River to Thebes and Luxor, then on to the Kalabsha temple and past Aswan. He relished exploring new territory; as he exalted to a friend, "There is nothing finer than being in the world and still out of it." The Parisian dealer Dikran Kelekian and his associate Maggiore met him on his return to Luxor and accompanied his party back to Cairo. There they joined forces with M. and Mme. Gaston Migeon, who were returning from Japan. Together they studied the old mosques, visited the Arab library and the museum in Cairo, and met "many intelligent" Arab, Syrian, and Egyptian collectors.[2]

At first, Freer focused his purchases on the Egyptian and Raqqa potteries, in his view, "the two earliest glazed potteries thus far exhumed in the world [and] the two most beautiful potteries in the world." Then in a burst of enthusiasm, he decided that for his collection to be complete, it must also include "stone and wood sculpture figures, unglazed, of certain Egyptian dynasties [of which he listed eleven]. I now feel these things are the greatest art in the world—greater than Greek, Chinese or Japanese." As his artistic horizon expanded, he exclaimed, "What Korin owes to Koyetsu and more, the Greeks owe to the Egyptians."[3]

After years of what he described as "weeding out and improving or devising ways of bettering my collection," he still struggled to define its structure. History and geography had become as important as beauty and harmony in his decisions on new purchases. He confided to Hecker, "Formerly, and correctly, my question had been what were the aesthetic qualities...always having in mind the very important consideration of harmony." Now he was convinced that to demonstrate a unity in the art of the East and the West, he must trace the threads of influence and outline the migration of aesthetic ideas. He searched for conclusive evidence in the objects, debated whether "Chinese wares had influenced those from Racca, Babylon and Sousa," or vice versa. Incredibly hardworking and thorough, Freer had a propelling need for accurate knowledge:

> It seemed to me that the question was too important to depend altogether upon the scanty ideas of others, for it was certain that a collection, such as mine would lose much of its interest to future scholars unless it was properly and as accurately as possible, classified.[4]

Ironically, his most important acquisition on that first visit to Egypt involved art only indirectly. Searching for old Egyptian potteries among the stock of the Cairo antiquarian Ali Arabi, he chanced upon a small group of manuscripts. "The beautiful writing first attracted my attention," he later wrote his St. Louis friend Bixby. Freer consulted the best Greek scholars in Egypt to attest to the age and authenticity of the manuscripts, and on their advice, he bought them.

It was a rare gamble in a field where he had no expertise or experience. The proud man hated to be duped. He considered Egyptian merchants "the worst gang of high and low scoundrels in the whole universe," and admitted that "lieing [sic] with Egyptian liars [is] making my hands and soul as dirty as theirs." The more he cogitated on the illustrious claims for the manuscripts' origin, the more he considered how foolish he would appear if they proved modern fakes. "Fearing that in my ignorance and credulity I might have been swindled," he rhetorically debated casting them overboard in the Red Sea as he left Egypt. On his return to America, he quietly submitted the pages to Professor Francis W. Kelsey, a Greek scholar at the University of Michigan and with relief learned that they were authentic and rare. The ancient texts are among the earliest extant copies of parts of the Bible. His eyes and judgment had not proved false. Named the Washington Manuscripts, the only part of Freer's collection that he formally published, he reproduced them in book form and proudly distributed gratis copies to "suitable institutions and scholars."[5]

A rare opportunity enabled him to extend his collection of Near Eastern art from pottery into painting. Col. H. B. Hanna had been trying for twenty years to find a buyer for his collection of Indo-Persian miniature paintings. Freer tracked him down in London, where it was for sale privately. "I fancy they represent an important link in the chain which connects the potteries of Syria, Persia, and Babylon, and the later art of China and Japan." It surpassed all his expectations, as he wrote Hecker, "It is doubtless <u>unique in the world</u>." Before making his bid, he checked with the experts, admitting, "I know nothing of the pecuniary value of Indo-Persian paintings." Within a month the entire collection and its relevant papers were his.[6]

On his second trip to Egypt in 1908, he went directly to Ali Arabi to extract from him information on the Biblical manuscripts.

> Old Arabi...is a marvelous scamp who calls me "of his family"...When he kisses my hand, crosses his

> breast and licks the ends of his fingers, I try to think of Allah and look serious. But the farce, the sickening coffee and the surrounding filth will give me bad dreams.

Freer loved the adventure. "Beats winning a big contract for cars quite out of sight."[7]

Frustration often matched success. At one point, he had in his hands "one of the great prizes of the whole world of pottery and another of bronze...owned by a wealthy Greek family [Sinando] and in the finest private collection in Egypt," but in "one hour they were practically mine, and the next hour millions would seemingly not be considered." The Greeks, he sighed, "beat the Japs as traders!" Experience was teaching him to work anonymously: "In early years I lost many good chances through lack of secrecy"[8]

Unlike other collectors who bought from dealers at home or ventured no farther than the bazaars of port cities, the intrepid Detroiter was often the first private citizen to venture into the foreign interiors. He undertook rough expeditions as a practical matter, keenly aware that as a new field was uncovered, competition increased and prices spiraled out of his range. Timing was crucial; his edge was that he was early to the source.[9]

After two profitable months in Egypt, he sailed to Syria, a remote area ripe for discovery and replete with challenges. The fastidious gentleman, accustomed to good service, intelligent company, and fine accommodations, adjusted remarkably well if sometimes grudgingly to the most unsavory conditions. He suffered stormy seas and poorly run ships, but he survived "by vigorous kicking" and managed to get "enough to eat, drink and...to keep about half clean." In early summer 1908, he wrote from Syria relishing his good timing:

> I am glad to be here now. Had I come sooner the beautiful in art would not have offset the filth and slime, morally and politically, in which I find myself. Had I come later certain opportunities to enrich my collection and increase my little store of esthetic information would have gone.

In only a week in Damascus, "this sweltering vortex of Arabs," he discovered how inaccurate the current information on Damascene potteries was. He also discovered in amazement examples of "stone cutting and carving of the best Greek period…Some heads, done 600 BC have fallen almost upon my head; and if the hellish Turkish officials, who are thicker and filthier than flies, do not confiscate my purchases and keep the Bakhshish as well," he promised he would return rich with treasures as well as information.[10]

With some trepidation, he moved into the interior of Syria to Aleppo, "that home of boils," where to his delight he found:

> [A] charming surprise—a beautiful ancient city, and in every way more attractive than I had fancied. It is the nearest city to Racca, an old-time caravan town filled with artistic treasure! The storehouse from which Kelekian, Kalebdjian and Noorian have drawn their supplies for years.

Freer claimed that only a half dozen Americans had preceded him there. Even the dealers feared the menacing boils (a painful skin infection), except for his Paris dealer, Tabbagh, "who was born here." Freer succeeded in contacting the "original discoverers of the arts of Racca," and purchased twenty pieces of pottery for the modest sum of 200 pounds, an investment which he proudly asserted would make his collection "absolutely the finest extant."[11]

In June he tried to get to the city of Racca, but millions of grasshoppers infesting the area between Aleppo and Racca had poisoned the water. His caravan could carry enough water for Freer and the soldiers, but it could not adequately supply the horses and camels. He would have to try another year and plan his next visit for March or October.

Another disappointment awaited him back in Damascus. Turkish officials had caught up with his treasures; they confiscated his boxes in Haifa and put the seller "behind the bars. It [was] his second offence!" Freer regretted his loss and the dealer's confinement but rationalized that they both had entered the bargain with their eyes open. He still had half his purchases secured and felt sure that the seller was "rich and clever enough to buy or fight his way out of jail." When advised that the American minister at Constantinople (now Istanbul) might appeal personally to the Sultan to release the goods, Freer declined. From the beginning, he had been uncertain of his own moral position in exporting art and would not risk disobeying "a foolish law, which is constantly transgressed." It might someday "reflect a shadow" upon his collection or the Smithsonian Institution, and he suspected that "the Orientals might sometime jump at the chance and make a great noise." His scruples, however, did not mute his outrage with the American government that, after its citizens risked fine and imprisonment to collect old pottery abroad, slapped a 60 percent duty on their imports.[12]

Turkish officials continued to annoy him in other ways as well. Secret coded cables flew regularly between Freer and Hecker, divulging little more than travel plans or requests for drafts of money, but the Turks refused to transmit them unless they were translated into a common language or signed by the American ambassador. And local officials shadowed him. When his ship left Syria and stopped at an old caravan port along the Turkish coast, Freer, the only white passenger aboard, disembarked to explore the town and found himself immediately tailed by a Turkish soldier. Together they covered the town, a few paces apart. In Constantinople he learned more disheartening news: the Turkish government not only made it difficult to export pottery, they now restricted new excavations.[13]

After his first trip to the Near East in 1906–1907, Freer had traveled east from Egypt to India and Japan (see Chapter 16). On this second trip in 1908, he traveled west from Egypt and Syria to Constantinople, Athens, Olympia, Corfu, Vienna, and Budapest. In Munich, he met Ernest Fenollosa for their last time together. In Paris with his old friends Raymond Koechlin and Gaston Migeon, he devoted hours to the collections at the Louvre on "closed days and early and late hours" when they could study and absorb in privacy.[14]

Sadly Fenollosa, who had been his mentor in Asian art for seven years, died suddenly in London that summer. Fortunately for Freer, his two years of extensive travel in the Near and Far East, as well as his association with Fenollosa and the French connoisseurs, had prepared him to pursue Asian art on his own.

He returned to Paris in May of 1909 to find his dealers armed with remarkable new shipments. Unrest during the Young Turk Revolution in July 1908, followed by the Ottoman counterrevolution in April 1909, had led to a dramatic influx of extraordinary Persian pottery and other objects of art. Freer capitalized on the opportunity and spent lavishly, more than $26,000 (nearly $700,000 today). Nine pieces of "ancient pottery," he claimed with his usual optimism, were of greater quality than any purchased recently by any of the French museums. He continued his treasure hunt in London, where he stumbled upon "the greatest collection ever exported from Persia...I have already bought 12 pieces finer than is owned in any Museum." In Berlin he inspected the famous Friedrich Sarre collection of Persian pottery five different times and quietly boasted, "The whole collection does not include a single specimen equal to anyone of at least eight of those recently bought by me in Paris and London, and in numbers my collection is easily three times larger."[15]

The competitive capitalist had indeed emerged as one of the world's major connoisseurs of Near Eastern pottery. From Europe he headed to the Near East for a third and last time. By 1909 his operation in Egypt included emissaries and agents who awaited his arrival. One had already secured half of a collection of Byzantine gold that once belonged to Emperor Theodosius (4th century AD). When the seller offered to buy the pieces back at twice the original price in order to sell the collection *en bloc*, Freer refused. The remaining gold pieces were eventually scattered into collections of J. P. Morgan, the Berlin Museum and others. With the purchase of "two great stone Hawks which would nobly defend my little group of Egyptian art when permanently housed" and a complete collection of Egyptian glass dating from approximately 1400 BC to 1400 AD, he concluded his mission in the Near East.[16]

In early 1910, Marcopoli and Company in Aleppo sold him pieces of "Racca" newly discovered in Syria, but after that his purchases in the Near Eastern field ceased. Competition and prices had caught up with him. Near Eastern art, especially pottery, had gained popularity among collectors. An exhibition of Muslim art held in Munich that year spread over fifty rooms. Objects were loaned from the imperial treasures of Russia, the Hapsburgs, and even from the Sultan's palaces in Constantinople, as well as from museums, private collectors, and art dealers all over Europe. Freer had already moved on to new territories.[17]

— 16 —

REVISITING JAPAN
1907

AFTER HIS FIRST TRIP TO Egypt in 1907, the perpetual student headed east to Japan in order to:

> [S]tep as rapidly as possible from Egyptian art, in its home, to Japanese art, in its home. This will enable me to compare under best conditions possible the best art of the two countries, and learn more accurately their differences, their qualities, their harmonies and discords. The stops on the way in Ceylon [Sri Lanka] and Java are to compare Buddhistic art which is the real middle ground, and is in a sense no interference.[1]

From Egypt, Freer sailed first to the island of Sri Lanka. The German steamer ship *Princess Alice* proved a happy choice. Kaiser Wilhem II's birthday fell during their voyage, and the crew put on a lavish display: a grand dinner, games, costume ball, and contests.

In Colombo, where as a tourist Freer had witnessed Christmas celebrations in 1894, he was now received as an honored guest, a prominent collector carrying the authority of the Smithsonian Institution. He joined 200 elegant guests at one of the grand events of colonial life, the St. Valentine's Day dinner and ball, held in a lovely palm garden where elaborate tables sat under the stars, Chinese lanterns and electric lights shimmered from trees and bushes, ladies gowns rustled, and "podians manipulating Bombay fans" mingled silently. He met Mr. John Still, the assistant archeological chief of the country, who arranged his week-long journey to the buried cities and Buddhist ruins from Sigiriya to Anuradhapura. In those remote "hellish places to reach," government facilities and personnel stood ready to serve and inform the eager student.[2]

As the spring monsoons approached, he departed Sri Lanka aboard the SS *Hamburg*. Nights on the ship were steaming hot. He managed to sleep on deck under a full moon until driven below by sudden winds and rain. After brief stops at the ports of Penang and Singapore, they docked at Jakarta. The port city held him only momentarily; quickly he found his way into the interior of Java.

A local preservation society of Dutchmen organized his visit to several ninth-century temples rarely seen by foreigners. Taking a Malay servant who spoke little English, Freer set off for Maos, Borobudur, Prambanan, and Mendut. His encounters with children and fishermen in the small villages charmed him, but his journey was challenging. Early one morning as his party attempted a difficult ascent to the Dieng Plateau on muddy roads, the ponies "gave out and balked" despite the brutal beating inflicted by their Chinese drivers. Sickened by the scene, Freer halted the party and instead took them to Djokjakarta, where Mount Merapi restored his spirit. "Beats Vesuvius and equals Fujiyama," he exclaimed in relief, and he proclaimed the sunset: "I think the most beautiful view of my life." Recovering his equanimity, he blamed the Dutchmen; there was much they either did not know or would not tell. He vowed to come again in a different season when dry roads would allow him to reach temples located above 9,000 feet, and when he could plan a few weeks in Thailand and Cambodia as well.[3]

The Dutch also failed miserably in arranging his departure from their colony. Freer had purchased a first-class passage on the Dutch Packet line from Jakarta to Singapore. He confidently marched on board and was escorted to:

> [A] cabin in the 2nd class containing five berths one for me the other four for fellow passangers [sic] of varied kind and color—not one white and all of uncertain sex—principally eunuchs, I guess…I got my money back rescued my luggage and walked the gang plank ashore.

The next ship did not depart for over a week. Blithely he spent that week "amidst the wonderful hills and jungles" of Java, where he happily claimed:

> The natives are charming, the landscapes the most beautiful I have ever seen the ground the most fertile, the gardens most fascinating, the homes the simplest, the people, excepting foreigners, the happiest and the temple ruins—well, they must be classed with the most important extant.[4]

Finally departing Java, he made brief stops in the Chinese port cities of Hong Kong, Canton (now Guangzhou), and Shanghai before landing in Japan. He had prepared well. Charles Morse, his Chicago friend, had provided a list of the best shopkeepers scattered throughout Japan. Fenollosa had given him letters of introduction and a twelve-page letter of advice on whom and what to see, how to gain access to the important private collections, and lists of dozens of temples with the specific artworks in each worthy of attention. Ushikubo of Yamanaka's in New York and Bunkio Matsuki of Boston had arranged to meet him in Japan.[5]

His ship landed at Kobe, where servants from his trip twelve years earlier awaited his bidding. A bevy of dealers also greeted the distinguished collector. His trusted guide Yozo Nomura, who had "grown very rich and is now prominent throughout Japan," had expected Freer to land at Yokohama, but within a few days, he too joined the group, who moved with the important American to Kyoto.[6]

Initially pleased by the reception given him by his "old-time Japanese friends," Freer became overwhelmed as dealers vied with each other to entertain and woo him. They whisked him from temple buildings to maple dances, to expositions, to a succession of curio shops and finally to dinners and evening entertainments. Staggered by the changes he witnessed in a Japan heady with prosperity after its recent victory over Russia, the sensitive American abhorred the huge warehouses, shipyards, and mammoth hotels that had replaced the little gardens and simple cottages of his earlier visit.

Worse, he became personally offended by an "incident which occurred there, was really very disappointing, and...other entertainment of embarrassing kinds, at Kobe and Kioto, disturbed me very much, in fact, quite sickened me of modern Japan." Such personal embarrassments he divulged to friends only orally, if at all. In writing he expressed valiant resistance to the assaults on his sensibilities: "The work I want to do must not be defeated even if at the cost of much personal disappointment and no little constraint of ideals."[7]

Faced with the problem of mollifying his offended client, the savvy Nomura, who had been educated in the United States, produced an urgent invitation from Tomitaro Hara, a wealthy school friend from his home province. Hara invited the American to his estate in Yokohama as his honored guest. Although suspecting that Nomura might have arranged the invitation, Freer chose to believe Hara's flattering tale of pursuit: "A prominent banker, manufacturer and collector…traced me from Shanghai, sent men to Nagasaki, where my ship did not stop, then to Kobe to meet and escort me." Leaving Kyoto immediately, he declared, "I care little about going back to dear old Kioto—the place is spoilt."[8]

Hara's estate embodied Freer's "old-time" vision of the finest in Japanese culture. Arriving after dark, his carriage wound through pine groves; "the entire roadway…along which I drove was lighted by coolies wearing white gowns and carrying huge white lanterns… as we passed, they closed in column behind the carriage and followed." At the top of a hill, Mr. and Mrs. Hara and their young daughter awaited their guest. For two glorious weeks, he remained at San-no-tani, their home, where the hills of the 200-acre estate, dotted with pine and bamboo forests, waterfalls, and ponds, overlooked Yokohama Bay. To this natural park over the next three decades, Hara imported ancient pagodas and villas from Kyoto, including a huge rambling daimyo castle built in late 1500 AD. Today, a large lotus pond replete with bridges and islands completes that private microcosm, now known as Sankei-en.[9]

Tomitaro Hara came from an old middle-class family, studied Chinese literature and poetry in Kyoto, and taught at a conservative women's college where he met and married the daughter of Zenzaburo Hara. Like his new father-in-law who had married the daughter of the richest man in Yokohama, he, too, took the name of Hara and was adopted into the Hara family. When the elder Hara died in 1899, the thirty-one-year old Tomitaro took over his silk business, expanded its market, and started his own silk farms. He added a bank, a hat company, and a linen company. He had begun to collect Japanese art in the late 1890s and welcomed aspiring artists to his estate.

In a man of ambition and vision so like his own, Freer found a true comrade. Hara poetically described their "keen interest which is only common to you & me, mysteriously born with the same bias & tendency of taste." He encouraged Freer to consider the guest house as his own home for as long as the American cared to stay and gave him unlimited access to the treasures in his go-down (art storehouse). Freer could come and go as he pleased; servants and horses awaited his call. He entertained his own guests, like fellow Yontodegan Charlie Swift and his family and Charles Morse and his party. Each day, treasures were brought from Hara's collection to Freer's guest house for his pleasure and study. He had the luxury of time to handle each piece and to make notes. Hara and members of his family or friends often joined him for the visual feast. Although Hara spoke little English and Freer no Japanese, they communicated in the language of art. Mr. Takahashi from the Yokohama Specie Bank served as curator and interpreter when necessary.[10]

That daily exposure to artworks, all previously unseen by Freer, gave him an invaluable education in the rhythm of Japanese artistic development, of the stream of schools and styles and of the foreign influences interacting and synthesizing with it. Each new collection Freer examined expanded his understanding. His knowledge had previously come from dealers whose biases were shaped by the objects they could acquire for sale, from the information and objects imported to France by Hayashi and Bing prior to 1900, and from Fenollosa whose assessment was molded by Kano traditions and scholarship circa 1880 and 1890. In Hara's Japan, Freer learned the native perspective on Japanese art history.

Relishing his new independence from dealers, he devoted his remaining two months in Japan to studying in museums, examining private collections in Tokyo, and then to exploring the temple art in Nara, Koyasan, and Kyoto. The perpetual student proclaimed: "I hope to learn much about certain forms of art work of which I know nothing," and two weeks later reported his progress: "The Household Department of the Government is opening up every temple, museum, palace collection in the country...Seeing the best and learning much." Hara also introduced him to the private world of the Japanese tea master–connoisseurs.[11]

The most influential of them was Baron Takashi Masuda. A generation older than Hara, he was an outspoken, pragmatic man who had chosen a modern business career over the government service expected of his samurai class. In his private life, however, he was traditional and conservative; he shared Freer's dismay at the Westernization of his country and the erosion of Japan's heritage. After their first meeting, the proud American wrote:

> I spent this afternoon with Mr. Masuda the richest collector of Japan and he invited a few other Japanese collectors to meet me...You should have heard their congratulatory remarks concerning the manner in which I bought the Ririomin Rakans [Arhats] from under "our feet" as they put it...they stand

> ready to make great sacrifice to get them back again. Fortunately for America, I could not return them even if I wanted—they are in the Smithsonian lot.

Baron Masuda ran Mitsui Trading Company, the largest corporation in Japan, and owned one of the finest art collections in the country. In 1896, he had initiated a large annual art exhibition and tea ceremony honoring a seventh-century Buddhist monk. In each of the many tea houses scattered across his vast estate, he stationed one of his businessmen/art collector/tea master friends to serve as hosts. Freer had entered the top echelon of Japanese connoisseurs.[12]

Art collecting in Japan was a dynamic vehicle for men rising in the business and political worlds. Japanese gentlemen at the higher levels of society gathered to study and to buy and sell art. They welcomed Freer, who contributed his expertise on the artists of the Momoyama period, the Rinpa School, and ancient Japanese pottery. He had collected the art of Kōetsu nearly a decade before he met Hara and Masuda. Intuitively he valued what appealed most to the Japanese connoisseurs. And they, in turn, recognized that their new friend, whose art collection was "owned" by the United States government, could help foster cultural and political relations between their two countries. They granted him privileges rarely accorded to a foreigner, but with rising ambivalence. He had already imported a number of their national treasures to America.[13]

Perhaps carried away by such heady acceptance, Freer cabled Hecker to wire $10,000 and wrote gleefully:

> [T]he doors of one of the temples here were thrown open to me and I was allowed to make selections from their treasures, but for spot cash only. I looked

> the collection through hastily and found besides much rubbish, enough good to make me risk the ten thousand...I realized the hazard to both my purse and reputation as a critic...which would naturally follow my going into such a game without an adviser like Prof. Fenollosa behind my back. However, I believed the game a big one and worth the risk of $10,000—Canfield's [gambling] games of old days were a hundred times safer.

He wired for $5,000 more and announced, "The spoils are mine." His diary comments are punctuated with exclamations: "exciting day" and "extraordinary morning" and then, ominously, "getting dangerous." He sensed something amiss. "Many suspicious things happened and the game is pretty clear now—Shocking !!!" Many of his purchases, he realized, were copies. He exposed the treachery of dealer and the priest. Demonstrating unusual equanimity, he wrote in his diary that the men had been "very rash and foolish—Extraordinary lies on all sides—but very exciting." Rather than despairing of his losses, Freer relished his detective work. When news of the fiasco spread, however, he spun it defensively to a Japanese acquaintance: "They utterly failed. I knew from the beginning, the whole situation and purchased only such things as I wished." In any case he did not pause to regret.[14]

In Japan, Freer was no rough adventurer. He embarked on an artistic expedition to the country's historic sites, armed with "heaps of Governmental letters directing all temples and museums...to exhibit to my satisfaction their art treasures." His entourage included Mr. and Mrs. Charles Morse; Miss Margaret Watson, a young woman who often accompanied the Chicagoans when they visited

Freer in Detroit; and Professor Grosse, the eminent German scholar who was spending three years in the Far East studying and collecting for the German government. Hara had planned to accompany them, but the new cocoons were coming in and the silk business demanded his attention. Instead he sent Freer a detailed list of fifteen places and the objects he must see. For three weeks the party inspected temples, shrines, museums, private collections, palaces, and castles as they moved slowly from Kyoto to Nara to Koyasan. At a respectful distance trailed the dealers.[15]

Opportunities for study were rich, but opportunities for making important purchases were poor. Accelerating demand for Japanese antiquities among Western collectors and the passion of wealthy Japanese for their nation's art were escalating prices. For instance, recently Masuda paid Count Inouye 35,000 yen for an important Buddhist painting that had been offered to Fenollosa in the 1880s for 200 yen. By 1915 a rare makemono (hand scroll) was offered for 353,000 yen. Furthermore, Masuda and Hara, both patriotic preservers of their native cultural heritage, objected to exportation of their national treasures to the West. Some collectors were willing and even eager to sell to the American, but many were not. Officials threw up unexpected roadblocks. As he urgently wrote Hecker for money because word had just come "today" that Kofuku-ji temple in Nara was selling a set of sixteen paintings, the sale suddenly evaporated. Freer adapted: "I am finding old-time paintings, sculpture and pots—practically none worth while can be bought, but that does not matter so long as I am allowed to see them."[16]

The Japanese frankly mystified Freer. As generously as he had been welcomed by private citizens and government officials, he was never sure of the ground he stood on. Entertainments and privileges were unexpectedly thrust upon him as frequently as doors were unexpectedly closed to him. He overcame insults only slowly; offers of extravagant hospitality he accepted warily. Life in Japan was not under his control. As he neared the end of his trip, he concluded: "The Japs are beyond my understanding—the more I see them the less I know them—high and low. The experiences of one day are no guide to the happenings of another."[17]

His experiences with the Japanese connoisseurs, however, left a powerful impact. "My old training in business taught me the value of time and how to use it, taught me self discipline too...I saw nearly all of the greatest Chinese and Japanese art in Japan—and saw it well too." He began to look beyond Japanese paintings and pottery to less competitive fields: Korean art and Japanese sculpture. His exposure to the rich splendor of the Chinese paintings in the tea masters' go-downs strengthened his interest in Chinese art. These new impressions, as he would say, he "digested by degrees."[18]

Unexpectedly, an important purchase in Asian art that year was captured by Frank Hecker from a man in Toledo, Ohio. Hecker wired Freer in Japan that the Horace N. Allen collection of ancient Korean pottery was for sale. After examining the catalogue of the collection and discovering that it contained many rare and even some unique pieces, Freer wired Hecker to buy it, suggesting that $5,000 would be a low price. Allen, the former American minister to Korea, had collected the pottery between 1896 and 1898 and guaranteed that every piece had come from the Korean Royal Tombs and that each was genuine Korai. Hecker wired that he had secured the 80 pieces for $3,000, and Freer applauded his business partner's "old-time habit of always getting rock bottom prices."[19]

He returned to an America in the throes of the economic Panic of 1907. The crisis spread from copper speculators to bankers to businesses. Investments halted, loans stalled, and money managers held their breath as stock prices fell over 30 percent. Freer's assets were tied up in stocks and bonds; as prices collapsed, he chose not to raise cash. He curtailed his art purchases. Early in 1908 he had to defer payment on the painting by Homer because his finances were so tight, a rare red mark in Freer's books. When J. P. Morgan and his Wall Street cronies ended the panic with an infusion of $25 million, the economy slowly stabilized, enabling the patient but persistent collector to continue his far-flung adventures.[20]

Freer limited his investments in Japanese paintings and pottery, but his keen interest in promoting the ancient art of Japan did not diminish. Before leaving Japan, he had proposed to Baron Masuda an ambitious project to increase interest in Asian art in America: "an Exhibition of first-class Japanese and Chinese art in New York... entirely without commercial influence." When Masuda arrived in the United States in October 1907, he invited Freer to act as chairman of the American Committee.[21]

At the first meeting of the committee in New York, Japan's new consul-general in New York announced that the leading gentlemen of Japan, in addition to sending fine examples of sculpture, bronze, paintings, and lacquer, stood ready to present to the city of New York "a pavilion in which to exhibit the treasures" and that the building would remain in New York as "a permanent mark of friendship." Always happiest behind the scenes, Freer consented to serve only as temporary chairman of the committee, but he worked tirelessly seeking sponsors to assure the project had a solid base. President Roosevelt agreed to serve on the Honorary Committee. Freer added prominent museum directors to the list, knowing they "would need the museums to house and secure the collection as it traveled to eight cities from Boston to St. Louis."[22]

Every other week Freer wrote Masuda apprising him of their

progress. Money became a problem when the museums in each city were unable to commit funds to cover the costs of insurance, handling, and lectures. Furthermore, providing space for the huge Japanese screens overwhelmed their personnel. The final blow fell in September 1908 with Fenollosa's sudden death. He was to prepare the catalogue and deliver the lectures. Freer was bereft not only of his mentor but also of his dream exhibition with his Japanese friends. Resigned and sadly disappointed, he admitted, "America lost her one great opportunity!" Like the Belle Isle Bicentennial memorial, another attempt at public service had failed. In response he retreated to the realm he could control, strengthening his private collection.[23]

In 1907 and 1908 Freer had focused on the arts of the Near East and Japan. The one culture most central to understanding Asian art lay between them: China. Through Matsuki and Yamanaka, Freer had purchased a smattering of Chinese art, and under Fenollosa's guidance, he had added to his collection of Chinese art. In Japan, he had studied a remarkable array of fine old Chinese paintings owned by the connoisseur/tea masters. Alert to the modest prices of ancient Chinese art, the entrepreneur saw opportunity. The connoisseur saw beauty and another East/West link. The adventurer saw a new field to explore. Freer set his sights on the Middle Kingdom.

— 17 —

PIONEER IN CHINA
1909–1911

In 1909 Charles Freer explored the urban edge of China's art frontier; the following year he led one of the first private expeditions to the interior of China. He was on his own, with neither mentors nor familiar dealers to guide him. For the next ten years, until his death in 1919, he gathered ancient Chinese art, progressing from the paintings and ceramics of the Tang, Song, and Yuan periods (618–1368) to the sculptures, ceramics, metalwork, and jade of the even earlier Han, Zhou, and the then legendary Shang dynasties (1046 BC to 200 AD). Only after his death did an expedition led by the Freer Gallery of Art in Anyang, China, confirm the existence of the Shang dynasty.

Freer set off for China hoping to disprove the widely held belief that paintings from the Tang and Song dynasties no longer existed in China. Most scholars assumed that the scroll paintings executed prior to the thirteenth century had long since disappeared, victims of mildew, white ants, and wars. Some ancient Chinese art had survived in Japan because as early as the seventh century, Japanese emissaries, priests, and artists had carried Chinese masterpieces back to their islands for study and inspiration. Hidden for centuries in the Japanese imperial warehouse Shosoin, rare Chinese paintings, ceramics, and sculptures passed through generations of priests and noblemen. Friederich Hirth, the author of the 1908 classic *Ancient History of China*, claimed that medieval Chinese art was available only in Japan.

Charles Freer not only defied common knowledge in his pursuit, he flew in the face of fashion. Most of his contemporaries in Europe and America favored an array of Chinese crafts and export ware: the pretty chinoiserie, lacquerware, sword guards, and netsukes. Like Whistler, some sought the colorful porcelain, especially the famous blue and white of the Ming and Qing dynasties (1368–1912). Freer had bucked the trend early, stating flatly in 1903 that he did not purchase porcelains and was only interested in fine early Chinese pottery. In 1909, the indomitable collector bent to a new purpose. He left Egypt for the last time to search in China for paintings, pottery, and sculptures from the Tang and Song periods. He took on a daunting task.

Prospectors for ancient art in China faced two challenges: Did the works still exist there, and if so, were they copies or originals? Literary records left by contemporaries of the earliest artists described remarkable paintings, but as Fenollosa wrote before he died in 1908, "We do not know whether any great T'ang masterpieces yet remain in Chinese collections; for an archeological exploration of China cannot even be said to have begun." Freer's Paris friend Koechlin warned in 1903 that imitations "have been produced in vast numbers since the XIIIth century BC—imitations so clever, indeed, as frequently to deceive the most practiced mandarin himself."[1]

Books on Chinese art were limited. Herbert A. Giles's *Introduction to the History of Chinese Pictorial Art* (1905) served as Freer's earliest bible. Laurence Binyon's introductory history, *Painting in the Far Eastern* (1908) followed, but not until 1910 did Fenollosa's widow finally issue his posthumous two-volume tome, *Epochs of Japanese and Chinese Art*. Of the three experts, only Giles had been to China. As late as 1910, Edouard Chavannes's book on his archeological mission to Longmen near the site of China's ancient capitals was not available in the United States; Freer had to request a copy from Bing's son in Paris. Freer's collection of Chinese art was still small. In his 1906 inventory of Chinese art, he listed no screens, only eighty pieces of pottery, and, of the thirty-six kakemonos, sixteen were Japanese paintings erroneously attributed to the Chinese artist Li Lung-mien.[2]

Charles Freer passed through China's ports first in 1907 on his way to Japan. In Hong Kong, he wandered through "native town," with Dr. E. A. Voretzsch, the German consul to China, visited temples in Canton (Guangzhou), wandered the old crooked streets of Shanghai with a guide, and wrote home: "In the old furniture shops and in certain bazaars, I bought Sung pottery of rare beauty, cheaper than I could buy copies in the foreign settlement." In his first glimpse of China's potential cache, he filled three shipping cases, including what he hopefully claimed were from the early dynasties, a "chow" [Zhou] bronze dog and a Han mirror. Fascinated by the natives who rode in carriages, traveled beyond their provincial homes, and mingled with apparent sophistication, he declared the Orient "is going first class." Alarmed that their economic enterprise would soon out-westernize the West, he added prophetically, "Let the Western world look out!"[3]

After examining the Masuda and Hara collections of ancient

Chinese paintings, Freer understood both the financial advantages and the artistic merits of turning his attention from Japanese art to Chinese art. He had seen enough on his brief visits in China's port cities to surmise that deeper penetration into the interior might reward him with undiscovered artworks. China would also provide a crucial link in the historical threads of his collections. As the forerunner of major artistic movements in Japanese and Korean art, it was at the center of the Far East, and its silk road was a vital connection to the arts of the Near East. He had hoped that Fenollosa would accompany him to China, but the scholar's death in 1908 left him to pursue his quest alone.

The hardy pioneer was not a foolhardy investor. His encounter with the fraudulent monks in Japan left him with a nasty reminder of dangers constantly presented by copies of old masters. From at least the Tang Dynasty to the present, the Chinese painter trained his hand, his eye, and his mind by studying and copying the work of an earlier master. More than just reproducing the visual image, he sought harmony with the spirit of the original master and attempted to imitate his "intention of the brush." Not until the Song Dynasty did painters traditionally sign their works. Freer's generation relied on analysis of style and subject matter for clues to authenticate the dynasty or the artist. The collector, especially the Western collector, faced constant risk without guarantee of reward.[4]

Braced by curiosity and the excitement of entering an uncharted field, Freer sailed from Egypt to China in 1909 and stayed for two months. Dr. Voretzsch read of Freer's imminent arrival in the Hong Kong newspaper and cabled him in Singapore an invitation to be his house guest. Freer accepted. The Voretzsch home, located just below the peak in Hong Kong, afforded him genial accommodations, a splendid view, and relief from the heat endured in the city below.

His host, a collector of Chinese art "of the right kind," applauded Freer's mission, sure that diligent search for art in China would lead to important discoveries. He arranged to have "men worth knowing from Canton and Hong Kong" call on Freer: "native experts and collectors as well as responsible dealers from whom I am already learning some of the facts which for so long I have wished." One taught him how the native experts tested Song pottery for "genuiness" and age.[5]

Two days later, Freer embarked for Shanghai, where Mr. D. Pecorini greeted him at the dock. The Italian official and his American wife were friends of Charles Coleman, and Freer's Capri friend had advised them of his arrival. To his delight Freer discovered that Pecorini was "an ardent collector of Chinese art, knows everybody worth knowing in Shanghai, has some office in the Chinese Customs under Sir Robt. Hart, and his wife is a devoted Whistlerite." Freer, however, had to refuse their offer of hospitality in "hot, sticky 'typhoonish'" Shanghai, for the only boat scheduled to Peking (now Beijing) for a week sailed that very day. He promised to spend time with them on his return; obviously with an interest in Chinese and Whistler's art, they were people, in his words, "worth while."[6]

His ship maneuvered up the Hai Ho river to Tientsin, where Freer secured the services of a loyal corps of servants, as he did wherever he went throughout the world. When Edgar Worch, the respected Paris dealer, suddenly became ill and had to return home, Freer engaged his guide, Nan Ming-yuen, exalting, "I have never known his equal in ancient things Chinese—in fact, in Chinese art he is fully Fenollosa's equal in Japanese art." Together they settled in Peking.[7]

Before leaving America, Freer had purchased from Bunkio Matsuki and from Worch sculptures purportedly extracted from central and western China. Nan soon put Freer in touch with the men who were excavating those early stone carvings. As the men arrived from the provinces of Shanxi and Henan with their loot of ancient stone and bronze, Freer bought directly from them. Diligently tracking down rare specimens hidden away in private collections, he soon discovered paintings he was sure dated from the Tang and Song periods, artworks that the experts claimed no longer existed.[8]

To protect his operation, he rented:

> [A] couple of rooms in the Tartar City where the natives think I am a buyer for some American Auction house. I allow no one with things to sell to see me in my hotel, excepting two or three reliable Americans, to learn my plans or the location of our claims. It beats California in '49!

Determined to divert suspicious competitors from guessing the real objects of his search, he bought entire lots of paintings, kept the pieces he valued, and quietly gave away "the worthless stuff." He cabled Hecker to send 2,000 pounds sterling, reporting that in one week, with appropriate secrecy and stealth, he had found in most unexpected places "more than twenty superb pictures…and by very famous artists." All of them he claimed were from the Tang and Song dynasties, secured for less than 10 percent of what he would have paid elsewhere. The old salesman was in his element. His precautions and his adventures played like a drama. He refused to deal through the International Bank for fear some Westerner might discover his activities and spoil his game. He could not imagine that anyone, at least anyone with sense and intelligence, could be in the heart of Peking and not be alive to the rich storehouse of art lying dormant in or near that city.[9]

While he huddled with his native dealers in Tartar City, his two faithful scouts, Ho and Pam, scoured the interior provinces for artworks that might interest him and reported weekly on their efforts. So involved was he in his transactions that he took only an occasional break to visit a temple, to see the Summer Palace, and to travel through the Nan-k'ou Pass to the Great Wall and to the Ming Tombs. These trips he made without the cautious Nan, who refused to leave Peking.[10]

To his surprise, private Chinese collections were opened to him as "freely as in Europe or America," including the one most famous in all of China, the collection of Viceroy Duanfang. Freer declared him "in many respects the keenest and ablest collector I have ever met," and his collection, "the best I have ever seen." As the governor of various provinces, the viceroy had direct access to excavations; and importantly for Freer, he was a scholar in the finest Chinese tradition, one who could decipher inscriptions on bronze vessels. The enlightened official, who had traveled in the West and was committed to modern education, was brutally beheaded during an army mutiny in 1911. Over the next decade Freer negotiated for parts of the Duanfang collection as increasing political turmoil forced his family to raise cash.[11]

Cagey about arousing curiosity and causing the prices to spike, in 1909 Freer halted his operation after four and a half weeks in Peking and made plans to return quietly a year hence, cautioning Hecker to keep his news "confined to an extremely select circle of our most intimate friends." He admitted, "I have worked night and day and have employed over a dozen men in the siege, and, now I feel that...the field will have been fully ploughed for this year." He had bought over 60 paintings.[12]

Declaring Peking "the greatest art storehouse I have ever struck," he packed and shipped eight cases of treasures and announced, "One needs a whole year to see the most interesting features of this great country." The scouts arrived from the interior with such an array of fine things that Freer and Nan filled a ninth case; and then on the morning of his departure, a man returned from Honan "bringing two marvelous bronzes which I must carry in my trunk to Shanghai." There seemed to be no end to the cascade of Chinese art Freer had loosened. With some smugness he concluded, "I have made important additions here which will bring my Chinese department on a level with the Japanese and Persian...Such things have never been seen before in America or Europe."[13]

In mid-October, the explorer braved 800 miles by train to the ancient southern capital Hangchow. Then by steamer he coasted another 600 miles along Poyang Lake, up the Yangtze River to Nanking, before he finally made his promised return to Shanghai. Pecorini again met him at the dock. After his usual rounds searching in all the furniture stores and visiting important private collections, including that of the coal and shipping merchant A. W. Bahr, he inspected goods held for him by the native art dealers. Each evening he dined with the Pecorinis and recounted his day's exploits.

Charles Freer was now America's foremost expert on Asian art. He carried with him the spirit of his late mentor Fenollosa much as he had earlier held close the spirit of Whistler. Before leaving Asia in 1909, he returned to Japan to participate in the memorial ceremony for the American scholar at the Mii-dera temple overlooking Lake Biwa in Japan, where Fenollosa's ashes had been interred. The *Detroit Free Press*, undoubtedly at Freer's behest, printed an elaborate description of the Buddhist service and tea ceremony complete with photographs. Invigorated by his experience in China, he returned to Detroit to reexamine his collection and correct some of his earlier attributions. Staking his reputation as much on the accuracy of his knowledge as on the specimens he purchased, the proud connoisseur was determined "that no future expert in examining the catalogue [of his collection] can drive a horse and cart through it."[14]

From Detroit, he worked his lines in China until he could return to the field. He wrote A. W. Bahr in Shanghai, expressing an interest in certain parts of his collection. Voretzsch, his Hong Kong host, bought paintings hoping to sell them to Freer. To news that a collection of Chinese pottery was for sale, one he had seen in Hong Kong and remembered as "exceeding in beauty and excellence any other group I have ever seen," he responded that the price of $600,000 gold was out of his range. Competition was increasing. European diplomats and businessmen were buying in his field. Aggressive Japanese dealers and the German scholars "are in the very heart of our pasture," he advised Charles Walcott at the Smithsonian. Ancient sculptures unguarded in the caves and temples of China lay vulnerable to profitable export. Since 1907, early stone sculptures had trickled out of China, "a half a dozen or so to Europe and a small but very interesting group of sculptures now at Boston." Nan Ming-yuen worked on behalf of his absent "dear Master." Many of the overtures Freer made while he was in China came to fruition only after months of subtle negotiations and years of patient waiting. When the owner of one temple he and Nan had visited in 1909 finally decided months later to sell a stone image, the battle was only half won. Discussions continued with "the village-men" who did not want to lose their treasure.[15]

Freer contended with his own nagging ethical problems. He knew many of the objects offered to him had been plundered by bandits. In purchasing the goods gained by unscrupulous means, was he simply abetting piracy, or was he nobly aiding preservation? Should he grab whatever he could find, then justify his actions by the care the treasures would receive under his guardianship and by the education they would afford to the thousands of Americans? Or should he righteously assist the Chinese government efforts to halt the loss of its artistic heritage? Freer chose both paths at different times in his life. For now, he and his agents combed China to gather what they could under the auspices of the Freer Collection and the Smithsonian Institution. By 1910 the savvy collector owned more than thirty stone sculptures.

Freer returned to China in the fall of 1910 convinced that the country's interior held great treasures of art. Determined to see its hidden riches of antiquity for himself, he planned an expedition to the ancient cities of Kaifeng, Luoyang, and Sian (now Xi'an)—a daunting and risky project. Hamilton Butler of the American Consular Service advised him that none of the three cities had foreign "hostelries," but Western missionaries were active in all three, so he would not be utterly isolated. He warned that the 200-mile trip from Luoyang to Sian could be maneuvered only by cart or pack train because the planned railroad had yet to be constructed. Freer would be on his own. He knew only vaguely what to expect, but he clearly knew his purpose: to study "sculpture, painting, pottery and allied arts of the Han, Sui, Tang and Song dynasties in power from 200 BC to the thirteenth century."[16]

On August 16, 1910, he sailed from San Francisco Bay, landing at Yokohama on September 2. After spending the first night with the Hara family at San no tani, he met his old guide Nomura in Tokyo and renewed his friendships with the Japanese connoisseurs. He stopped at the curio shop of Baron Masuda's brother and made the rounds to other art shops with his Yamanaka agents, Ushikubo and Kita. He had allowed only a week to canvas the Japanese art market and to quiz his Japanese friends on recent developments in China.

In Shanghai, his fame had preceded him. Chinese and Westerners awaited him with great expectations; their pottery and paintings were set aside for his inspection. John C. Ferguson, an American missionary, educator, and recently an art "expert" who had lived in China for almost twenty years, introduced him to private collectors. In Peking, with Nan at his side, he reassembled his old organization, the same entourage of scouts, dealers, and experts, the same rickshaw coolie, and the same little house in Tartar City.[17]

For his proposed journey to the interior, he needed official sanction and support. Fortunately, the new American ambassador to China, William J. Calhoun, a Chicago railroad lawyer, and his wife were interested in art and even somewhat knowledgeable. When Secretary of War J. M. Dickinson and his wife arrived, Freer's name was added to the list of distinguished guests invited to receptions, dinners, and special tours, including one to the Imperial Winter Palace. These official obligations, which the reticent collector usually dreaded, were a practical pleasure enabling him to meet foreign ambassadors and important Chinese officials, many of whom offered him their assistance in arranging his expedition. All, he noted with satisfaction, were "the people here best worth knowing."[18]

Such deference paid to a private citizen created curiosity within the diplomatic community. Rumors spread about his extensive investment in artworks in 1909 and about his impending trip inland. Speculating that "they think me either a saint or a fool and I fancy they are trying to learn which," Freer fostered the secrecy he loved, giving none of them a clue to his real plans. From Marcel Bing, who had just returned to Peking from a similar expedition to the provinces, Freer learned that flooding often made the roads impassable and, more alarming, that Bing's party had been attacked by bandits. Left penniless but with their plundered art treasures untouched, they sold two horses for cash to buy their way back to Peking. With typical optimism, Freer assumed that the government had arrested the bandits and now guarded the road more carefully.[19]

Finally, on October 20, his little expedition set out with only the most essential people: the coolies who transported their goods; his guide, Nan; a cook; a photographer; two "rubbers (stone copiers); and one personal servant. They carried their beds, cook stove, and provisions. For the two-month trip, the Chinese government provided Freer with a special passport and a military guard. The viceroy of Henan province had sent word to his subordinates along the way to show the American every courtesy and had presented Freer with an official document to use anywhere in the province if he felt in need of help. "The document looks like fire cracker wrapper, but, I fancy, it is as powerful as an iron-clad." He arrived at Kaifeng, chief city of the province, with feet and legs sore from "the worst roads under heaven."[20]

For five days he traipsed through ancient temples filled with Song Dynasty remnants. To his amazement they were "freely shown to the foreign visitor." Overwhelmed at first by the ancient riches, he gradually understood how much had been lost or destroyed. Although spared military destruction, Kaifeng, once a city of two million inhabitants, had suffered for centuries the ravages of an overflowing Yellow River. The famous imperial pottery kilns had been obliterated. "During the time of my visit, which lasted about one week, over 400 buildings fell down owing to undermining caused by high waters of recent floods." Neglect compounded the decay. Dismayed, he described the plight of the artworks in one old wooden temple:

> The roof has fallen in, the rear wall of the building is demolished and under the debris there are magnificent life-sized bronze figures, life-sized marble figures, life-sized wooden figures, and some life-sized figures made of pottery beautifully glazed—all going to destruction…and nothing is being done to protect them.[21]

From Kaifeng, the Freer party ventured by rail 180 miles, detouring around a collapsed bridge, to Luoyang. The city stood on the site of the ancient capital which, according to Freer, dated from the "commencement of the historic period, say BC 781" and ruled with the exception of only a few years until 907 AD He thought he had found the very roots of the Chinese civilization. (We now know recorded Chinese history began over a thousand years earlier.) At the height of its power, Luoyang's walls stretched 25 miles on each side of the metropolis and included the river gorge of Longmen. When Freer entered in 1910, the walled city had shrunk to one square mile. Once again, he was greeted as an honored guest:

> A superb body of highly intelligent gentlemen gave me the finest dinner of my life, in the Yamen—Government Palace. More style, more elegance, and greater refinement than I have ever seen anywhere before. And because of the mud, water, and filth in the streets of this ancient city, all of the guests had to be carried in chairs on top of poles carried

> on men's shoulders some of whom waded to their
> thighs in mud.[22]

He then followed the steps of Chavannes and a few other scholars to the caves at Longmen. Although only ten miles from the city, the arduous journey over the barest excuse for a road required more than a day. The lieutenant governor of the province insisted on furnishing him with a sedan chair and eight bearers as well as mules and carts for the trip. After two days of preparation, Freer and his party left for the famous caves. Sometimes covering as much as three-quarters of a mile in less than two hours, his mule train twisted through narrow river valleys scattered with garden farms and burial grounds.

Longmen, which means Gate of the Dragon, is a gorge carved by the confluence of the Yi and the Lo Rivers. On both sides walls of limestone are dotted with hundreds of cave temples. Some of the chambers were ten to fifteen feet deep and high, others penetrated the steep cliffs to a depth of 40 and even 200 feet, and the mouths of some reached to 75 feet in height. Over many centuries, artists had sculpted Buddhist figures and incised elaborate designs on the ceilings, sides, and floors. The larger temples held as many as 15,000 figures; most held several hundred. Freer exclaimed to his old Yondotega friend Cam Currie, "I quiver, thrill, and wonder like an idiot…I am not exaggerating! These supreme things compel reverent and constant attention."[23]

Each new experience elicited from Freer's romantic soul not only rapture in his sublime moments, but also from the student in him, a compulsion to evaluate:

> To the Grecian, Indian, Persian and Egyptian designs and ideals, the Chinese artists added rhythm, space division and flowing lines, finer, in my opinion, than can be found elsewhere. It will be interesting to know what the experts of future centuries will say, comparatively, concerning this art and that of Greece and Egypt.[24]

Few Westerners had even heard of Tang sculpture, let alone classed it with the venerable creations of the Athenians and the ancient Egyptians. But then no other American and fewer than a dozen Europeans had ever seen the wealth of art in which Freer basked at Longmen.

Even the Chinese paid little attention; few came to wonder or worship before the ancient stone deities. During his two weeks at Longmen, he saw only three pilgrims. One, a bent, leather-faced old woman, shuffled silently into a temple where Freer and his associates were working. She muttered a few words before the Guanyin bodhisattva and then went directly to the river, where she lit a pack of firecrackers before disappearing. A few days later, two mandarins knelt before the Amida Buddha in one of the larger temples, clapped their hands, and then, after only a minute of silent reverence, they left. Aware that they were men of rank, Freer hastened to invite them to tea. To his amazement he learned that for the sake of those few brief moments, they had endured a hard journey of hundreds of miles to honor their ancestors who had been stone carvers in the temple.[25]

The only buildings at Longmen were two groups of temples built during the 17th and 18th centuries. Most were constructed of brick, but Freer chose a wooden temple in the older group for his temporary residence. Each morning he and his men rose at 5:00 a.m. and worked steadily until they retired at 8:30 p.m. for the evening. For the equivalent of ten cents a day, Freer hired young local men to scale the steep cliffs; inspect each grotto, many of them hidden in high grass; and report to him on their contents. Some grottos were empty, while others required Freer's personal investigation. When necessary, he rode the backs of coolies over difficult terrain or across the river if it might prove worthwhile. His photographer recorded each important or interesting carving, statue, or aperture. His stone "rubbers" painstakingly made ink impressions of rock details and inscriptions too subtle for the camera's eye. While his technicians worked, Freer examined and studied.[26]

The cave-filled valley unfortunately provided an ideal hangout for bandits. Through the narrow gorge passed a steady flow of local traffic heading to and from Luoyang, mostly merchants oblivious to the antique art surrounding them. Travel along the rutted paths was laborious, limited primarily to wheelbarrows laden with coal, grain, stone, or even human passengers. The ruffians hiding in the caves picked their moment, struck with lightning speed from above, and just as quickly disappeared with their bounty.[27]

Just before Freer's arrival, two people had been murdered in the area. Two days after he settled into his temple home, "a grand big, fine looking chap who had a bearer walk before him and carry a crimson umbrella with stick 15 feet high" arrived with an entourage to inspect his camp. He was the local mandarin assigned by officials in Peking to assure the safety of Freer's party. He doubled the number of soldiers in Freer's guard; as soon as he himself was safely out of the dangerous territory, he sent half of his own bodyguards back to march the length of the site shooting off their rifles as a warning. Freer seemed unconcerned, but his comrades were terrified:

> My cook sleeps with the new bread-knife I bought in Peking, my interpreter wraps countless blankets about him when he lies down, the photographer never sleeps, my servant wept last night when the temple cat mewed outside.

Each night, guards kept watch at the temple courtyard and at the temple gate beyond. They caught several culprits during the two weeks and killed one of them, an unfortunate sacrifice because their superiors preferred to question live ones rather than bury valuable sources of information. The grand mandarin called on Freer every other day to check on his security arrangements.[28]

Freer's records give no evidence of what objects, if any, he brought back from his two weeks working in the caves. We know he struggled with the issue of plundering. He knew that his bodyguards, in their eagerness to please him, would steal whatever rare object caught his eye, even from the temples. Before his expedition to the interior, he had asked permission through Ambassador Calhoun to export some large stone statues, admitting that he was "ashamed to ask for so great a favor [but] it was now or never." After seeing what existed in such abundance at Longmen, he considered again applying pressure to transport some of those superb sculptures to America. The need to protect his honorable reputation and the fear of jeopardizing the artwork he had already gathered in Peking stayed his hand. Still he was torn; he had seen enough destruction by floods, vandals, and neglect to cause him grave concern for their survival.[29]

On another issue, however, he was not ambivalent. He noted with indignation the difference between the courtesy the Chinese accorded him and America's disgraceful laws excluding Chinese immigrants (Chinese Exclusion Act of 1882). He had experienced the best in the Chinese people from his coolies to the "very agreeable" soldiers and "practically all educated Chinamen—How much we misunderstand the Chinese in America!"[30]

Floods forced him to abort his exploration of Sian, the third ancient capital. He returned to Peking after only a month's absence. With typical resilience, he resolved to go there next year when he could also include Datong, site of "the second and only other Lung-men on earth." Freer's enthusiasm and endurance, however, exceeded that of his men. His photographer and two rubbers volunteered to accompany him only "for a consideration" (money), but Nan, his cook, and his servant had seen and walked enough. They refused any part in further adventure.[31]

Back at his operation in Tartar City, barely sparing a moment to catch his breath, Freer launched immediately into a whirlwind of activity. He gathered reports from his scouts, negotiated with dealers, met with private collectors, and reported to Hecker: "I am buying principally, extremely fine things...three superb bronzes...T'ang and Sung paintings—and from the interior finer sculpture than has ever heretofore left China." He dispatched his runners back to Henan province to negotiate purchases for him and to Mongolia to secure a rare bronze object he had heard was for sale. He worked aggressively to stay ahead of competitors crowding into his territory. With alarm he watched prices escalate. Since his trip in 1909 and even since his arrival in September 1910, the news of his successes had attracted European buyers, "and while they are getting very little of the sort I hunt for, they are booming prices terribly and are causing owners to hesitate to sell."[32]

How much of its artistic heritage still remained in China was an unanswered question. Only a few years earlier, experts had claimed that no ancient Chinese art had survived there; yet in 1910, the interior cities and private collectors were spilling out treasures of ancient paintings, sculpture, and pottery. Was the source nearly exhausted, or had they just tapped the tip of an iceberg? No one really knew—certainly not Freer, a solitary hunter. Would his opportunities evaporate after a year to two, or would even greater riches leak out for decades? Adding suspense to the challenge, the Chinese government could at a moment's notice suddenly close the port to exportation of art objects. Even items painstakingly gathered on private expeditions might be locked up at dockside. Freer had earlier encountered such frustrations with customs officials in Turkey. It was all part of the game.

From the moment of his arrival in China in September until the day he had to leave in February, Freer's operation in Peking accumulated art. The agents who had greeted his arrival with five cases of goods for his selection continued their work while he traveled to Longmen. One secured eighteen fine paintings and then set off again to buy a private collection that Freer described as "ancient painting, pottery and bronze all suitable for my collection and at reasonable prices." By December of 1910, Freer had filled eleven cases with over 200 objects for shipment to America.[33]

As the cold winter settled over northern China, he decided to move south, but first he took three days to inspect the Imperial collection at Mukden. The chief official familiar with the taste of foreign visitors showed him only Ming decorated porcelain until he insisted the official open other closets filled with older "genuine Ting Yao pottery." From Mukden Freer went to Shanghai, where dealers, agents, and private collectors awaited his arrival. The men he had dispatched to the provinces inland from Shanghai returned laden. From "Pang Lai-ch'en, the greatest native picture collector…

selling in order to settle his rubber losses, on the Chinese New Year February 1st," Freer bought what he called "my crowning acquisition of paintings...adds a matchless note to the group."[34]

Now thoroughly at home in the Far East and eager for more adventure, he had no plans to return to America. He intended to continue south to Hong Kong and on to Cambodia to study Buddhist temple sites at Angkor Wat, a prelude to a future expedition through Southeast Asia to gather artworks and add one more link in the chain of his collections. From Cambodia the indefatigable hunter planned to return to Peking and launch his spring expedition to more remote provinces. Unfortunately, alarming news came before he could leave Shanghai.

His sister Emma had suffered another stroke, and his brother Watson had been injured in an accident with a runaway horse. Freer promptly cabled his family that he would leave immediately for home. Watson assured him that both were recovering, and his attendance was not necessary. Relieved that his gesture of concern was declined, he preferred pursuing his activities in China to providing passive moral support in Kingston. But then more serious news arrived. A plague had broken out in North Manchuria and was spreading south. A spring trip to the interior cities would be impossible until the plague had passed. Concerned that he might be quarantined in Hong Kong or Shanghai, Freer abandoned the journey to Angkor Wat and sailed almost immediately to Japan.[35]

An appropriate culmination to his adventures awaited him in Tokyo. The circle of tea master/connoisseurs held a reception in honor of Freer's remarkable expedition to the interior provinces of China. Marquis Inouye, Baron Takahashi, and Viscount Kaneko each gave speeches complimenting his pioneering work. The gentlemen insisted that Freer speak.

> I talked an hour on comparison between early Chinese and Japanese art, based on recent investigation made by myself in China and Japan. A most audacious performance on my part—think of an American with cheek enough to draw comparisons on Chinese and Japanese art before an audience made up almost entirely of Japanese experts. I told them that they having drawn us together, would have to suffer for their kind persistence.

For all his modesty, Freer was a widely respected connoisseur of Asian art. Few experts challenged his authority. The day after the reception in Tokyo, Baron Masuda assembled many of the same men at his home to plan their own expedition into China, along Freer's route. In imitating Freer, they paid him the ultimate Oriental compliment.[36]

Charles Freer returned to America elated, in the prime of his physical and mental powers. He had only begun to uncover the artworks buried in the hinterlands of China and Southeast Asia. With uncharacteristic pride, he expounded on his experiences to the press and confided to friends his plans for another expedition.[37]

A month later, a stroke shattered Freer's health and his dreams. He never returned to the Far East; he never again traveled outside the United States. For the next eight years, digging deep into his reserve of resilience and optimism, the renowned connoisseur promoted Asian art, strengthened his extraordinary collection, and began construction of his museum.

PART FOUR: ENTREPRENEUR'S LEGACY

— 18 —

ILLNESS
1911–1912

"Taken ill at 6:30." Freer wrote that single note in his diary on May 28, 1911, just weeks after his triumphant return from Asia. Forced by the plague in China to cut short his travels, he had returned to Detroit earlier than expected; his home was still torn up by workmen constructing a second art gallery for his expanding collections. He had settled into the Pontchartrain Hotel and had continued his customary trips and calls on friends.

Ptomaine poisoning from food he had eaten in the hotel dining room hit him first. Two days later he suffered a stroke. Undoubtedly quoting the doctor's diagnosis, he described it to his Capri partner, Tom Jerome, as a "cerebral effusion in a comparatively mild form." To an acquaintance in China, he described it blandly as a nervous breakdown following his trip. He lost the use of his right leg and could barely raise his right arm. Nurses attended him around the clock; a masseur gave him daily rubs. Confined to bed, he gamely made notes in his diary in an unsteady, childlike scrawl, but the letters he dictated to his friends were factual, optimistic, and pure

Freer; his mind had not been affected.[1]

By July, he claimed that he had so amazed the doctors with his rapid progress that they allowed him to complete his recuperation at the Hecker cottage on Mackinac Island. Accompanied by his retinue of nurses, masseur, and doctor, he sailed north with Frank Hecker aboard his partner's yacht. From July through September, his letters repeated the litany. "I will probably be quite well again in a month or two." But his progress slowed. When the early fall winds blew across the north Michigan island, Freer returned briefly to Detroit. His house was still in turmoil; so with his nurse in tow, he sought refuge for the next two months in the Berkshire Mountains of Great Barrington, Massachusetts, close to his Kingston roots.[2]

Only years later did he admit to Charles Walcott at the Smithsonian that his paralytic stroke came in the wake of a serious illness, an illness he kept a close secret during his life and which remained hidden for nearly a century. His death certificate in 1919 stated that he had suffered from syphilis for eight years, a critical fact in understanding the circumspect Mr. Freer.[3]

At the turn of the19th century, although a disease of plague proportions, syphilis was shrouded in ignorance and shame. Like the AIDS epidemic a century later, it was associated with sexual activity and not mentioned in polite society. At that time, there was also no cure for syphilis. For centuries, the treatment had been rubbing on the body or even injecting mercury or iodides. A popular quip was "Spend one night with Venus and a lifetime with Mercury." In 1906, the Wasserman blood test provided the first definitive diagnosis for syphilis; and in 1910, the arsenic drug Salvarsan promised better treatment for the symptoms. There was no cure until 1943, when military doctors realized penicillin could heal syphilis.

The early syphilis symptoms might disappear without treatment, allowing sufferers to deny the disease. In stage two, affecting only half of patients, symptoms like a headache, a sore throat, the lack of energy, and lesions or a rash were followed by a latency period of months, years, or a lifetime as the bacteria infected vital organs. Only a small number of syphilitics entered the tertiary stage, often plagued by personality changes described as manic or nervous derangements, and ending in death. The scrupulous Charles Freer fell gradually into that last small category.

How he contracted the dreaded disease and how long he lived with it we can only speculate; needless to say, he left no written record. Was it on the 1895 trip to Japan where he wrote of "things one doesn't mind trying?" Or perhaps after his retirement cavorting among the locals on Capri or visiting the "clubs" in Manhattan with his artist friends? In 1898 when he spent weeks recuperating in Hot Springs, Virginia, was he reacting to symptoms of syphilis? We have no evidence. After the stroke, his diary noted the services of a "rubber" for the first time, suggesting he had mercury treatments. Rubbing the mercury ointment into the skin, a messy and time-consuming procedure, required a trained person. In any case, syphilis was a silent chord in his life, perhaps compounded by sexual tension.[4]

Almost a century after his death, rumors that he was homosexual surfaced, based on conjecture and third-hand reports from families who knew of him. They are circumstantial clues. Charles Freer had carved a fine line between insider and outlier in Detroit. Amid his circle of hard-driving industrialists, he created the Yondotega Club for elevated fun among male comrades. In a society ruled by men with social wives and numerous children, he remained a bachelor, but one among many gentlemen bachelors. He set himself apart as an art connoisseur; his passion for beauty expressed the softer side of the striving capitalist. If he did have sexual relationships with men, it is certain that in his Detroit social circle he could not be other than closeted. The horrors visited on Oscar Wilde during his trial and conviction for sodomy in 1895 would have terrified him. That onetime friend of Whistler had given a lecture in Detroit in 1882 that Freer probably attended; he certainly knew Wilde's writings on beauty's power to uplift society. It is unthinkable that Freer, never the reckless type, would jeopardize his position and reputation by flaunting moral probity as it was then understood.

Any internal conflict he might have suffered, he covered with a conventional exterior. He enjoyed the society of men and women. On his escapades with F. S. Church years earlier, he wrote sly references to certain women, but after his journey around the world in 1895, he saw little of Church. The escapades stopped, perhaps spurred by cautious self-control. At the summer colonies of his artist friends, he befriended their models, often beauties with acting aspirations and sometimes the artists' lovers. As a go-between in their liaisons, he participated in their intriguing milieu and may have cultivated for himself their reputation as gay blades and frequenters of brothels, but likely from a safe distance.

For Dewing, Saint-Gaudens, and Stanford White, male "sporting" was an accepted evening entertainment. They formed the "Sewer Club" and rented private rooms for their activities. They collected books of erotica, favored nude paintings of nubile girls, and covered their philandering tracks with encrypted notes and secret addresses. Mistresses are assumed to be the hidden pleasures, but they also wrote each other homoerotic letters embellished with phalluses. The cautious Freer recorded no evidence of his participation; instead he left notes on poets he read, like William Henley and Walt Whitman, who extolled the bonds men shared. Like art, their poems were uplifting. Henley praised the masculine "unconquerable soul," and ended his most famous poem "Invictus," "I am the master of my fate; I am the captain of my soul," words of discipline by which Charles Freer lived.[5]

That Freer and Tom Jerome, a fellow "Yon," created a household together on the Isle of Capri, gives currency to his homosexuality, but not proof. Spending time abroad where he enjoyed the sybaritic pleasures of their home and garden amid a bohemian lifestyle certainly made it safer to share intimate male friendship or more. In any case, it didn't last. The two remained friends and co-owners of the home, where Tom Jerome lived with a beautiful mixed-race woman named Yetta until his death. Freer moved on.

His relationships with women were circumspect. He had firm opinions: praising "a lady free of the false side and so many little objections which happen to so many otherwise estimable ladies," or protesting "the modern American woman with her fancies of independence, rights...and other diabolical tendencies." He could jest about "my well known objection to women." Yet when he was only 49 years old, he lamented, "my own interest in passionate paths might have been greater. But, I fear in our old days, we are all losing the instinct to love, [instead] enjoying old men's dreams." The two women he described with greatest emotion were safely unattainable. "Romaine Brooks—a corker on Capri"—was a lesbian. Belle da Costa Greene, the director of the Morgan Library and a sharp-tongued professional woman, kept him at a distance. In his later years Charles Freer developed platonic relationships with strong, intelligent, capable women devoted to him; most were decades his junior. Some were suffragists, their tendencies apparently not "diabolical."[6]

Neither syphilis nor homosexuality is mentioned in the Freer papers that survived. The coterie of loyal women who surrounded him in his last years would surely have destroyed any evidence of a stain on his reputation. His doctor stated the cause on his death certificate; only then was syphilis acknowledged and then buried. One of his acolytes, Agnes Meyer, still protective of her hero fifty years later, recalled his "numerous relationships with the opposite sex," and blithely claimed his illness was congenital syphilis, a form contracted in the womb that in 1854 would have led to early death.[7]

Whatever the history of his illness, in the autumn of 1911 the 57-year-old collector was ensconced in the Berkshires with his nurse. His resilient optimism had always countered his problems in the past, but the persistence of this attack devastated him. Fresh from his exhilarating adventures in China, his curious mind was as alive with projects as his body was numbed by weakness. He longed to continue his travels, but he could barely hold a pen, could read for only a short time, and his stamina for examining art objects dissipated after an hour. To his agent Dattari in Egypt, he admitted that "illness prevents consideration of buying for my collection." Cruel punishment for the art explorer.[8]

A few guests called at his Massachusetts hideaway. Watson and Anna spent three days with him, but most of his friends stayed away to spare his strength. He gamely ventured with his nurse down to New York City to visit his dealers, but he had little will to buy. When the colorful New England fall turned to gray winter, he returned to Detroit. Scholars called on him, eager to hear about his China discoveries. Dr. Wilhelm von Bode arrived from Germany and Dr. Wilhelm Valentiner came from the Metropolitan Museum in New York to examine his collection in the spacious new gallery he had created as an experiment in lighting and design for his future museum. After two hours of study, however, he was exhausted and discouraged. The complete recovery he so resolutely believed in would not come.

In early November he wrote Thomas Dewing, "I am holding my own and the doctors are planning a little experimenting with me… this may unfit me for a week or two." The treatment was administered on November 23. It was probably arsenic-based Salvarsan, discovered the previous year. The drug was dangerous and required a skilled administrator. Arsenic powder had to be expertly dissolved and injected into the buttocks; it might take a week to be absorbed and relieve the pain, the weakened muscles, and the abscesses. It seemed to work. Six days later Freer left his bed, dressed, and ventured downstairs. Two weeks later his nurse left, and he began going to his office for four or five hours a day. He attended the board meeting of the Yondotega Club, his first social outing in seven months. His handwriting was again sharp and clear.[9]

Thereafter, Freer's body vacillated between strength and weakness; his outlook bounced between optimism and realism. His limp might be permanent and his muscles weak, but he stubbornly counted on complete recovery from his illness. Each year he hoped the next would bring strength and travel. Sometimes he waited patiently, taking rest as a remedy; other times he desperately sought out new doctors, new treatments, or new climate, pursuing a cure with the same tenacity he had pursued goals all his life. For the next eight years, he suffered not only from fatigue and restricted mobility but also from frequent bouts of "an extreme attack of nervousness and nausea." Striking him without warning, they were caused by the disease, the arsenic and mercury, or a combination.[10]

He remained in Detroit through most of 1912, managing to get away occasionally. In New York City, he called on Dewing and Tryon, whom he had seldom seen during his globe-trotting years.

Asian art scholars journeyed to Detroit to examine the objects that had finally arrived from China. Denman W. Ross, trustee of the Museum of Fine Arts, Boston; Frederick Gookin of the Art Institute of Chicago; Berthold Laufer, who had led an expedition to China for Chicago's Field Museum; and Langdon Warner, the young Harvard man curating at the Boston museum—each spent a day or two conferring with the celebrated connoisseur in his Ferry Avenue home.

Early in 1912, he permitted the first exhibition of the Freer Collection in Washington, D.C., to be installed in the Smithsonian's new National Museum of Natural History. He chose a broad array of bronze, sculpture, pottery, and glass; a few Japanese paintings; and numerous Chinese paintings hung opposite works by Whistler, Dewing, Thayer, Tryon, and one by Homer. Berthold Laufer delivered the opening address and wrote the catalogue. It was a grand affair and was greeted with respect by the press. Freer could only plan and monitor. His former coachman—now "curator"—Stephen Warring and the Smithsonian officials did the work in Washington. Freer attended for just one day in April.[11]

Confined in Detroit under doctors' care during most of 1912, Freer felt a growing dissatisfaction with his life there. For the last decade, since the failure of the Bicentennial memorial proposal, he had gradually divorced himself from his Detroit connections. His interest, his ambitions, and his challenges lay outside Michigan. His involvement with Whistler, his work on the Smithsonian gift, his long months of travel in Asia had taken him well beyond Detroit. Since 1907 he had spent barely half of his time in the city. Illness now left him moored in his adopted hometown, and he bemoaned how much it had changed. The noise and congestion irritated him; the automobile and factory smoke appalled him; the brash, young men walking the streets grated on his sensibilities. Just as he had lamented changes in Japan, Freer longed for Detroit's "old time" ambiance. Modern mass production and cheap cars had produced new attitudes and new leadership. He had little in common with Henry Ford, who supposedly said, "I wouldn't give five cents for all the art in the world." In dismay he reported to Jerome, "[T]he old-town has lost nearly all of its charm. It is a busy, smoky, seething town...I personally go about in the town but little."[12]

Detroit held his house, but it was no longer home. To Bixby in St. Louis, he admitted that he was "not quite within this busy spot, nor quite without it." His friends at the Yondotega remained his only link, and even their hold had weakened. He had resigned as president of the club in 1910 because of his extensive travels. Reluctantly he had facilitated the purchase of a parking lot adjacent to club for the members' automobiles but insisted on walls to hide the eyesore. By 1913 he wrote the new president, Cam Currie, in distress, "I am getting less and less interested in trying to preserve the old time Yon ideals—they seem no longer the spirit of the place—only ghostly visions." Many of his Yon peers had died or moved away. Freer's response was to leave too.[13]

— 19 —

LIFE IN NEW YORK CITY

1913–1914

FREER GAVE NOTICE TO HIS servants, temporarily closed his house, and departed for New York City in early January 1913. Stephen, his former coachman, remained to look after his collection. For the next year, the distressed collector settled in the Plaza Hotel in New York and the Berkshire Inn in Great Barrington, Massachusetts, only occasionally visiting Detroit. With Dewing at his side, he haunted the New York galleries much as the two men had done together during the 1890s; they called on artist friends and combed through dealers' shops. The Yamanaka firm and his contacts in China kept him informed of art works available for purchase. New York restored him mentally while he awaited physical recovery.

The Armory Show opened in February 1913, and everybody, including Freer, flocked to witness the new wave in art. The American Ashcan artists like George Bellows and John Sloan hung their bold, realistic paintings, but the Europeans Vincent van Gogh, Camille Pissarro, Marcel Duchamp, and Henri Matisse stole the show. The exhibition must have left the seeker of beauty appalled.

For once he recorded no comment. He had seen modern art in Munich in 1901 and dismissed it then as "aberrations." Whether Freer realized it or not, the Armory Show threatened the importance of his own American art collection. Far removed from the subtle, ideal images created by Tryon, Dewing and Thayer, this new artwork challenged their vision and buried their fame. Even Whistler's popularity was fading. Some New York collectors bought at the Armory Show, but Freer saved his gold for the Prince Kung exhibition of Oriental art held in New York at the same time.

Before escaping Detroit, his mind still spinning from his China adventures, Freer had embarked on an ambitious new project: to guard the art treasures still hidden in the interior of China against marauding, unscrupulous profiteers. Facing the fact that, at least for the moment, his acquisition trips to Asia had ceased, he proposed an American School of Archeology in China, specifying that:

> [T]he school...from where expeditions could be sent into adjacent countries...should be equipped for research in archaeological, aesthetic and literary directions...and looking to the creation in China of a great National Museum and the protection of China's marvellous [sic] ancient monuments.

As early as April 1912, he had discussed the idea with the young Boston curator Langdon Warner. Freer offered to contribute half of the cost of a preliminary trip to China if the Boston museum contributed the other half. When Boston procrastinated, he took the proposal to the Smithsonian; they agreed to fund $10,000 for an eighteen-month survey under Warner's direction.[1]

Freer presented his idea to the council of the Archeology

Institute of America at its meeting on December 21, 1912, and they appointed a committee of three, the two senior officers of the Smithsonian and Freer, to report on the advisability of establishing the school. His initiative may have been spurred by competition. On December 17, 1912, Frederick McCormick, a news correspondent who had spent the last thirteen years in China, wrote to Freer of his own plans for an institute in New York City with similar goals.[2]

On January 5, 1913, newspapers made public the plans for an American School of Archeology in China. Freer wisely invited McCormick and New York investment broker Eugene Meyer, a fellow Asian art enthusiast, to join the executive committee. Meyer and Freer pledged to underwrite the project budget of $500,000. Freer supervised the project down to the finest detail; he advised Warner on preparing for his journey and plotted his itinerary. For the next two years, they worked to increase understanding between the East and the West and to halt the plundering of Chinese art.[3]

Aesthetic scavengers had been raiding China since the end of the Japanese-Russian War in 1905. Small pieces of sculpture easily removed from their niches found their way to Japan, Europe, and America. Statues were ripped from temples and caves; large statues were pried loose and dismembered for easier transport. Chaos created by the Revolution of 1911, the collapse of the Qing dynasty, and the faltering new Republic increased the pillaging. Paul Mallon, a sensitive, knowledgeable French art dealer on a journey through China in 1912–1913, saw convoys of wheelbarrows carting Buddhist heads down from the mountain sites; iconic treasures were offered to him for the equivalent of a dollar apiece, two dollars if the noses were intact.[4]

Most of the men involved in the preservation effort had profited from plunder, even as they deplored careless destruction. One of the most famous plundered objects was a life-size statue from the late Wei or early Tang period purchased by the Paris couturier Paul Poiret. Three years later that statue became part of the Freer collection as a gift from Eugene Meyer. Today we may ask, at what cost and for whose benefit was that statue "preserved"? The answer is complex.[5]

Their moral red line was fuzzy. Meyer and Freer asserted that the current political turmoil left the Chinese unable "to assume proper care of a collection of valuable objects." McCormick publicly advised governments and private institutions to return "stolen Chinese antiquities to China," yet he advised Freer:

> If we can carry out the ideas and plans which I am suggesting it is likely that President Yuan Shihk'ai would gladly consent to the storing on loan for decades to come in American museums of perhaps her most valuable antiquities.

Langdon Warner was charged with establishing both a Chinese National Museum and an American school; yet he promised the school would furnish American museums with informed curators, a chance to excavate in China, and opportunities to add to their collections at cost prices. He encouraged the new Cleveland Museum of Art "to step in and make a killing," before the Europeans stole the opportunity.[6]

Their proposed American School in China struggled with increasing costs and Warner's inept management. When the United States government agreed to China's promise to set aside $100,000 gold from the Boxer Rebellion indemnity for the creation of a national museum in Peking, the school seemed doomed. World War

I sealed its end. Once again, Freer's attempt at noble public service had failed. One enduring benefit from their efforts, however, was Freer's friendship with Eugene Meyer and his wife.[7]

Agnes and Eugene Meyer matched his passion for Asian art. Eugene, a wealthy entrepreneur, had made his fortune in copper. Aggressive and broad-minded, Meyer's interest in the Far East was spurred by both commerce and culture. The young couple had spent their honeymoon touring Asia, and Eugene was currently working on a scheme to sell Maxwell cars in Japan. Less than a week after their first meeting in January 1913, Freer moved to the Meyer country home in Mount Kisco, New York, for ten days of quiet solitude, walking and driving through the suburban countryside. He paid his host a high compliment when he wrote, "You are a Han man!" and later described him as "the salt of the earth and a man who never forgets a friend." Meyer replied in kind: "I regard your friendship as one of my chief pleasures in life." Freer respected the quiet, dedicated man who combined public service with fortune making; he trusted his judgment in both finance and fine arts.[8]

The relationship between Agnes Meyer and Charles Freer was more emotional. She responded to him as Freer had responded to Whistler, with reverence. Thirty years her senior, he was one of many father figures in the life of the handsome, dynamic, young woman. She published articles about Freer as her mentor and friend, crediting his inspiration and influence on her life. (She seldom mentioned the importance of her husband's relationship with Freer.) Of their first meeting, she wrote:

> I met Mr. Freer, by chance, at an exhibition of Chinese paintings...But what, after all, is Chance? Our common interest was found to bring us together,

> as there were so few people at that time who cared as deeply as we did about the long and brilliant history of Chinese culture.

Describing him as her "hero" she continued, "We both knew, as one often does know at a first encounter, that we had begun a momentous experience." With the dramatic, effervescent Agnes, Freer could give free rein to the artistic side of his nature and express his most intimate feelings. In combining business acumen with aesthetic passion, the Meyers reflected both sides of Freer's nature. They became among his closest confidants during the last years of his life.[9]

In May 1913 Freer returned briefly to Detroit to open his galleries for their first visit. An attractive friend of Agnes's, the artist Marian Beckett joined them to spend four days examining his extraordinary art collection. Inspired by their interest, Freer put on a grand display. An equally inspired Agnes later wrote:

> And what a revelation it was to be the guest of this remarkable man! Our host's sense of form and beauty pervaded everything, from the courtly manner in which we were received at the front door…to the careful exhibition of the paintings, one by one, hung on a screen which isolated each one from the vast surroundings of the long gallery.
>
> When the light began to wane, Mr. Freer asked Stephen, his butler-curator, to place before us two Japanese screens in a bold design which could still be appreciated in the faint light of a setting sun. As we sat on the floor, leaning on big comfortable pillows,

> Stephen poured us some vintage champagne which we sipped slowly and appreciatively as we admired the pine-clad mountain scenery of the screens until it faded away under the deepening twilight.

After their departure, Freer wrote that his gallery seemed "empty and lonely" and chided, "It was wicked of you all to fly so soon." With typical thoroughness, he sent to each one a list of the paintings seen and the name of each artist. His galleries did not remain "empty and lonely" for long. The widow Louisine Havemeyer followed fast behind the Meyer party.[10]

Freer saw the Meyers frequently during the summer and fall of 1913, both in New York City and in Mount Kisco. He called their estate his "new nirvana," his American San no tani. Miss Beckett and another attractive artist friend of Mrs. Meyer's, Katharine Rhoades, often joined their party. Beautiful women and beautiful surroundings brightened his life, but serious purpose was never far from Freer's mind. He spent as much time in forceful discussion with the group of men associated with Eugene as he did in charming conversation with the lovely ladies. With Eugene, he debated Warner's progress in China, investigated business propositions in Detroit, and compared investments in art. Freer frequently alerted his friend to shipments of art arriving at the dealer houses in New York. On Eugene's next excursion to Detroit, he was accompanied by the artist-photographer Edward Steichen; the three men spent three days absorbed by the objects of the Freer collection.[11]

As the summer heat stifled New York, Freer again moved his headquarters to the Berkshire Inn, from which he could still make occasional runs to New York. In December 1913, his illness unremitting, he reopened his home and settled again in Detroit to receive another new treatment, probably Neosalvarsan, a less toxic synthetic arsenic compound. It required "absolute rest and quiet." There he remained for most of 1914 as recurring bouts of illness forced him to bed for periods of a week to ten days, under his doctor's watchful care and attended by his nurses, Miss Ida Franks and Miss Leitch. He gave up his downtown office, admitting, "I cannot get around the streets of this now bustling place as easily as formerly." A small building he had constructed between the former stable and his home now served as his office. Isolated from his old life in Detroit society and from the art world in New York City, it was a lonely, demoralizing existence. Gamely he wrote Bixby, "My health is none too good, there is no use in 'kicking' so I wear the conventional smile and announce that 'All's well.'"[12]

When the gambler Richard Canfield decided to sell his Whistler art collection, one that Freer had enthusiastically encouraged and second in size to his own, Freer's ambivalence was palpable. He replied to his old comrade, "While I regret the loss to my collection, I consider it wiser for you to accept the offer made to you… than to await uncertainties here." Henry Clay Frick captured the two jewels: *Rosa Corder* and *Comte de Montesquiou*. Tragically, a few months later, Canfield fell in a subway station and died that night of a fractured skull.[13]

Freer's focus remained on collecting Asian art, but he chafed at being held hostage to only the objects offered by dealers in America, a sore solution for the man who prided himself on pursuing in person the ancient artworks buried in the homes and valleys of Asia. Holding fast to his dream of traveling again, he maintained his network in China. Nan Ming-yuen, "my old business associate and Jack-of-all trades in China, whom I adore," dodged the perils of the Revolution to scout for him. A. W. Bahr, the American businessman in Shanghai, bought from mandarins with cash flow problems and shipped their goods to America. From Bahr, Freer selected a few things. Dealing with the American missionary, educator, and entrepreneur John C. Ferguson, whom he had met in Shanghai, was more complicated. His brash attributions and his questionable aesthetic taste tried Freer's patience; but he had command of the Chinese language, then rare among Westerners, and claimed important political connections in China.[14]

Shortly after returning to China with Freer's specific instructions on what kinds of art to buy, Ferguson cabled:

> BRUMMEISEN TUANFANGS KUKAICHI MUSITAMOS JOZACHAR KNEIFEN IDEOLOGIST CANTHORSUM BOENWAS DIVOROLLA CONDUCIVE

Translated from their code, it meant that he could buy from the famous Duanfang collection a hand scroll, *Nymph of the Luo River*, attributed to Ku K'ai-chih. The artist was one of the very earliest documented in Chinese history, comparable to Giotto in the West. Laurence Binyon had claimed the only other surviving work of Ku K'ai-chih for the British Museum. Freer made remarkably little fuss over such an extraordinary addition to his collection; he may also have been wary of Ferguson's claims.[15]

When the collector was stuck in Detroit for more treatments, Eugene Meyer selected items to send to Detroit on approval as Howard Mansfield had done many years earlier. But Meyer was an active businessman; his time to shop and visit was limited. On his trips to New York City, Freer increasingly devoted his attention to the ladies, Agnes Meyer, Marian Beckett, and Katharine Rhoades, whom he called the "Three Graces." They affectionately hailed him "General," a tribute to his earlier association with Whistler's ladies, who had dubbed him "General Utility."

Agnes became his confidant; she and Freer gossiped, consoled, complained, and exalted together. Although still a young wife with an ambitious husband and two small children (joined in the next few years by two more babies, including Katharine Graham, later owner of the *Washington Post*), Agnes found time for her elderly friend. Together they studied artworks, primarily Chinese. With Freer's encouragement, Agnes began a scholarly treatise on the Song Dynasty painter Li Lung-mien and struggled to learn the Chinese language. She kept him informed of all news and intrigue. They spiced their serious study of art with a saucy study of their peers and competitors.[16]

One of the most intriguing people Agnes brought into Freer's life was her friend Belle da Costa Greene, the director of the Morgan Library. A bold woman armed with a keen mind, a sharp tongue, and utterly unpredictable manners, she enchanted the conservative Freer. In the words of a contemporary curator and friend:

> It was necessary to take Belle Greene as she was. One had to be ready and strong, for one never knew beforehand what pyrotechnics she might produce. This very unexpectedness, dreadful as it might be and often was, was one of her fascinations.

A competent administrator and a thorough and knowledgeable student, she had years earlier won the confidence of J. P. Morgan; few men intimidated her. In the company of her friends Bernard Berenson, the West's most famous art historian, and his wife, she arrived in Detroit in February 1914 for her first introduction to the Freer collection. Effusively she wrote:

> I simply lost my mind and heart over his early bronzes…and the paintings Gowd oh! Gowd!—I liked the rolled ones infinitely better than those in the wood…I could hug him (Freer) a million times for the joy he has given me today.

Her critical comments were just as unrestrained. The Peacock Room she thought "a nightmare, never have I beheld anything so horrible." And of her host she wrote: "Poor Freer shamed…very often in his 'English' and I blushed and nearly perished with shame with him at his oft-repeated 'Amurrican' and 'modren.'" She had no kinder words for Mary Berenson, whose lack of knowledge about Chinese art appalled her. But Bernard she described as "simply adorable," an affection perhaps colored by her reported romantic liaison with him.[17]

The erudite Berenson, who had first seen the collection ten years earlier with Fenollosa, acknowledged Freer's connoisseurship by stating that nowhere in the Western world could Chinese art:

> [B]e studied in its variety and completeness as I found it at Mr. Freer's. He showed us a hundred masterpieces which for their intrinsic aesthetic merit deserve to rank with any other hundred that could be selected from the entire range of the world's art…I regard Mr. Freer's collection as one of the few greatest treasures of art in existence and certainly the greatest in our country.

Agnes warned that "B.B." hoped Freer would publish his own evaluation, thus giving Berenson "the pleasure of going for you in print & overwhelming you with his ready and mellifluous vocabulary"; or, she speculated, he hoped Freer would commission him to write about the collection at a fat sum. Freer agreed to "go slow" when Berenson next approached him.[18]

After a visit in December 1914, he described Belle as "my graceful and lighthearted companion…though young in years she seemed ripe like old wine…How lustrous and luxurious not to mention intelligent and appreciative!!" He rejoiced in having her alone amid his collection without the competition of Berenson, and when she left, he sighed, "my domicile is again in darkness and my household gods are in tears." Admitting to living "at a mad pace…under the stimulus of my enchanting phenomenon," he wistfully asked, "How will it end—in miraculous cure or like the echo of a cricket's cry?" Belle, however, was inspired more by the collection than by the infirm collector; she remained no more than an acquaintance in Freer's life.[19]

Freer could collect art only sporadically, well supplied by his dealers but hampered by increasing prices as well as his decreasing energy. His purchases of Japanese paintings had essentially ceased because he "found it possible to buy at lower prices much finer examples by the early Chinese." When some of the most famous collections in Japan, gathered by men Freer had known and respected, went to the auction rooms, Freer's comment was: "What prices!!"[20]

The trauma of World War I consumed his old friends in Asia and Europe. Hara entreated Freer to sail to Japan to regain his health in the beauty of his estate, to which his guide Nomura added: "If you live at San no tani, they are sure they will forget this tumultuous foolish world while you will forget your illness." Instead, Freer dispatched young scholars like Osvald Sirén and Langdon Warner and colleagues like William Bixby to Japan with personal letters of introduction to his Japanese friends so they could profit as he had from their native connoisseurship. To his French friends he sent catalogues of exhibitions and news of Oriental art in America, hoping to lift their war-torn spirits.[21]

For Charles Freer, the chaos of war was a distant tragedy, but his disease was ever present. Overcoming his ill health obsessed him. Letters to business associates as well as to his friends and often mentioned his health first. Underneath a jocular optimism lay steely determination: "I am as usual—banged up, but still in the game." To his Yon friend Cam Currie, he announced that he felt "spunkier," and was not yet ready to have his name carved "on the cold stone tablet in the Yon garden." But weak muscles and unruly nerves plagued him. By the end of 1914, constant throat problems and tonsillitis (a second-stage symptom of syphilis) had reduced his voice to a rasping whisper. Desperate to find a cure, he sought relief in a new climate. Once again, he gave notice to his servants and closed his house. This time he went west.[22]

— 20 —

COLLECTOR REVITALIZED

1915–1918

COUNTING ON A NEW ENVIRONMENT to work magic, Freer sought his cure in the sun and sea breezes of San Diego, California. He boarded the Santa Fe train on January 13, 1915, for a nearly ten-day trip via Los Angeles. His goal: "to return with a man's voice." To avoid strain and responsibility, he informed very few people of his plans or his whereabouts. During the next six months, he was alternately restless, demanding, hopeful, dissatisfied, and invigorated.[1]

In San Diego, he settled first at a tourist hotel to mingle a bit closer to "the real western types—whose character I enjoy." When he attempted to join his sister-in-law Anna Hecker Freer at the elegant oceanside Hotel Del Coronado, he met embarrassing rejection. The hotel manager, fearing the gentleman's weak voice might be a sign of tuberculosis, refused him accommodations. Peevishly, Freer responded that after all he was happy to avoid the Detroit crowd and really cared to see Anna only "occasionally." The treatment of his throat problem prohibited unnecessary talking, so he retreated to books like Henry Knibb's *Song of the Outlands* and spent leisure hours at the 1915 Panama-California Exposition in Balboa Park. In April, he moved to Arrowhead Springs, a resort in the mountain foothills north of San Diego to try an intensive rest cure. For three weeks he devoted his days to salt and eucalyptus rubs, steam baths, and quiet walks.[2]

Somewhat restored but far from cured, he journeyed north to San Francisco for several days to inspect its Panama-Pacific International Exposition. On his way home from China in 1911, he had met with the exposition's officials and joined their advisory committee. He had loaned twenty-five paintings to the exposition, including sixteen Whistlers and several Tryons. But when he saw them hanging in the Palace of Fine Arts amid "a bewildering, silly maze…and not a single Thayer!" he curtly recommended removing 75% of the pictures and properly hanging the remaining 25%. In a glum mood, he returned to Arrowhead Springs to restore his spirits.[3]

Four years had passed since his stroke and his debilitating illness. He had to face the permanence of his physical limitations. California had not brought him more stable nerves, stronger muscles, or a "man's voice." He had found periodic relief from the symptoms of syphilis but no cure. Expeditions and pleasant association with connoisseurs in foreign countries were no longer possible, and the American School in Peking, a legacy potentially as significant as the Freer Gallery of Art, had collapsed. A turning point came at the end of his stay in California. He acknowledged his fate and reframed his attitude. Art was the catalyst, and P'ang Yuan-chi, a dealer he had known in Shanghai in 1910, was the agent.

New merchants had entered the art market on New York City's Fifth Avenue as Freer headed west. Worch opened a branch of his Paris shop on Fifth Avenue to challenge Yamanaka's longstanding monopoly. C. T. Loo, an enterprising emigre from China and the most influential Chinese art dealer in Paris, filled an elegant gallery with objects from private collections brought *en bloc* from China. His elaborate network of suppliers in China included "Dealer's Clubs," an aggregate of scouts with goods stashed in large tea houses in the port cities. For his first New York season in 1915, he exhibited a remarkable collection of Chinese paintings owned by P'ang Yuan-chi of Shanghai. A cousin, P'ang T'zu-ch'eng, accompanied the collection, which included fine scrolls attributed to the great masters like Ma Yuan and Kuo Hsi (Guo Xi).[4]

The ailing collector had departed for California before Loo opened the P'ang exhibition, but he provided the dealer a list of collectors to invite to the sale and praised the "splendid paintings" P'ang had earlier sold him. Through his New York contacts, Freer followed the progress of Loo's sale. Agnes Meyer and Katharine Rhoades penned him glowing descriptions of the artworks. Eugene Meyer advised hard-nosed negotiations with the dealer. Freer replied that P'ang's prices were too high and refused to bid. He had a distinct advantage; he had seen the paintings in private collections in China before P'ang owned them and knew the dealer paid only "a few silver dollars" for the paintings he now priced at 10,000 gold dollars.

While Freer wanted to see him prosper, he did not want to support prosperity "on too huge a scale." Furthermore, he felt no urgency. As he wrote Agnes in March 1915, "I know positively [the gold of America] is still drawing ancient treasures out of the Forbidden City!" and advised her to be wary of wily Chinese merchants: "How bland and saint-like their methods and with what sweet composure they bury one's last copper into the canyons of their silken robes." If Frick or Rockefeller, the only ones able to pay the prices set by P'ang and Loo, decided to jump in, then America would still be the winner. Frankly, he knew that few American buyers competed with him for the ancient art of China. Confidently, he waited for P'ang to come to him with lower prices.[5]

On cue the cousin, P'ang T'zu-ch'eng, arrived in San Diego in May accompanied by C. T. Loo and Kuan Fu-ts'u, a "real expert and shrewd," whom Freer had known in Shanghai. After two days examining the paintings, Freer narrowed his selection to twenty-four, and on the third day, he settled on thirteen for purchase. In the strictest terms, he cautioned all involved to remain silent about the large sale: "I don't want it known that I am buying anything or busying myself with anything." His restrained purchasing of the last four years had ended; his collector's spirit had quickened. Buying art revitalized him far more than the famed California climate.[6]

On his way home in June 1915, he stopped in Chicago to confer with the scholars Gookin and Laufer. Gookin followed him to Detroit to assist in documenting and cataloguing the collection of Asian paintings. Two weeks later Freer met with representatives from the Cleveland Museum of Art and the Metropolitan Museum of Art as an unofficial adviser on the formation of their Asian art collections. Ready for action, he returned to New York City.

The city's dynamism had been part of his life since 1913. He could wander in the galleries along Fifth Avenue and in the halls of the Metropolitan Museum, attend scholarly lectures, spend an afternoon with his dealers Yamanaka and Knoedler, or look in on sympathetic collectors like William T. Evans, a fellow donor to the Smithsonian. Dewing, Tryon, and occasionally Thayer called on him, as did Zeichiro Hara, a son of his old friend in Japan and now a student at Columbia University. The young artists Misses Beckett and Rhoades attended him, and Agnes praised him for returning looking "so well and strong again." At the Meyers's home in Mount

Kisco, Edward Steichen made photographs of the clean-shaven, dapper collector. The twinkle in his eyes had returned to counter the limp in his gait.[7]

New York City accorded him the recognition he had found so satisfying in Paris and Tokyo. The friendships of the Meyers, Louisine Havemeyer, and her brother-in-law Samuel T. Peters, a wealthy coal dealer and trustee of the Metropolitan Museum, enriched the last years of Freer's life. To them, he gave generously of his time and his expertise. After the Japan Society exhibition of Asian pottery, he predicted bright prospects ahead for the cause of Oriental art: "Fresh converts are falling into line and I hope that our pottery show will add to the number." Peters encouraged Freer's participation in the museum's expansion in Oriental art.[8]

Louisine and her late husband Henry, the sugar baron, had known Charles Freer since their early print collecting days. In 1906 the couple saw the Freer collection in Detroit for the first time. Fenollosa had gleefully anticipated the meeting: "I think it will make H. O. H.'s few hairs stand up, to see it. It's a charitable thing to keep him in mind that people do exist who know something, besides himself." The strong-minded Louisine, who later went to jail briefly as a suffragist, continued collecting after her husband's death in 1907. Freer took her under his wing, declaring, "her taste is most exquisite," and her appreciation of Oriental things "more thorough than any other lady I have ever known." He spent arduous hours examining her collection and helping her weed out pieces of modest value.[9]

For Eugene and Agnes, Freer was a mentor. Agnes, ever eager to buy, struggled with her husband's pragmatic restraint. When the P'ang collection arrived at Loo's gallery, she feared her busy husband would "grant Pong [sic] three minutes to line up his treasures...

offer him about 98 cents for the lot and tell him to take it or leave it." When P'ang declined Meyer's offer, Eugene sent a list of the paintings they wanted to Freer in San Diego and left the settlement to him. Three of the paintings on Meyer's list Freer had already selected for himself. One he could not part with, but the other two he passed on to the Meyers at his cost and advised them to buy two other Song paintings. With a "great Ma Yuan" Agnes had secured from Yamanaka the same year, she triumphantly announced she now owned five superb Chinese paintings. Under Freer's guidance another collection of Asian art "of the right sort" had blossomed in America. Before his death, Marcel Bing had sent a collection of bronzes and jade from war-torn France, and Meyer again turned all negotiations over to his friend. This time Freer paid the full asking price, in part because of Bing's "personal love of the group." The man who treated dishonest or dishonorable agents with cold disdain and an empty hand responded to those he respected with benevolence and a generous purse.[10]

Freer now returned to Detroit only to open his collection to important guests, to confer with his cataloguers, or to initiate new projects, such as mounting his hanging scrolls on framed panels. Pressed to prepare his cherished art objects for his future museum, he assembled experts to do the demanding work he could no longer tackle himself. He stayed in a hotel so he could dedicate his home to preparing his collection for transfer to Washington. Grace Guest, an art teacher at Miss Liggett's school who researched and catalogued the Near Eastern art, gained enough expertise to become an assistant curator when the Freer Gallery of Art opened. Men with established reputations assisted periodically: Langdon Warner, Berthold Laufer, Frederick Gookin, the author/lecturer Dana Carroll. With Freer they worked to verify the attribution of each art object and to place each within its original historical context, a formidable task in those early days of Asian art scholarship.

His dogged focus on accuracy meshed with his mission to educate future generations. In 1915, he wrote, not quite accurately:

> The years of acquisition were full—have passed—with them I am content. But now comes identification, classification, explanation for those unborn and living for whom the first work was done.

Written before cousin P'ang called on him in California, he only thought his acquisitions had ended. His zeal for converting future generations to Eastern art, however, had shifted to a higher gear.[11]

He became a godfather to Asian art collections in museums scattered from Minneapolis to St. Louis and from Cleveland to New York City. The time was ripe. Between 1915 and 1918, when Freer worked with them most actively, masterpieces of Asian art were priced below even mediocre pieces of European art. The fall of the final Qing dynasty in 1911 loosened art treasures from temple, imperial, and private storehouses. Langdon Warner warned: "Dealers in China say all good objects are being shipped to New York City and that costs had skyrocketed... [there is] little in Shanghai...bandits out, government suspicious, and travel limited." Freer prodded museum officials:

> Interest in the finer arts of China is making tremendous headway throughout England, France, and Germany, as well as in this country, and I strongly advise you to lose no opportunity to secure fine specimens for your Museum.

The competitive entrepreneur and passionate connoisseur was back "in the fray."[12]

Freer had advised the medieval scholar Wilhelm Valentiner at the Metropolitan Museum in New York on the acquisition and exhibition of Asian art, and for his services, the Met's trustees elected him an honorary fellow for life. When Sigisbert Chretien Bosch-Reitz was appointed the museum's first curator of Oriental art in 1915, he traveled to Detroit to examine the collection of America's foremost expert. Freer declared the young Dutchman "intelligent, broad visioned, sympathetic, and charming." When Freer learned that the museum coveted a pair of Song Dynasty jars he had just optioned to buy, he withdrew his offer. "I would very much prefer to see the pair of jars permanently in the Metropolitan Museum," he explained, because the pots "would be seen by a much larger number of students." That extraordinary pair of jars had graced a table in front of the throne of the empress dowager.[13]

F. Allen Whiting became the director of the Cleveland Museum of Art in May 1913, charged with developing an entirely new museum. As the museum board debated how much to emphasize Oriental art, Whiting wrote Freer, "Your opinion is bound to carry weight with the trustees." Freer promptly invited the trustees and their wives to visit him in Detroit to inspect his collection and promised to loan thirty artworks for their inaugural exhibition. Buy only "fine" objects, he cautioned, and scrutinize donations: "The mouth of every gift horse, should be scientifically examined."[14]

The Minneapolis Institution of Arts had no Asian art when it opened in 1915, so Freer, a nonresident member of the board of trustees, loaned to its inaugural exhibition paintings by Whistler, Dewing, and Tryon. He advised the museum to buy from P'ang and from Kelekian, and by 1917, he was loaning them Japanese paintings for exhibition.

At the St. Louis Art Museum, his influence was more personal. Its president was his old car company comrade William K. Bixby, whom Freer had warned early that "the majority of collectors make the enormous mistake of spending the first ten or twelve years of their collecting in gathering trash, and the balance of their life in getting rid of it." Over many years, the two men had shared an appreciation first for the paintings of Tryon and Dewing, then Whistler, Near Eastern art, and finally Chinese and Japanese art. Bixby acknowledged: "You gave me the start in art work and art collecting." Freer advised him on the "class of Oriental things to acquire" with the museum's Oriental Art Fund.[15]

Two museums were conspicuous by their omission from his crusade: the Museum of Fine Arts, Boston and the Detroit Museum of Art. Already well established in the Oriental art field before Freer began collecting, Boston did not need his help. The museum and the Boston Brahmins associated with it may have intimidated him. By the time he returned from his first trip to Asia in 1895, Fenollosa had been dismissed in disgrace. Freer conferred with Edward Morse on pottery and examined his collection in 1900; and although he traveled to the Boston area frequently, his letters and diaries mention no visits to study the museum's important Asian art until 1902. Boston's new "guru," Kakuzo Okakura, arrived in 1904. The autocratic, outspoken Japanese whom his former teacher Fenollosa once considered "one of the greatest living experts on Oriental art" was welcomed warmly by Morse and Boston society. He had little need for the solitary collector in Detroit. When Freer offered to share with the Boston museum four magnificent antique wooden panels he had bought at the 1903 Gillot sale, Okakura suspected they had been very recently carved. Sarcastically Freer asked the curator to find him more carvings from "the man making them" and happily kept all the panels. Langdon Warner explained the situation simply in 1914, a year after Okakura's death: "Mr. Freer as you know did not like Okakura."[16]

Freer's more compatible connection with the Boston Museum was through one of its trustees, Denman Ross, a Harvard-educated bachelor who collected Whistler as well as Asian art. They toured the museum together in 1902 as Freer was thinking of his own museum. Ross invited Freer to Boston several times, sought his advice before traveling to the Far East in 1912, and encouraged his support of Harvard's Fogg Museum, where Freer served on its Visiting Committee and donated paintings to its collection.[17]

With the Detroit Museum of Art (now Detroit Institute of Art), Freer maintained a guarded truce. Although he had donated to the museum his prized collection of Storm van's Gravesande prints, he remained critical of its ethnological focus geared to appeal to the city's various ethnic groups. Unimpressed with its longtime director, Armand Griffith, and outraged by its leading patron, James Scripps, Freer spent modestly supporting art in Detroit. He was generous when praising it was warranted; and he served at various times on the museum's acquisition and funding committees in an effort to promote the paintings of Tryon and Dewing, but his loyalty to his hometown museum was ambivalent at best.

Meanwhile, the upheaval in China continued. As many fine paintings, especially of the Tang and Song periods, and other beautiful objects arrived in America, Freer reported in early 1916 that "Mr. Loo has enjoyed a prosperous winter, and other Chinese merchants now here are all wearing smiles." Resigned to never seeing China again, Freer tapped into a network of interrelated dealers, Seaouke Yue, K. T. Wong, and Li Van Ching (as Freer anglicized their names) among them. Their maze of fathers, sons, uncles, and cousins in China all seemed to own fine collections of art or to have access to them.[18]

Yue, on his first trip to America in 1916, was introduced to Freer by the P'angs. He had gathered a large collection of antiquities from private owners in both the north and south of China. Freer made his selections and then sent the dealer to the Meyers, the Peters, and to museum officials. After selling all his goods and promising to scour China for "famous antiquities and ancient paintings, etc.," Yue returned with the rare jade "Great Serrate Baton" from the renowned Duanfang collection. It joined Duanfang's famous "Red Sword" already in Freer's collection. Yue's gift of an "antelope horn skin-scratcher" so pleased Freer with its "beauty, rarity, and historic association" that he promised it would go to Washington. Saluting their partnership, Freer wrote, "Our united efforts—yours in discovery and mine in preservation, should be of value to humanity."[19]

Li, whom Freer described as "a very strange person—even for an Oriental," lived next door to the senior P'ang in Shanghai. Without bothering to come himself to wheedle, flatter, and cajole like the other Chinese merchants, Li shipped "fine T'ang and Sung paintings," for the collector to choose the ones he wanted to buy. Wong, the third of this valuable trio, acted as a "side-partner in America" for dealers in China in addition to serving his three or four "old time customers," and Wong's father searched China for Freer's special requests.[20]

Determined to protect his life's mission, Freer warned that "New York is overrun with all kinds of people from Europe and the Far East, as well as from America, with things for sale," especially vilifying a "certain crowd of Japanese and Chinese outcasts [who] unload rubbish" manufactured in New York City. They threatened his efforts to educate Americans. In a country so uninitiated to the rare beauty of the ancient Asian art, he feared its people might be misled by bad art and fail to understand the message in his future museum.[21]

Mentally Freer was active, but his persistent illness limited his travel. He never saw the success of his proselyting efforts in the St. Louis, Minneapolis, or Cleveland museums. Philadelphia, however, lay closer. In late 1918 Freer made a pilgrimage to see the collection at the University of Pennsylvania Museum, one more museum he had assisted. Describing his "fascinating adventure," he praised the objects: "highly significant…intensely elemental in form and fused with emotional fulfillment…expression of feeling as well as external artistic craftsmanship." Its collection was one realization of his dream to expose Americans to the beauty of Asian art. He could see the waves ripple beyond his own pond. Sadly, however, as he strengthened his collection and raised the standards of other collections, his body continued to weaken.[22]

— 21 —

FINAL PURSUITS
1915–1918

As Freer's health inexorably declined, his personal life constricted. He stayed in touch with his oldest friend, Frank Hecker as well as with Watson and Anna, but he rarely saw his Yon stalwarts like Cam Currie. Charles Morse, his colleague in Chicago, had died in 1911; Tom Jerome, his partner on Capri, died in 1915; and Freddie Mann, who had traveled in Egypt with him, died soon thereafter. Charles Freer's greatest loss, however, came with the death of his sister, Emma. Up to the very end he had provided her with every possible comfort. She spent summers at the New Jersey seaside, and it was to Ocean Grove that Freer rushed in August 1915, when her life began to slip away. Coming so shortly after he returned reinvigorated from California, he was stricken anew. In his grief, he wandered on the beach the night of her death in search of solace and acceptance of her fate. Wistfully he wrote, "The moon lit ocean gave approval."[1]

Some of the starch in Charles Freer's fiber left him after her death. For two weeks following the funeral, he lingered in Kingston.

Not since he had departed in 1876 to seek his fortune in Logansport, Indiana, had he stayed in his hometown longer than the time required to conduct his business and be on his way. He settled into a private cabin at Yama Farms Inn, a resort near Kingston, where he could stroll in the nearby woods. Fittingly, its formal name was Japanese, Yama-no-uchi. Agnes's friend, the tall, willowy brunette Katharine Rhoades and her mother were his guests. Even that haven he found "too trying for an old man"; he suffered from "too much nerves—not enough strength." With Katharine in tow, he moved to the Stuyvesant Hotel in Kingston and "walked to old places of boyhood out Lucas Ave." His brother Will had died in 1910. Only the invalid Watson, attended by a male nurse, and Anna still lived on their farm near Kingston. Divorced from Detroit, his family in Kingston dwindling away, Freer became unmoored, almost rootless.[2]

As the disease carried him on a roller coaster of highs and lows and sapped his strength, Katharine, a 30-year-old artist and poet became his companion. The 64-year-old collector clung to "K," his term of endearment for her. As his confidant, his secretary, his alter ego, and at times his nurse-aid, she bore the brunt of his criticism and shared in his joys. Always the proper gentleman, he could safely write "My beloved Agnes" to the wife of his good friend, but he dared not address the unmarried Miss Rhoades, "my other third in such endearing term." She frequently spent the morning or afternoon with him; she addressed his Christmas cards and made several attempts to paint his portrait. None satisfied him and none survives.[3]

Katharine accompanied him on inspection trips to his home in Detroit, where experts were cataloguing the collection for his museum. Chinese students assisted during their college vacations, but for translating signatures, seals, and inscriptions on the Chinese paintings, he imported Asian experts. Freer, ever the perfectionist, relied on them to separate much of "the chaff from the wheat" by using literary evidence to detect counterfeits.[4]

Katharine was also at his side in New York City when, in another desperate effort to regain his health or at least find relief, he submitted his failing body to a new treatment by a new doctor. Starting in November 1915, Dr. George Draper gave him a series of "painful spinal injections." Each one incapacitated him for 24 to 48 hours. Confined to his room at the Plaza Hotel, he required nurses and a "rubber." It was a difficult winter. For six months he endured weekly unspecified injections, noting in his diary simply "1 I" or "2 I." Even rides through Central Park in a motor car left him exhausted. Agnes Meyer and sympathetic New York friends sent him flowers and dispatched butlers with baskets of healthful fresh fruits and vegetables. They brought cheery conversation to their dear friend, who was often hard to please.[5]

The constant tension between hope and reality exacted a toll on Freer. Although he claimed that his doctors in New York were "accomplishing more than I thought possible," after 1916 his increasing debility from syphilis imposed unwelcome limitations. He admitted to Agnes that this recent siege of ill health had been long and "the result uncertain." Longing to retreat again to sunny California, he asked to have suitable rooms at the Arrowhead Resort altered for his extended stay. His chauffeur and car arrived in San Diego. His progressing illness, however, made that journey impossible. He remained in New York City with the Meyers, Katharine, and his doctors.[6]

In the 35-year-old Dr. Draper, from a cultured, gifted family of social standing in New York City, Freer had found not only a competent physician but also a sympathetic friend and a budding connoisseur of art. As the doctor applied his physic to Freer's body, the collector planted in him an enthusiasm for Asian art. Draper was a worrier and a perfectionist, his seriousness softened by a subtle, dry sense of humor. A tall, slender man, brilliant and articulate, he was a skilled storyteller with a penchant for interesting famous patients, most notably Franklin Delano Roosevelt, whom he later treated for polio. One of the early specialists in psychosomatic medicine, he underwent analysis with both Sigmund Freud and Karl Jung. Freer trusted him implicitly and followed his directives to the letter. They teamed well. When the collector gave his new friend a Chinese painting of Shen Hung, the "master of medicine," the doctor responded in words that echoed Freer's:

> [Impossible] to articulate my feeling...nothing could have touched me more...something wonderful stirring quietly on my emotions...power and beauty of Chinese painting...intellectual and emotional experience.

Dorothy Draper, famous in her own right as an interior decorator, shared her husband's new enthusiasm. The Drapers became part of Freer's shrinking entourage. With a keen understanding of his patient when the injections no longer seemed effective, he advised Freer to get outdoor air and do moderate exercise away from the city. From youth to old age, Freer found his tonic in nature.[7]

During his visits to the Berkshires in 1913 and 1914, he had bought property high on a hill rising behind Great Barrington. A magnificent site, with dense pine forests scattered amid open meadows, his virgin land stretched across the hillside. The horizon opened in three directions, his own San-no-tani. Typically, he described it as his "small garden spot...a few pine trees, lots of rocks, and a view stretching straight to Nirvana." His long-nourished dream of a rustic mountain cabin, hatched years ago as he and his friend Church trekked through the Catskills, might finally become a reality.[8]

In the summer of 1916, following doctor's orders, Freer threw himself into building what he called "a bungalow" on his hilltop site. He negotiated property lines and supervised the group of men hired to cut back weeds and trim trees for a road. He staked out the dimensions of the building with his contractor. Just as he had in building his home in Detroit, he participated in every decision and oversaw every detail. Unsurprisingly, his scrutiny frequently provoked the local workmen. When two Polish men hired to burn the scrub brush quit after two days, he hired Italians and then fired them.

Each morning he motored from the Great Barrington Inn to "the Heights" to inspect the progress. George Alger, his business secretary in Detroit, arrived with his family and Freer's car. Katharine Rhoades stayed at the Inn with Freer. Dr. Draper made his long-distance house calls a social visit and brought his wife. Watson and Anna, the Meyers, the Heckers, and Louisine Havemeyer formed a stream of visitors. Dealers came with their wares. One day Freer worked on India-Persian miniatures, on jade the next day, another day on small bronzes or Chinese paintings.

When America declared war in April 1917, the harsh reality of World War I touched Freer personally. Eugene Meyer volunteered his services to lead the War Finance Corporation, and with Agnes, moved to Washington, D.C. With an ill man's inwardness, Freer felt most keenly the loss of his physician to the war front. Dr. Draper became Captain Draper and left first for Washington, D.C., and then for France. Freer wrote him wistfully: "You and Shen will continue to fight my old enemy, even at the disadvantage of distance." Shen, the painting of the medicine master, had become his talisman.[9]

He reported regularly to Draper in minute detail on his physical condition, just to "keep in touch with headquarters." In one letter he outlined a recent attack:

> I arose at seven A.M., and the moment I stood erect - dizziness…warned me to return to bed, and instantly I obeyed. A half hour later, when raising my head slightly, nausea came, lasting about five minutes, followed by slight vomiting…recognized the importance of a horizontal position, relaxation and quiet.

In another he reported his recovery: "Slowly but surely regaining better control of my right leg and, excepting the constant dullness in my head, (no dizziness) I am feeling nearly normal." Dr. John Munn Hanford attended him, but Freer wanted to know the decisions came from Draper. As his concern over his health mounted, he treated his body ever more cautiously. Fearing overexertion, he did less and less. He now found relief in art, his life's blood.[10]

Jade became his newest passion. Its subtle qualities are difficult for the uninitiated to fully appreciate, and the Chinese collectors reluctantly released that most cherished object last. From his dealers, Freer had learned to understand jade and where to find the best pieces. Along with bronzes, paintings, small statuettes, sculptures, and always pottery, jade loosened his purse strings during and after the winter of 1916–1917. As the quality of art available from China rose, Freer continued to buy, but with discipline.

In 1916, the Tang stone Bodhisattva Kwan-yin that the Paris dressmaker Paul Poiret had purchased from Paul Mallon was put on the market. Denman Ross offered to pay a quarter of the purchase price if the Boston Museum would buy it, but neither the museum nor another donor stepped forward. In December, Freer, in the company of Agnes Meyer and Katharine Rhoades, saw the statue at Kelekian's shop in New York. Freer chose not to spare the funds demanded by that single masterpiece. Eugene Meyer bought the Kwan-yin statue and persuaded Freer to accept it as a gift for the Freer Gallery of Art. Fearing some mocking publicity in "grotesque exaggeration" of its price and because there was "no one in charge capable—outside of Lodge—to erect, surround etc., etc., so important a work," Freer insisted that Kelekian store the statue and not announce news of the purchase. "Lodge" was John E. Lodge, the curator of Japanese and Chinese art at the Museum of Fine Arts, Boston since 1916. He would soon become Freer's nemesis.[11]

With Katharine or Agnes, the elderly gentleman also slummed in the "junk shops," as he called the numerous import shops in New York. While he slowly walked down one side of the long display tables, his accomplice searched through the objects on the other side; they competed to discover amid the rubble a piece of fine workmanship or rare age. One day a local dealer visiting Freer at his spacious Plaza Hotel room offered him, among other things, a pair of lovely white pottery vases. Freer liked them immensely but absolutely refused to pay the $1,500 asked by the dealer. During one of her own forays into the "junk shops," Agnes spotted one of the vases and bought it for $250, then gleefully presented it to Freer. Were there numerous such vases floating around New York, or had she spotted the singular prize? Such were the challenges he loved about collecting.

His optimism and determination, however, could not overcome one brutal fact: the tonic of loyal friends, a hilltop bungalow, a sympathetic doctor, and even buying art could not give him the recovery he so desperately wanted. His time was running out.

— 22 —

THE FREER GALLERY OF ART
1902–1919

CHARLES FREER COLLECTED ART NOT for mere possession and certainly not for profit; he collected partly for prestige, but mainly for posterity. His collection was the legacy of his life. It bore his personal imprint, expressed his values, and harbored his dreams. He nurtured it like a child, conscious of its need for purpose, balance, authenticity, protection, and growth. With equal care, he planned the museum to perpetuate his vision. Since 1902, he had been creating in his mind what would become the Freer Gallery of Art.

As the idea of a permanent museum took root, he pictured a "proper" setting, suitable in spirit to the works of art, harmonious and subtle in design. Under the influence of Whistler and Fenollosa, he grasped the potential of linking the arts of East and West in his museum. When he signed the deed in 1906 conveying his art collection to the United States government, he thought his friend Stanford White, the leading architect of the day, would design the building. Unfortunately, a month after the deed became final, White was fatally shot by the jealous husband of his paramour. It was an artistic as well as a personal loss for Charles Freer.[1]

Two years later the new Smithsonian Secretary Charles Walcott pushed Congress to establish a National Gallery of Art; and as part of the project, he asked Freer to draw up plans for his museum. The collector sketched a vague outline: a building 800 feet by 300 feet with eight exhibition rooms of equal size open to a central hall and a second floor lighted by a skylight. Congress failed to fund Walcott's initiative.[2]

In 1909, Freer spent a month examining Europe's finest museums. He studied architectural styles; he investigated methods of heat, light, and ventilation; he observed room arrangements and facilities for students. He considered using the "Tudor-Gothic" style of London's South Kensington Museum (now the Victoria and Albert Museum); but after seeing its Italian Renaissance addition, he liked that too and declared, "I hope to better it from every point." In Germany he decried their gloomy, vast halls that devoured the works of beauty, leaving them lifeless and obscured. From each stop he learned more about what to avoid in his future museum than what to emulate, complaining to Hecker: "The great aim here seems to be pretentiousness, confusion and ugliness." He was determined that his own museum would provide an environment comparable in quality and compatible in mood with the art he had collected. In short, it would express the aesthetic he shared with Whistler and the eminent connoisseurs in Japan.[3]

His adventures in China from 1909 to1911 preempted further planning for his museum, but by 1912, with his restless mind trapped in a disabled body, Freer again focused on his building. Without consulting an architect, he laid out his ideal museum. Since the first inventory submitted in 1906, his collection had nearly doubled to over 4,000 objects, the increase generated overwhelmingly by his Asian art. The scheme, therefore, should be weighted toward the display of Eastern art. On Plaza Hotel stationery, he sketched a square building reminiscent of the famous Byodo-in in Uji Japan, with wings on each side, one for Japanese art and one for Chinese art.

When the first building site in Washington was exchanged for a smaller but preferable spot next the original Smithsonian building, he adapted his plans and settled for a simple two-story structure shaped like a quadrangle around an inner court. The Japanese and Chinese exhibition rooms would face each other across the courtyard, along two sides of the building. The rear side of the building he reserved for the Whistler collection, including a special room designed for the Peacock Room.

A section of four small rooms in the front he assigned to the other American artists, one room each for the works of Dewing, Thayer, and Tryon, and a fourth for a miscellaneous group of works by noted artists like Winslow Homer, John Singer Sargent, and Childe Hassam. In each of the American artists' rooms, twelve to sixteen pictures would hang on permanent display. Freer specifically outlined where each painting would hang. The architectural style he now favored was Italian Renaissance. His one overriding criterion remained: the building would function for the art it contained. His years of study and his exposure to the elegant displays of art in Japan had taught him the value of uncluttered space as the best stage for art. Further, he insisted on a practical museum, well lighted with ample facilities for uninterrupted study and research.[4]

His parameters set, he chose another longtime friend, Charles A. Platt, an etcher and landscape artist, as his architect. Although lacking the brilliant genius of Stanford White, Platt proved a judicious choice. He had much in common with his client; he was a close communicant with both nature and art, an experienced traveler with breadth of vision, and a perfectionist. A member of the colony of artists surrounding Saint-Gaudens and Dewing, Platt had outlined gardens in Italy for Freer to visit on his grand tour in 1894. Recently Freer had introduced Platt to the Meyers, who commissioned the architect to design their new home in Mount Kisco. He liked Platt's "big, frank methods of reasoning and expressing ideas that makes [sic] him so helpfull [sic] and efficient" and admitted he enjoyed "being bossed by a wide-visioned master." When the architect willingly undertook the task of reviewing the entire Freer collection of artworks, Freer declared him a man of "rare patience and endurance."[5]

The two men consulted frequently on the project in 1913 and 1914. Together they visited Henry Clay Frick's home as well as public museums. Freer had not originally intended to have the building erected during his lifetime, but under pressure from the Smithsonian, he allowed the project to go forward. The building plans were approved by the United States government in 1915, and Freer increased his bequest from $500,000 to $1 million to cover inflation. Platt completed the final drawings by mid-1916, and construction began October 2, 1916. When construction costs inevitably exceeded budget, Freer unflinchingly gave an extra $70,000 to avoid unwarranted compromise.[6]

Curiously, Freer retired to the background once construction on his building began. From the time the final site was selected until the museum was nearly complete, he did not go to Washington to inspect or supervise it. Agnes Meyer and Dr. George Draper, both in Washington during the war years, reported to him as it took shape. Even marking its progress with his closest friends failed to entice him. In the man who had stood sentinel over the smallest detail in constructing and decorating his home in Detroit and creating his bungalow in Great Barrington, such a distant attitude toward the most expensive, most important, and most permanent building he erected was remarkable. No evidence among his papers explains his physical detachment. Perhaps the Smithsonian officials insisted on acting as overseers, but Freer would not likely have abrogated personal responsibility unless he chose to. Psychologically, was he not yet ready to sever the umbilical cord with his art collection and accept the physical evidence of its home after his death? His feelings must have alternated between fulfilling pride and wrenching sorrow.[7]

Ten years earlier, the donation of his artworks had been a grand and exciting plan for the distant future; by 1916, the imminent transfer of those artworks promised an increasingly painful separation. Given his innate optimism, death did not seem to concern him in the corporeal sense, but the end of his life did mean the end of his control over a collection of art that had been his life's work. In 1906, he had left his gift to the nation tied securely with many strings. Faced with the reality of its survival without his guidance, he stubbornly resisted any changes after he was gone.

In his original deed, Freer specified that no work of art could be added or deleted from the collection after his death. Only under pressure and with agonizing struggle did he relax his restrictions on its future. He had not anticipated the financial bonanza his investments had delivered over the last thirteen years. His estate, specifically Parke-Davis stock plus its dividends, had multiplied so substantially since 1906 that allocation of the excess cash needed to be addressed. In his new will, dated May 13, 1918, he assigned any residue of the estate to the Smithsonian. The income from such residue should, if an "exigency" existed, provide for the care of the building and the collections. (The original deed had put the full burden of maintaining the museum on the Smithsonian.) Otherwise, the residual income should be used for "the encouragement of the study of the civilization of the Far East," and any further remainder might be used to purchase "works of American painters, sculptors and potters," provided the works immediately become the property of the National Gallery of Art, not a part of the Freer Collection or even exhibited in the Freer Gallery. The unity and harmony of the collections he had created should remain unaltered.[8]

A second, more traumatic task assaulted the ill connoisseur: choosing a curator to manage and control his collection after his death. Once again, planning in 1906 had been exciting; he considered possibilities for a curator as early as he thought about a building.

The first concrete candidate was a newcomer to Asian art and a most unlikely choice. Not surprisingly, Freer settled on a close confidant with sympathetic values. In 1917 Charles Freer tentatively proposed to Dr. George Draper that he become curator of the future Freer Gallery of Art. In response to Draper's report on the progress of the building under construction in Washington, Freer wrote:

> Concentrate on what it will some day hold and what influence from the things within will eventually emulate and, with Shen, consider your share, not only of its message, but also perhaps of your own active collaboration.

Perhaps unwilling to disappoint his friend and patient or simply too busy to take the idea seriously, Draper allowed Freer to persist with it. Walcott pressed Freer to formally name a curator and visited Freer in June 1918 to discuss the issue in person. Freer confirmed his choice of Draper and agreed to inform the doctor, who was then at the European war front, of his decision.[9]

He had parried the harsh reality of relinquishing control by proposing Draper as curator and Katharine Rhoades as assistant curator, two people not only close to him personally but also whose training in Asian art came exclusively from him. In August 1918, praising Draper's war work in France, Freer quixotically commended it as "a proper forerunner to the one of after the war in which we are mutually interested up to our chins."[10]

Katharine Rhoades knew all aspects of the collection as nearly through his eyes and mind as anyone else. Together they unpacked each new shipment, studied each piece, and listened to the experts. She witnessed his first reaction, his studied reflection, his reasoning with external facts, and his final willful conclusion as each object was offered to him. As circumspect as the man she served, she brought to her mission the sensitivity of an artist as well as the loyalty of an acolyte.

From 1917 to 1919, she devoted herself almost totally to the collector as he lived the emotional drama of his disease. She described his acute sensitivity as "tremendous—& tremendously fine," and regretted only that she herself was neither finely enough tuned nor spiritually developed enough "to respond accurately to the changes in feeling & acting which that sensitiveness demands." Reminiscent of Freer's experience as Whistler neared death, she wrote:

> An extraordinary and wonderful atmosphere has surrounded the General…the beauty of his spirit. Sometimes he seemed to have found such spiritual contentment - & exaltation, that I wondered & almost feared that the earthly self had completed

> itself...[followed by] a great contemplative mood—full of power—quietness of strength & attainment of philosophic ideals.

But she also lived through his periods of being "horribly upset" and confided to Agnes, "Each time such a situation arises it seems to become more critical...& my greatest thought is its effect upon the General's health of body & mind."[11]

Even Agnes, with all her strength and bravado, cowered in the presence of the ill man. She wrote in her diary after making a mistake: "Quand meme it was stupid of me I shall know better next time & I fully deserved the look the General gave me." As early as 1917 the two women had their hands full helping their "General" maintain his equanimity. They had accompanied him to the opening of an exhibition of Chinese paintings from the Freer collection in Chicago, and Platt, hoping to get new ideas for the Washington gallery, met them there. Agnes lamented that "it was agonizing to forestall any incident which might upset him," but they failed.

> The General had his usual run in with the hotel but was somewhat appeased when he managed to get a man fired. He is not getting stronger physically or temperamentally. K. has an extremely difficult job.[12]

His trips to Detroit became a trial; its strident modernity jarred his unstable emotions. He railed against "noisy-low browed dancing during dinner at hotel," and changed hotels more than once. Even his beloved Yondotega Club failed to uphold his standards. After an unpleasant experience at the club, he wrote its president, his old friend Cam Currie:

> I ought to, I know, express to you words of kindness concerning that Yondotega dinner—a dinner of alluring prospects—but sombre [sic] ending—and its [sic] hard to interpret the atmosphere in which one's heart breaks, but life goes splendidly on.

No record remains of the offending incident. Other small problems had earlier brought protest from Freer: a rusty gate, an unworthy candidate; but this new disillusion brought total rejection. He resigned from the club. The rough draft of his formal letter remains among his papers; filled with corrections and rewritten phrases, showing his struggle to put into words the high ideals he meant his act of resignation to exemplify. He hoped to wrench the club into mending its ways. Instead the old man was patted on the head and given an honorary position; that too he defiantly refused, he preferred integrity to empty honor. He chose to remain "without the gate."[13]

Amid the disappointments and strain of his persistent illness, the invalid found one task particularly rewarding. From among his "reserved list" of art objects not designated to go to Washington, he selected "specimens" to give to friends and family. Instead of leaving the job to his executors as he had planned, Dr. Draper encouraged him to do it now, and salutary advice it was. Freer derived great satisfaction from choosing an item particularly appropriate for each recipient and had the pleasure of receiving in return their letters of gratitude.[14]

Finally he sought solace in the mountains, investing his waning energy in the bungalow on his hilltop lot in the Berkshires. In the joys of its spectacular vistas and healing nature he pinned his hopes for renewed strength. He spent days walking the land, burning the brush, and harassing the builder with his inspections and suggestions. With Katharine as his constant companion, he fed his soul as well as his body in his emerging nirvana. By late 1918 his lifetime dream was nearly realized, but alas, he never lived there. As with his dreams throughout his life, the pursuit was as vital to him as the capture.

Tragically for this reticent, dignified man, he had to battle unpredictable "enemy" demons aroused by late-stage syphilis. He became more nervous and cantankerous; people irritated and offended him more frequently. He moved from the Plaza Hotel to the Gotham Hotel. Unable to find a chauffeur who pleased him, he assigned that job to his secretary George Alger. When Alger resigned in frustration, Freer turned all the accounts and records over to Katharine. Stephen Warring became the masseur and chauffeur as well as curator and butler. Warring seemed to bear stoically the strain of catering to the ailing old man, but Katharine, because she was so constantly with the "General," suffered acutely. She became ill herself and left for a few months. Freer went to a sanatorium. The injections no longer offered relief. There was no cure.

During the winter of 1918 and 1919 the "enemy" felled him with increasing frequency. He was confined to bed, and nurses were platooned around the clock. Agnes, his sister-in-law Anna, Katharine, and Dr. Draper rotated the responsibilities of calling on the invalid in his rooms on the top floor of the Gotham Hotel overlooking Fifth Avenue. With each new attack, Freer's hold on life became more fragile. Friends hedged in their letters: "if he recovers." Agnes wrote in her diary in February, "The General has been near death's door…I firmly believe that he will come back completely." She kept his room filled with garden flowers.[15]

Louisine sent her butler with nourishing soup, eggs, apples, and rice pudding. In April, she found him seated by the window, plagued by the heat and the noise below, "a wasted sufferer waiting for the call, the shadowy substance of the man." He suffered nightmares and strange visions—sometimes a great fire appeared before him; other times he could not comprehend what he saw. He found some comfort in cradling an ancient piece of jade in his thin hands, stroking the smooth, hard finish as it had been stroked by appreciative Chinese mandarins centuries ago.[16]

Still he did not give up. He kept hoping to get back to Detroit to oversee the preparations of his collection for its transfer to his museum. He wanted to see his hilltop bungalow. As his body wasted away, his spirit stubbornly took optimistic flight. Each week he wrote that surely the next week he would be strong enough to travel. In his last letter to Watson, penned in a strong hand on May 30, he thanked his brother for a recent note that "gave me personal expression of your feelings and doings." The dying man proclaimed, "Bully for you and bully for Anna [for your efforts at Maple Farm] are putting you back on your feet. Keep up the good work" and reassured his brother:

> I am receiving the best of care in every way, and have no kicks up my sleeve...My visions, which come often, however, include many of my favorite mountains and hill top views, and I suffer neither pain nor sorrow - all seems calm and much very beautiful so, all is well. Love to all, Charlie.[17]

As Charles Freer struggled to hang on, the Freer Gallery of Art neared completion. Decisions on the final disposition of his collection became imperative. Worried about his mental and physical states, Freer's closest friends gathered to counsel him. Frank Hecker attended him on issues of finance and business; on matters of art Agnes, Katharine, and Dr. Draper took command. Watson and Anna visited, as did Louisine and his Yon friend Cam Currie. His circle of concerned friends urged him to reconsider the restrictions he had imposed on his museum. They rightly feared the strings with which he had bound his gift would limit the future value of his legacy. Six months before his death, he still insisted that the deed for his collection retain its original form, doggedly determined to preserve the integrity of his creation.

In May 1919, cajoled by his friends, he was persuaded to draft a codicil to his will. He allowed his funds to be used "for the promotion of high ideals of beauty and, to that end occasional purchases shall be made of very fine examples of Oriental, Egyptian and Near Eastern fine arts." Setting the strictest limits on future acquisitions, he stipulated that such objects were to be examined and approved by Katharine Rhoades, Mr. and Mrs. Eugene Meyer, and Mrs. H. O. Havemeyer in consultation with the Fine Arts National Commission. In the absence of such an opportunity to buy Asian art, the money could be used to purchase American art for the National Gallery, not for the Freer Gallery. Opening the door to future acquisitions just a fraction more, he permitted gifts to the Freer collection from the Meyers, Mrs. Havemeyer, Hecker, and Platt, "each of whom has already contributed important art objects to that part of the National Collection at present in my care."[18]

Without question Freer envisioned the addition of only a relatively small number of remarkably choice pieces. In his cautious retreat from control, he acknowledged the possibility of uncovering fine art still buried in Asia; yet he protected the harmony of his collection by leaving behind a rear guard of his loyal friends. Caught between protecting his creation and the possibility of new discoveries, he gambled grudgingly. That farsighted bet, instead of petrifying his museum in 1919, enabled it to become the power in Asian art it is today. Exploration of antiquities in the Near and Far East had barely begun in 1919. Today the Asian art in the Freer Gallery of Art, after 100 years of remarkable acquisitions, is acknowledged as among the finest in the world. Freer, however, prohibited any future purchases of American art; that collection remained frozen in 1919.

Meanwhile, his most traumatic decision, naming the man to direct his museum, had unraveled. Dr. George Draper had returned to his medical practice in New York in 1919 and gently but firmly declined Freer's naïve idea of making him the curator. Draper's passion lay in his own challenging profession. With the building's anticipated completion barely twelve months away, choosing the curator was critical. At the urging of Agnes, Katharine, and the Smithsonian's secretary Walcott, Freer made one final attempt to designate his successor. On May 14, 1919, in the company of Agnes and Katharine, he discussed the prospects with John E. Lodge, curator of Chinese and Japanese art at the Museum of Fine Arts, Boston. When Boston trustees Denman Ross and William Sturgis Bigelow suggested that Boston retain Lodge "in an advisory capacity" if he accepted the Freer Gallery position, Freer agreed. On June 4, he formally proposed that Lodge accept the "Keepership (or Curatorship)" of the Freer Gallery of Art, with Katharine Rhoades as the assistant curator. He commended the Bostonian as:

> [T]he person best qualified and equipped to assume this charge: to take care of the collection itself; to further scholarly research; to deepen the appreciation of the objects in the collection as well as the

> ideals which govern them, and to administer the necessary directive functions in connection with their storage and exhibition.

He assured Lodge that he need not end his association with the Boston Museum and, in fact, encouraged him to maintain it:

> I should wish that the scope of your activities would include a continuation of your relationship with the Boston Museum in an advisory capacity, and also to allow for future associations with other leading art museums both American and foreign.

Freer envisioned that the man in charge of his institution would be a leader in the Asian art field throughout the world. Lodge responded with his acceptance and enclosed the proposal voted on by his museum's trustees. It stipulated "that Mr. Lodge be granted such leave of absence as he may deem necessary to organize the Freer Collection and act as its Keeper or Curator." Lodge further clarified his own understanding of his position:

> The administrative welfare of the Boston Museum collections of Chinese and Japanese Art, and the Freer collection is put into my hands, with full responsibility and proportionate power to do my best for both.

Clearly the Bostonians and Lodge assumed that his primary responsibility would remain at Boston, with the Freer position as an adjunct.[19]

Freer read that letter with disbelief and then with fury. Irate that anyone should consider overseeing his collection simply on a "leave of absence," indignant at Lodge's assumption that his post gave him "unlimited authority over the collection," and incredulous that the man would attempt to hold both curatorships simultaneously, Freer demanded "to drop the entire matter as it stands and treat it as a closed incident." He never named his successor.[20]

Although he avoided seeing his building in person and naming its director, he controlled details that he feared the dollar-conscious government might starve. Designating $200,000 of Parke-Davis stock "solely for the purpose of hiring a competent curator," he assured his gallery the guidance of a well-paid administrator unhampered by the stingy restraints of Congress or jealous competition from other parts of the Smithsonian. He allocated money for the creation of the courtyard garden with appropriate statuary and a separate fund for its care and maintenance. He insured the purchase of suitable display cases and furniture to protect against skimping on the interior. He made a bequest directly to the University of Michigan to fund research "regarding the art objects embraced in the collection of oriental art... [to increase] knowledge and appreciation of oriental art." With impressive foresight, he used the power of his purse to assure the highest quality in his future museum.[21]

During the summer of 1919, a burst of pleasure came into his life when large shipments of Chinese antiquities arrived from both Yue and Wong. Stephen Warring traveled to New York to assist in the unpacking. Agnes, Anna, Katharine, Dr. Draper, and Louisine all gathered to inspect the treasures. Freer rallied to make the final acquisitions for his collection and to help his friends choose among those the old man passed over. It is tempting but wrong to see Freer as he sensed his own inevitable end, buying with greater abandon, buying paintings, pottery, jade, and sculpture in grand lots just to make sure he had covered the field before his death. Not Freer. With all the strength he had, the principled connoisseur studied each piece in each shipment. He agonized over questionable pieces with the same care so characteristic of him when he was younger and stronger; he still had a keen eye for the qualities of a fine "specimen." A few months earlier, Freer had penned in a strong longhand letter his evaluation of two pieces of pottery Agnes had sent him:

> The glazed incense burner is a corker—just the kind, in decoration, needed to connect the chain Han to T'ang of potteries in my group so I bought it.
>
> ...The unglazed vase which I returned...is also a wonder in form, and at first glance gave me heavenly thrills - but close inspection brought chills!!! And as I tested it along side of masterpieces, I found, by degrees. that it resembled too closely for comfort, the fakes now being made by Kano Tessai in Tokio and by a follower of his at Nara: both of whom are marketing their imitations principally in China.

The dealer and its owner both claimed that the returned vase was very old; Freer defiantly wrote "if they are right then another like it may never be unearthed," but he followed his own judgment and declined.[22]

His pen strokes weakened. By August 1919, his angry outbursts increased. Agnes described one day when she alone dared face him during one of his frenzied attacks:

> The General stormed around his rooms, shouting, smashing his heavy cane against the furniture in an attack of sheer madness…I opened the door, walked rapidly toward him before he could hit me with his cane, pinned my eyes with all my young force on those insane eyes that terrified me, and said quietly, very quietly, "good morning, General."…Gradually those mad eyes began ever so slightly to focus…with a deep sigh of relief, as if he were escaping from some intolerable burden.[23]

He had moments of repose too. On August 15, Eugene Meyer stopped in to visit and found Freer asleep. After examining the jades alone as Freer slept, he left a note addressed, "My dear General," commending once more his old friend's contribution in bringing together the East and the West. A month before he died, Freer, in a moment of serenity, assured a fellow "Yon":

> In these days of continuous illness I am happy to say that I am without pain or sadness and I really believe that the illness, although interfering with muscular activity, stimulates and exhilarates the mind.[24]

On September 12, he made his last entry in his diary: "Anna spent afternoon." On September 25, he died.[25]

Charles Lang Freer was buried beside his family in the Wiltwyck Cemetery in Kingston; his simple headstone matches theirs. The New York, Detroit, and Kingston papers ran laudatory if modest obituaries. He slipped away as privately as he had lived his life.

The men most keenly cognizant of Freer's rare accomplishments were his fellow connoisseurs in Japan. In honor of their great American friend, whose early appreciation of Hon'ami Kōetsu had demonstrated his profound understanding of Japanese art, they erected a memorial in Japan. Appropriately, they chose a site in the garden of the Buddhist temple dedicated to Kōetsu near Kyoto.

A small, secluded temple, one of literally hundreds in the area, Kōetsu-ji lies hidden quietly on a hillside. A simple path leads from a narrow road down the hill, meandering between the hut-like temple buildings sheltered in the privacy of bushes and trees. Near the center of the grounds where several paths converge, a natural stone rises amid the foliage. The words carved in Japanese and translated into English proclaim it the Memorial of Charles Lang Freer. The setting in nature would have pleased Freer as much as it pleased the Japanese. Erected by Masuda, Hara, and Yamanaka with the support of their friends who knew and respected the trailblazing American connoisseur, the memorial was dedicated in a simple Buddhist ceremony on May 9, 1930.

The extraordinary man had, in his own way, connected West and East.

EPILOGUE

THE FREER GALLERY OF ART opened to the public on May 2, 1923, to general applause. The elegant building, low and square with the harmonious proportions and human scale of Florentine Renaissance style, mirrored the taste of its donor. Massive bronze doors behind three tall arches admitted visitors to an oasis of art; peacocks strolled in the garden court around a splashing fountain. The rooms were arranged as Freer had planned. A visitor could walk to the left of the courtyard through Chinese art or choose the right side through rooms of Japanese art; either way led to the Whistler rooms nestled across the back. Spare, handsomely crafted cases held pieces of pottery or displayed a partially unrolled makemono. Kakemono panels hung on the walls, elegant screens unfolded and Buddhist statues stood, just a few of each to avoid the feeling of clutter. So it remains today minus the peacocks.

Langdon Warner saw a certain makemono displayed at the Freer Gallery's opening and recalled his first experience with it in the ambiance of Freer's Ferry Avenue home:

> I remember long hours spent over the great table in the new fire-proof room, where one bent over that same scroll, armed with a huge magnifying glass,

> and fortified by a different glass, at one's elbow, filled with the nectar found only in that house. Books of reference were fetched, more paintings brought for comparison.[1]

The ambiance of the new museum was similar. No glass of nectar rested at the visitor's elbow, and no proud host stood by bursting with tales of the scroll's strange history, of adventures in some shop hidden down a dusty, smelly back alley in Peking, of smugly stepping into his rickshaw with fat Nan panting at his side, the precious scroll tucked securely under his arm. But the spacious skylighted rooms, the intimate atmosphere, and the carefully selected objects on exhibition resembled the intimacy of his home. Library books and other objects in storage were available by appointment. Like a ghost, Freer cast a mood on his museum as he had cast his imprint on his collection.

Freer's taste was so far ahead of his time that much of the art world did not catch up to him until after World War II. Most of his contemporaries thought that embroideries, carved lacquerware, snuff bottles, brightly colored porcelain, and cloisonné vases were Chinese art and that Japanese art was tea jars, woodblock prints, and netsuke. In Near Eastern art they knew of little beyond mosque lamps and tiles. While others collected showy objects crafted with technical brilliance, Freer had looked for ancient, often faded expressions of an artist's soul.

The farm boy who became a pioneering art connoisseur left not only an extraordinary collection, he also left an idealism embodied in an institution. When Katharine Rhoades was asked to clarify Freer's phrase "for the promotion of high ideals," she defined it as "maintaining certain standards of belief, of judgement, and of conduct…he demanded orderliness, accuracy, comprehensiveness." High standards had marked the quality of the man as they would mark the quality of his gallery. In Berthold Laufer's assessment, he was "the first great collector to make a concise and clear distinction between two things - the industrial art and the liberal arts of the Orient…We are therefore indebted to Mr. Freer not only for what his museum contains, but just as much for what is brilliantly conspicuous there by its absence." The intimacy and focus of his museum reflected his belief that "while great museums have both their place and use…small collections, setting forth perfectly a single unit, will prove more available and influential in the end." His collection was not to be lost among the endless corridors in a large, metropolitan museum.[2]

For all the glorious beauty of the objects in the Freer Gallery of Art, it is not a sensuous place; no extravagant feast awaits the glutton's eye; no riotous display of color, no fanfare dazzles its public. It is a scholarly retreat with all the warmth of a monastery, a secluded spot for contemplation where the committed are restored and the willing novice is converted. And that too is the way Freer wanted it. He counted on the objects to arouse passion in the sympathetic viewer as they had in him. Langdon Warner described Freer unwrapping scarf-bound packages pressed on him by a dealer: "At first he was questioning and doubtful, even respectful of other's opinions, but soon the tide would sweep him off his feet and he would declaim and lecture and snort over a bowl, till he ended by paying the inevitable price for his fancy." The museum still invites such passionate discovery.[3]

Freer harbored the zeal of a religious reformer. He willingly rode the back of a sweating coolie through flooded, muddy waters to reach a mecca of art. He chose to sacrifice the mundane pleasures of the idle rich on Capri to labor in remote fields of art. To share the beauty he loved, he gave nearly all his worldly wealth. He had a puritan discomfort with pure pleasure. "Have a look at every fine thing the gods permit, and think kindly of the absent sinners," he had implored Osvald Sirén when the young scholar traveled in China. Proud of his success and prosperity, Freer did not shrink from the fortune he amassed and the art he gathered, only at deriving solely a selfish pleasure from them. He needed to serve a purpose. From the beginning he had conceived his museum as a didactic institution; the perpetual student wanted to expose Americans to the finest in art and to teach them that the finest artistic impulses existed in the East as well as in the West.

In his crusade, he carried not only the fervor of faith but also the conviction of right. His conclusions came slowly, confirmed by study, and he held to them tenaciously. Sympathetic friends to whom he showed his treasures wisely refrained from expressing contrary opinions. Sirén wrote of him:

> Freer was at the time generally recognized as *primus inter parens* among collectors of Far Eastern art in the Western hemisphere, and he did not like to see or hear any adverse opinions about dates or attributions, which could tend to shake the principles of his *musee imaginaire*.

Essentially a romantic in an era of limited scholarship, Freer judged artworks with his eyes and his intuition. "Harmonious standard," "subtlety of expression," and "refinement of subject matter" weighted his decisions to buy and to keep an art object. Inevitably new authorities contested his opinions.[4]

A lengthy debate followed Freer's death in which Agnes and Katharine played strong roles. John Lodge of the Boston Museum continued to be a candidate for curator, along with art critic Royal Cortissoz and archeologist Carl Bishop. Finally in 1920 the officials and friends to whom he had entrusted his legacy appointed Lodge as the first curator of the Freer Gallery of Art. Contemporary critics acknowledged Freer's initial assessment of him: "the safest and soundest man for this very difficult position." The epitome of the taciturn New Englander, Lodge thought long and carefully before uttering even a few pointed remarks. Expansive in neither expression nor personality, by nature pessimistic and dubious, he scrutinized the objects in the Freer collection with a magnifying glass and a ready red pencil.[5]

As he prepared the collection for the opening exhibition, Lodge examined and reclassified the objects he had inherited, changing the attributions on most of them. Paintings which Freer and his scholars had assigned proudly to a specific painter of the Song Dynasty were presented at the gallery's opening as "Ming" or merely "in the manner of." Langdon Warner cringed at such "damning," but reluctantly admitted that "Mr. Lodge's cautious label is the only way out of a very doubtful position":

> The bronzes which, we were taught to believe, descended from the mythical ages of Chou and Shang and miraculously defied the certain, gnawing chemistry of the earth in which they were embedded, are now more reasonably ascribed to Han - perhaps a mere two thousand years ago. How full of righteous indignation our dealers will be!

Some reviewers of that opening exhibition objected, criticizing the selection of "only such paintings as could legitimately lay some claim to the period they represent, with the result that one finds a few superb paintings, some less good, and a whole mass of pleasant but quite undistinguished pictures hung together as a representative collection."[6]

In the 1920s, when Lodge evaluated the thousands of objects under his care, scholarship on Asian art was still rudimentary. Many of his attributions have again been changed, a large number of them reaffirming Freer's original attributions. The Bostonian E. S. Morse made corrections on the Asian pottery before the gallery opened. On some pieces his corrections stand, but on a remarkable number, later scholars confirmed the attribution asserted by Freer. The collector's stipulation that no object could be removed from the collection served a purpose: valuable pieces that might have been discarded remained. Freer would have quietly enjoyed his vindication.

Whether Freer, on the basis of scant information, gave each object a proper attribution is less important to us today than how early and skillfully he selected what to buy and what to keep. Out of the present collection of over 14,000 objects, nearly 10,000 came from his final bequest; the other 4,000 have been purchased over the last hundred years with the funds he provided. The times in which he lived as well as his own errors and aesthetic prejudices drove his selections. He eschewed most Ming and Qing paintings; he virtually ignored porcelain. The earliest Yamato-e paintings he could not afford, and few Shang bronzes had been unearthed. Those gaps subsequent curators filled. Fortunately he relented in his last months to allow additions to his Asian collection. Strengthened by training and scholarship, future curators gathered from excavations and the chaos of wars treasures Freer had never dreamed of owning.[7]

In the 1920s academics explored the ancient Chinese capitals with new scientific tools, and by the 1930s major exhibitions increasingly displayed ancient Chinese art in Paris, London, and other Western art centers. Even then serious collectors and dealers concentrated mostly on bronzes and ceramics. Gradually, under the guidance of scholars like Laurence Sickman and Sherman Lee, some museums acquired paintings and sculpture, but not until the early 1950s did the American art community recognize the fine arts from Japan and China as comparable in execution and beauty to sculpture and painting in the Western tradition. Freer's leadership and foresight had paved the way a half century earlier.

When the Freer Gallery of Art opened in 1923, the only comparable institutions at that time were the Musée Guimet in Paris, the Imperial Museum of Tokyo, and Oriental departments of museums in Boston, London, Berlin, and Cologne. Freer knew intimately most of the men who had developed those collections. Without exception, those museums accomplished through the efforts of many individuals and often with substantial help from their governments what Freer accomplished alone. His independence gave his institution its uncommon strength. Because he was early in recognizing the beauty and value of ancient Asian art, he and his endowment enabled the United States government to establish a world-class museum.

Admittedly Freer's quixotic mission to prove a universal aesthetic force linking the arts of the East and the West missed its mark. In his antipathy to the emerging modern art, he stubbornly refused to allow his museum to make any additions to his American art collection. The dynamic artistic movements of the 20th century soon left the Gilded Age tonalist artists he championed as the "deepest in artistic truth" sadly dated. He succeeded in preserving *the* collection of Whistler's works, but he froze the Western half of his mission. The Eastern half, however, has strengthened for a century. His museum perpetuates the force of the trailblazing collector who introduced the West to the East through art.

Before the Freer Gallery opened, the American public had little knowledge of the man or the collection they were to inherit. Freer had recoiled from any publicity. Commentators marveled that "very little has been written of him, and no photographs of him have ever been published, even in his own city." Information on his collection during his lifetime was equally meager, but today we should broadcast the jewellike excellence of the Freer Gallery of Art.[8]

Freer was unique. By combining in one man an eye for quality, a passion for learning, a willingness to go places where few others ventured, a stubborn self-reliance, and a commitment to preserve his collection as a whole, he set himself apart. Other American collectors possessed some of those qualities; none possessed them all. Among the Japanese, whose Asian collections surpassed Freer's, few kept their collections intact. The Masuda, Hara, and Inoue collections were scattered through auctions. Alone among his contemporaries, Freer built a superb collection of ancient Asian art and preserved it "for the benefit of future generations."

The Freer Gallery of Art stands today as unique as the man who created it over 100 years ago.

APPENDIX

CHINESE DYNASTIES (abbreviated)

Neolithic and Xia periods, ca. 8000 – 1600 BC

Shang dynasty, ca. 1600 – 1100 BC

Zhou dynasty, ca. 1100 – 256 BC

Qin dynasty, 221 – 206 B.C

Han dynasty, 206 B.C – 220 AD

Period of Disunity

Sui dynasty, 589 – 618 AD

Tang dynasty, 618 – 907 AD

Song dynasty, 960 – 1279 AD

Yuan dynasty, 1260 – 1368 AD

Ming dynasty, 1368 – 1644 AD

Qing dynasty, 1644 – 1912 AD

JAPANESE PERIODS (abbreviated)

Jōmon period, ca. 10,000 – 300 BC

Nara period, 710 – 794 A.D

Heian period, 794 – 1185 AD.

Kamakura period, 1185 – 1333 AD

Muromachi (Ashikaga) period, 1333/36 – 1568 AD

Momoyama period, 1568 – 1600 AD

Edo period (Tokugawa), 1600 – 1868 AD

Meiji period, 1868 – 1912 AD

Source: Asian Art at the Princeton University Art Museum, Copyright 2019 The Trustees of Princeton University.

ENDNOTES

Prologue

[1] Charles Watson Freer, Kingston, New York, Interview, April 17–18, 1975. Newspaper clipping, dateline New York, 27 May 1913, Scrapbook, Freer Gallery of Art Archives (FGA).

1 – Leaving Kingston

[1] Ruth P. Heidgerd, comp., "The Descendants of Hugo Freer, Patentee of New Paltz" (New York: The Huguenot Historical Society, 1968), p viii. Marius Schoonmaker, *History of Kingston, New York* (New York: Burr Printing House, 1888), p 72. Charles Watson Freer, interview.

[2] *Journal of the Senate of the State of New York*, May 8, 1845, p 644.

[3] *Kingston City Directory* (Kingston, New York: 1871, 1872, 1873).

[4] *New York Times*, 2 October 1976.

[5] Frank J. Hecker, *Activities of a Lifetime,* (Detroit: privately published, 1923), p 21–23. "The Recollections of Frank J. Hecker," *Detroit Free Press*, 13 September 1921, Scrapbook, p 27, FGA.

[6] Frank J. Hecker to Abel A. Crosby, 19 December 1874, Frank J. Hecker MSS, Burton Collection, Detroit Public Library (DPL).

[7] Gerald M Best, *The Ulster and Delaware: Railroad Through the Catskills* (San Marino, California: Golden West Books, 1972), p 25–31.

[8] "Recollections of Frank J. Hecker," *Detroit Free Press*, 1921.

[9] Letter Book, 17 August 1876; Freer to Hecker, 23 August 1876, Hecker MSS, DPL.

[10] Herbert Corey, "Charles Freer," newspaper article, 6 July 1913, Scrapbook, p 9, FGA.

[11] *Logansport Journal,* 19 September 1904, Scrapbook, FGA.

[12] Hecker to "My dear Mr. Ketchem," 22 October 1877; Hecker to James Joy, 31 October 1878, Hecker MSS, DPL.

[13] Hecker to C. H. Buhl, 18 August 1879, Hecker MSS, DPL.

[14] Hecker to Buhl, 11 October 1979, Hecker MSS, DPL.

[15] Buhl to Freer, 31 October 1879, Hecker MSS, DPL.

[16] Grove Webster to Hecker, 23 November 1879, Hecker MSS, DPL.

2 – Detroit Industrialist

[1] Thomas A. Arbaugh, "John S. Newberry and James H. McMillan: Leaders of Industry and Commerce," *Tonnencour, Life in Grosse Pointe* (Grosse Pointe Historical Society, 1997), v 2, p 72–82.

[2] William W. Lutz, *The News of Detroit, How a Newspaper and a City Grew Together* (Boston: Little, Brown & Co., 1973), p 33.

[3] Robert Conot, *American Odyssey* (New York: William Morrow & Co., 1974), p 66.

[4] Arbaugh, *Tonnencour;* Geoffrey G. Drutchas, *Michigan History*, March/April 2002, "The Man With A Capital Design," p 30.

[5] Silas Farmer, *History of Detroit and Michigan* 2 vols. (Detroit: Silas Farmer & Co., 1884) v 1, p 813, *Michigan Centennial History*, v 1, p 540. Albert N. Marquis, ed. *Book of Detroiters* (Chicago: A. N. Marquis & Co., 1908), p 15. Melvin G. Holli, *Reform in Detroit: Hazen S. Pingree and Urban Politics* (New York: Oxford University Press, 1969), p 37–44.

[6] Charles S. Moore, *Washington Past and Present* (New York: Century Co., 1929), p 226.

[7] Katharine Nash Rhoades, "An Appreciation of Charles Lang Freer," *Ars Orientalis*, v 2, 1957. See Hecker, *Detroit Free Press,* 13 September 1921, and *Activities.*

[8] Hecker, *Activities,* p 25.

[9] Freer to Hecker, 7 April 1883, 11 April 1883, 19 April 1883, 26 April 1883, Hecker MSS, DPL.

[10] Freer to Hecker, 26 April 1883, Hecker MSS, DPL.

[11] Freer to Hecker, 7 April 1883, Hecker MSS,DPL.

[12] Freer to Hecker, 16 April 1883, 19 April 1883, Hecker MSS, DPL.

[13] Freer to Hecker, 21 April 1883, 24 April 1883, Hecker MSS, DPL.

[14] Freer to Emory Clark, 4 August 1919; Freer to Cameron Currie, 22 March 1915; San Diego newspaper clipping dated 20 January 1915, Scrapbook, p 15, FGA.

[15] *Detroit Free Press,* "A Thriving Industry," 29 March 1885, p 1.

[16] Charles L. Freer Diaries, 1889–1919 (1890 and 1899 are missing), FGA.

[17] *Dau's Blue Book for Detroit* (New York: 1885). See Charles S. Moore, *Detroit As She Is* (Detroit: Mabley & Co., 1889).

[18] Charles Watson Freer, interview.

[19] *Kingston Daily Freeman*, Kingston, New York, 21 June 1910.

[20] Charles L. Freer, Letterbook, 14 October 1901, FGA.

[21] Thomas W. Brunk, Notes to author, 2016.

3 – Apprentice in Art

[1] *The Art Amateur*, 2/191; 24,3, American Periodical Series, Hathi Trust digital library, circa 1879; Farmer, *History of Detroit and Michigan*, v I, p 359. Clayton, Wallace E. *The Growth of a Great Museum: An Informal History of the Detroit Institute of Art* (Detroit: Founders Society, Detroit Institute of Art, 1965). Farmer, *History*, "Art, Artists, and Inventors," v 1 p 360. Edward Strahan [Earl Shinn], ed.; *The Art Treasures of America*, 3 vols. (Philadelphia: George Barrie, 1879).

[2] Fitzroy Carrington, ed., *Prints and Their Makers* (New York: Century Co., 1912). Frederick Keppel, "Personal Characteristics of Sir Seymour Haden P.R.E.," p 194. John J. Jordan to Freer, 30 October 1889, Gravesande file, FGA.

[3] Frederick Keppel, *The Golden Age of Engraving* (New York: The Baker & Taylor Co., 1910), p xxvi.

[4] Keppel to Freer, 6 July 1887, Keppel file, FGA.

[5] Carrington, *Prints*, p 184.

[6] Keppel to Freer, 6 July 1887, 21 August 1887, FGA.

[7] Howard Mansfield, "Charles Lang Freer," *Parnassus*, v 7 (October 1935), p 16.

[8] Ibid.

[9] Daniel E. Sutherland, *Whistler, A Life For Art's Sake* (New Haven, London: Yale University Press, 2014), p 236.

[10] Mansfield to Freer, 26 June 1894, Mansfield file; Freer to Richard A. Rice, 8 June 1892, FGA.

[11] Detroit Museum of Art, *Historical Report*, May 1891. Thomas W. Brunk, "Notes" to author. Hawkins Ferry, "Representative Detroit Buildings, A Cross Section of Architecture, 1823–1943," *Detroit Institute of Art Bulletin* v 22, no. 6, (March 1943), p 46–62. See also Clayton, *Great Museum*, p 12–18. Farmer, *History*, v 1, p 360.

[12] Holli, *Reform in Detroit* (New York: Oxford University Press, 1969), p 149.

[13] James McNeill Whistler, *Mr. Whistler's Ten O'Clock Lecture,* delivered 1885 (London: Chatto and Windus, 1888).

[14] Clayton, *Great Museum,* p 18. Detroit Museum of Art, *Historical Report,* May 1891. Voucher box, 1887, FGA.

[15] Jordan to Freer, 30 October 1889; Freer to Jordan, 2 October 1893, 9 March 1893; Freer to Keppel, 12 August 1893, FGA.

[16] Freer to Jordan, 2 October 1893; Rice to Freer, 25 December 1889; Freer to Mansfield, 15 January 1894, FGA.

4 – A New Lifestyle

[1] *New York Herald,* 18 February 1906; Church to Freer, 29 October 1889, FGA.

[2] Church to Freer, 28 June 1890, 29 October 1889, FGA.

[3] Freer to Charles Phillip, 3 October 1892, FGA.

[4] Freer to Hecker, 16 October 1892, FGA.

[5] Freer to Church, 10 November 1892, 23 February 1893, 15 August 1894, FGA.

[6] See Geoffrey G. Drutchas, *A Great Village: The Founding Generation of the Yondotega Club, 1891–1945* (Digital Edition, 2017).

[7] Freer to Emory W. Clark, 25 November 1916, FGA.

[8] *Book of Yondotega Club* (Detroit, 1892), DPL; *Book of Yondotega Club 1900,* (Detroit, 1900), DPL.

[9] Freer to Stephen Y Seyburn, 25 March 1902, FGA. Swift oration, 1 January 1915, quoted in Drutchas, *A Great Village*, p 49. Church to Freer, 2 October 1889, FGA.

[10] Freer to Currie, 22 March 1915, FGA.

[11] Thomas W. Brunk, *The Grand American Avenues*, Chapter 3, "Woodward Avenue," (San Francisco: Pomegranate Artbooks, 1994), p 71. Julia Angell, *Christian Science Monitor*, circa late 1922, copy at FGA. Freer to Eyre, 25 May 1892, FGA.

[12] See Thomas W. Brunk, "The Charles L. Freer Residence: The Original Freer Gallery of Art" *Dichotomy* (University of Detroit Mercy School of Architecture), v 12, Fall 1999. Freer to Darling, Brothers and Burger, FGA.

[13] Freer to Lady Superior at House of Good Shepherd, Letterbook 1:116, FGA.

5 – American Artists

[1] Aline B. Saarinen, *The Proud Possessors: The Lives, Times and Tastes of Some Adventurous American Art Collectors* (New York: Random House, 1958), p 123. Tryon to Freer, 14 May 1889, FGA.

[2] See Lula Merrick, "Tryon, Devotee of Nature," *International Studio* vol. 77 (September 1923), p 489–504. Also see Charles H. Caffin, *The Art of Dwight W. Tryon* (New York: Forest Press, May 1909); Henry C. White, *The Life and Art of Dwight W. Tryon* (Boston: Houghton Mifflin, 1930); Linda Merrill, *An Ideal Country: Paintings by Dwight William Tryon* (Washington, D. C.: Smithsonian Institute, 1990).

[3] Tryon to Freer, 5 March 1891; Freer to N. E. Montross, 25 November 1892; Tryon to Freer, 23 November 1891, 27 March 1891, FGA. Brunk, *Dichotomy*, p 49.

[4] Tryon to Freer, 27 March 1891, 21 April 1892, FGA. White, *Tryon*, p 83. Freer to Charles J. Morse, 19 August 1904, FGA.

[5] Church to Freer, 14 December 1891, FGA. Homer Saint-Gaudens, *The American Artist and His Times* (New York: Dodd Mead & Co., 1914), p 139.

[6] See Susan A. Hobbs and Barbara Dayer Gallati, *The Art of Thomas Wilmer Dewing: Beauty Reconfigured* (Washington, D.C.: Smithsonian Institution, 1996); Susan A. Hobbs, with Shoshanna Abeles, *Thomas Wilmer Dewing: Beauty into Art: A Catalogue Raisonné* (New Haven: Yale University Press, 2019) 2 vols.

[7] Dewing to Freer, 13 March 1892, 19 March 1892; Freer to Dewing, 7 June 1892; Freer to Harrison S. Morris, 2 October 1893; Freer to Rice, 8 June 1893, 20 September 1892; Dewing to Freer, 15 February 1892, 23 February 1892, 14 November 1892, FGA.

[8] Freer to Tryon, 3 August 1892; Dewing to Freer, 17 August 1892, FGA.

[9] Church to Freer, 3 February 1888; Freer to Montross, 18 August 1892, FGA.

[10] Freer quoted Thayer in his letter to Montross, 3 October 1892, FGA.

[11] See Thomas Brumbaugh, "A Seated Angel by Abbott H. Thayer," *Wadsworth Atheneum Bulletin*, vol. 7, (Spring and Fall 1971), p 52–64.

[12] Freer to Halsey C. Ives, Letterbook 1: 224 and 1:32, 1892; Freer to Dewing, 19 July 1893, FGA.

[13] Freer to Mansfield, 3 March 1893; Thayer to Freer, 3 March 1893, 30 March 1893, FGA.

[14] Freer to Church, 23 March 1993, FGA. Freer to LeBrocq, 22 March 1993, quoted in Brunk, *Dichotomy*, p 52. Freer to Mr. Morrison, manager, Hotel Brunswick, New York City, 17 November 1892, FGA.

[15] Tryon to Freer, 4 January1897, FGA. Brunk, *Dichotomy*, p 66. Freer to Tryon, 18 May 1893, 9 June 1893, 27 August 1893; Freer Diary, 1893, FGA. Freer to Tryon, 17 June 1995, quoted in Linda Merrill, *An Ideal Country*, p 23. Freer to Tryon, 7 September 1894, Abbott H Thayer Papers, Archives of American Art.

[16] Dewing to Freer, 20 December 1893, 10 January 1894, 19 March 1894, 10 April 1894; Freer to Dewing, 9 August 1894; Dewing to Freer, 14 October 1895; Freer to Hecker, 24 July 1895, 4 August 1895, FGA.

[17] *Exhibition of Paintings by Abbott H Thayer* (Pittsburgh: Carnegie Institute, 1919), p 8. Thayer to Freer, 29 May 1893, 20 May 1893, 1 August 1893, FGA.

[18] Thayer to Freer, 1 May 1896 (?), 28 August 1901, 3 March 1893, FGA.

[19] Freer to Harrison Morris, 4 October 1896; Freer to Wilson Eyre, 2 October 1893, FGA.

[20] Freer to Eyre, 17 November 1892, FGA.

6 – Whistler

[1] Freer Diary 1890, FGA; "A Day with Whistler," *Detroit Free Press*, 3 March 1890.

[2] Frederick Keppel, *One Day with Whistler* (New York: Frederick Keppel & Co., 1904), p 6.

[3] Deanna Maroun Bendix, *Diabolical Designs, Paintings, Interiors and Exhibitions of James McNeill Whistler* (Washington, D. C.: Smithsonian Institution Press, 1995), p 180. "A Day with Whistler," *Detroit Free Press*.

[4] "A Day with Whistler," *Detroit Free Press.* Peter Schjeldahl, "Mom's Home" *New Yorker*, 31 August 2015, p 93.

[5] Frederick A. Sweet, *James McNeill Whistler* (Chicago: Catalogue, Chicago Art Institute, 1968), p 21. Suzanne La Follette, *Art in America* (New York: Harper & Bros., 1929), p 174.

[6] Stanley Weintraub, *Whistler, A Biography* (New York: Weybright & Talley, 1974), p 236. Elizabeth Robbins Pennell and Joseph Pennell, *The Life of James McNeill Whistler* (Philadelphia: J. B. Lippincott Co., 1908/1921), v 1, p 233.

[7] Thomas Lawton, and Linda Merrill, *Freer: A Legacy of Art* (Washington D. C.: Freer Gallery of Art, Smithsonian Institution, 1993), p 41. Freer to Whistler, 31 March 1890; Birnie Philip (BP) II 14/1, Glasgow University Library (UG); Freer to Whistler, 28 April 1890, BP II 14/3, UG. William Bell, Whistler's secretary to Freer, 6 June 1891, FGA.

[8] B. Whistler to Freer, 19 March 1892, 29 January 1892, FGA. Freer to Whistler, 9 January 1894, UG F438. See also Linda Merrill, ed., *With Kindest Regards, The Correspondence of Charles Lang Freer and James McNeill Whistler, 1890 - 1903* (Washington D. C.: Smithsonian Institution Press, 1995).

[9] Freer to Mansfield, Letterbook 1:136, 1892; Whistler to Alexander Reid, 1892, Letter #224, FGA.

[10] Whistler to A. Reid, 15 June 1892, 26 June 1892, n.d. FGA.

[11] Freer to B. Whistler, 6 May 1892, BP II, 14/10 UG; Freer to Whistler, 2 August 1894, BP II, 14/8, UG.

[12] Freer to Jordan, 19 July 1893, FGA.

7 – Boom and Bust

[1] Freer Diaries, 1890, 1892, FGA.

[2] *New York Times,* 16 July 1892, p 6.

[3] Freer to Tryon, 3 August 1892; Freer to Church, 3 October 1892, FGA.

[4] Freer to Dewing, 7 June 1892; Freer to Tryon, 10 November 1892, FGA.

[5] *Detroit Free Press*, 23 February 1893.

[6] *New York Times,* 16 July 1892, p 6; 28 July 1897. See also Arbaugh, *Tonnencour.*

[7] Conot, *American Odyssey*, p 101; Holli, *Reform in Detroit,* p 37–44.

[8] Holli, *Reform in Detroit,* p 71; John C. Lodge, *I Remember Detroit* (Detroit: Wayne State University Press, 1949), p 128.

[9] Holli *Reform in Detroit,* p 57–60. See *Journal of the Common Council. 1893,* p 1152, 1894, 376, and Detroit newspapers published during the last half of February 1893.

[10] George Beard, *American Nervousness, Its Causes and Consequences, a supplement to Nervous Exhaustion (Neurasthenia),* (New York: G. P. Putnam's Sons, 1881). Freer to George Freer, 24 June 1894; Freer to Will Freer, 26 June 1894, FGA.

[11] Freer to Hecker, 21 September 1894, FGA.

[12] Freer to Hecker, 29 September 1894, 9 October 1894, 17 October 1894, FGA.

[13] Keith N. Morgan, "The Patronage Matrix: Charles A. Platt, Architect, Charles L. Freer, Client," *Winterthur Portfolio*, Summer–Autumn 1982, v 17, p 121–134.

[14] Freer to Hecker, 30 October 1894, FGA; Whistler, *Ten O'Clock,* lecture.

[15] Whistler to Freer, 18 July 1894, 3 April 1894, FGA.

[16] Freer to Hecker 16, November 1894, FGA. See letters in Merrill, *Kindest Regards,* p 101–103; Freer to Whistler, 23 November 1894, BP II, 14/27, UG. Whistler to Freer, 23 November 1894, FGA.

[17] Freer to Hecker, 16 October 1894, 19 October 1894, 16 November 1894, FGA.

[18] Pennell and Pennell, *The Life,* v 2, p 152. Freer to Hecker, 16 November 1894, FGA.

[19] Freer to Hecker, 16 November 1894, 25 November 1894; Whistler to Freer, 23 November 1894, FGA.

8 – Escape to Asia

[1] Freer to Hecker, 28 November 1894, 20 December 1894, 25 December 1894, FGA.

[2] Freer to Hecker, 6 January 1895, FGA.

[3] Freer to Hecker, 6 January 1995, 9 March 1895, 27 January 1895, FGA.

[4] Whistler to Freer, 23, November 1894, FGA. Freer to B. Whistler from Calcutta, 18 March 1895 BP11 14/13 UG. Freer to Hecker, 15 March 1895, 9 April 1895, 20 April 1895, FGA.

[5] Whistler to Freer, 23 November 1894; Freer to Hecker, 18 February 1895, FGA.

[6] Freer to Hecker, 9 March 1895, 18 February 1895, FGA.

[7] Freer to Hecker, 15 March 1895, FGA.

[8] Freer to Hecker, 7 May 1895, FGA.

[9] Freer to Hecker, 28 April 1895, 7 May 1895, 10 June 1895, 27 May 1895, FGA.

[10] Freer to Hecker, 27 May 1895, 7 May 1895, FGA.

[11] Freer to Hecker, 26 June 1895, 27 May 1895, FGA.

[12] Freer to Tryon, June 17, 1895, from Amo-no-Hashidate, Abbott H, Thayer Papers Archives of American Art as quoted in Nichols Clark, "Charles Lang Freer: An American Aesthete in the Gilded Age", *American Art Journal* II (October 1979) p 65.

[13] Ibid.

[14] Freer to Hecker, 24 July 1895, FGA.

[15] Freer to Hecker, 4 August 1895, FGA.

[16] Ibid.

9 – Exit From Business

[1] Freer to Will McMillan, 1 August 1896, FGA.

[2] Freer to William K. Bixby, 23 May 1896, 8 July 1897, FGA.

[3] Freer to Bixby, 31 July 1897, 6 September 1897, 29 September 1897, 6 October 1897, 13 October 1897, FGA.

[4] Freer to Bixby, 6 May 1898, Freer to James McMillan, 11 January 1899, FGA.

[5] Lee Glazer, *Charles Lang Freer, A Cosmopolitan Life* (Washington, D. C.: Smithsonian Institution, 2017), p 14.

[6] Freer to Bixby, 27 June 1900; Freer Diary, 1900; Freer to Hecker, 21 July 1899, 27 June 1899, FGA.

[7] Freer to B. Whistler, from Calcutta, 18 March 1895, BP II, 14/30; Freer to J. Whistler, no date BP II, 14/8, UG. Freer to Keppel, 30 July 1896; Freer to Mansfield, 3 March 1893; Freer to Jordan, 19 July 1893; Freer to R. E Plumb, 16 October 1896, FGA. Freer to J. Whistler, no date BP II, 14/8, n.d. 1897, BP II, 14/28, UG.

[8] Freer to Dewing, 18 May 1896, FGA. Freer to Whistler, 31 March 1897, in Merrill, *Kindly Regards*, p 115.

[9] J. Whistler to Freer, 24 March 1897, FGA. Freer to Whistler, 6 April 1897, in Merrill, *Kindly Regards*, p 116. Freer to J. Whistler, n.d. 1897 BP II, 14/30, UG.

[10] Freer to Hecker, 28 July 1899; Voucher box #8, FGA.

[11] Freer to Stanford White, 2 July 1900, 6 June 1900, 7 November 1900, FGA. County Records Book 209, p 45, Great Barrington, Vermont.

[12] Freer to Hecker, June 1899, FGA.

[13] Freer to Hecker, 7 July 1899, 28 July 1899; Freer to Eyre, 9 September 1901, FGA.

[14] Freer to Hecker, 6 September 1900, FGA. See *Century Magazine*, "Home of the Indolent" 1998. *House and Garden*, v 11 #8, August 1902.

[15] Freer to Hecker, 6 September 1900, 19 September 1900; Freer to Tryon, 1 November 1900, FGA.

[16] Freer to T. Jerome, 26 January 1900, FGA; *Detroit News*, n.d., Scrapbook, FGA. *Detroit Tribune*, 6 May 1905.

[17] Freer to Stanford White, 25 November 1899, FGA.

[18] *Detroit News*, 24 February 1900. S. White to Frederick MacMonnies, 26 February 1900; Freer to S. White, 6 March 1900, 19 September 1900, FGA. *Detroit Free Press*, 25 February 1900; *Detroit Tribune*, 26 February 1900.

[19] Dewing to Freer, 27 July 1898, quoted in Susan A. Hobbs and Barbara Dayer Gallati, *The Art of Thomas Wilmer Dewing: Beauty Reconfigured* (Washington, D.C.: Smithsonian, 1996), p 68. See also Letterbook 11:191, 225, 370, 395, FGA.

10 – Discovering Asian Art

[1] Freer to Charles J. Morse, 9 March 1897, 5 April 1900, FGA.

[2] John LaFarge, *An Artist's Letters from Japan* (New York: Century Co., 1897 [1890]), p 7.

[3] Fenollosa to Edward Morse, letter quoted in Walter Muir Whitehill, *Museum of Fine Arts, Boston: A centennial History* (Boston: Belknap Press, 1970), v 1, p 113.

[4] Ernest F. Fenollosa, *Epochs of Chinese and Japanese Art, An Outline History of East Asiatic Design,* (New York: Frederick A. Stokes Co., 1910), v 2, p 70–75.

[5] Lawrence W. Chisolm, *Fenollosa: The Far East and American Culture* (New Haven: Yale University Press; 1963), p 120; quote from the "Ninth Report of the Secretary of the Class of 1874 of Harvard College," p 42.

[6] Howard Mansfield, "Lecture for Ladies Day at the Grolier Club in New York City," 10 April 1896, typewritten; Ledger of accounts, 5 November 1992, FGA.

[7] Freer to Mansfield, 7 November 1892; Rufus E. Moore to Freer, 3 November 1892; Ledger of accounts, house financial materials 1892, FGA.

[8] Louis Gonse, *L'Art Japonais*, 2 v (Paris: A. Quantin, 1883); Ernest F. Fenollosa, *Review of the Chapter on Painting in Gonse's "L'Art Japonais"* (Boston: J. R. Osgood & Co., 1885), reprint from *Japan Weekly Mail*, 12 July 1884. Laurence Binyon, "National Characteristics in Art," typewritten copy, p 1, FGA.

[9] Fenollosa, *Review*, p 25, 24, 35.

[10] Freer to Takayanagi, 2 November 1892, 17 February 1893, FGA. "Kiri" means gold.

[11] William M. Milliken, interview with author, 13 January 1976; W. M. Milliken, *Born Under the Sign of Libra* (Cleveland: Western: Reserve Historical Society, 1977), p 7–14. Folder sheets; Freer to Hecker, 27 May 1895, FGA.

[12] See Letterbooks 3:543, 18 May 1895, and 3:380, 26 October 1895, 2:168, 2 December 1895, FGA; *Prominent Americans Interested in Japan and Prominent Japanese in America*, pamphlet (Japan and America 1903) (internet), p 89–91.

[13] Freer to Matsuki, 1 August 1896; Freer Diary 22 July 1896; Freer to H. Shugio, 31 July 1896, 16 December 1896, June 1900; Freer to Matsuki, 16 October 1896, FGA.

[14] Freer to Matsuki, Letterbook 5:64, 17 October 1898, 23 November 1899, FGA.

[15] Fenollosa, *Review*, p 5.

[16] Fenollosa, "An Outline of Japanese Art" 2 parts, *The Century Illustrated Monthly Magazinè*, v 56, pp 62–75, 276–289. Freer to E. S. Morse, 13 December 1900, FGA.

[17] Freer to C. Morse, 9 March 1897, 24 January 1901, FGA.

[18] Freer to Gookin, 1 June 1898, 31 October 1900, 22 January 1901, FGA.

11 – The Collection

[1] Whistler to Freer, 29 July 1899, FGA.

[2] Freer to Hecker, 28 July 1899; Whistler to Freer, 12 August 1899; Freer to Chapman, 1901, Letterbook 8:249; Whistler to Freer, 29 July 1899, FGA.

[3] Freer to Whistler, 27 June 1900, FGA.

[4] Freer to Bixby, 1 November 1900, 7 November 1900; Marchant to Freer, 19 December 1899, FGA.

[5] Whistler to Freer, 19 October 1900; Freer to Hecker, 16 October 1900, 1 December 1900, FGA. Freer to Whistler, 1 December 1900, in Merrill, *Kindest Regards*, p 132.

[6] Written in Freer's hand on Carlton Hotel stationery, Whistler miscellaneous file, undated; Freer to Marchant, 27 June 1901, FGA.

[7] Whistler to Freer, 10 February 1901, FGA. Freer to Whistler, 6 March 1901, BP II, 14/17, UG.

[8] Freer to Whistler, 20 June 1901, in Merrill, *Kindest Regards*, p 143–44.

[9] Freer to Hecker, 28 June 1901, 15 July 1901, FGA. Freer to Whistler, 21 July 1901, in Merrill, *Kindest Regards*, p 146.

[10] Freer to Hecker, 21 July 1901, 15 July 1901, FGA.

[11] Freer to Whistler, 20 June 1901; J. Whistler to Freer, 10 July 1901; Freer to Whistler, 21 July 1901, in Merrill, *Kindest Regards,* p 143-148.

[12] Freer to H. H. Benedict, 26 November 1901; Marchant to Freer, 3 December 1901; Freer to Marchant, 19 December 1901, FGA.

[13] Whistler to Freer, 25 October 1901; Freer to Bixby, 7 February 1902, FGA. Freer to J. Whistler, 6 February 1902, BP 11, 14/22, UG.

[14] Freer to Marchant, April 1902, FGA; Financial materials, FGA.

[15] Letterbook 9:246, FGA. Freer to Whistler, 20 February 1902, BP II 14/20, UG. Freer to Hecker, 6 May 1902, FGA.

[16] Freer to Hecker, 6 May 1902, 13 June 190; Freer Diary, 12 June 1902, FGA.

[17] Freer to Hecker, 3 June 1902, 30 May 1902; Freer Diary, 1902, FGA.

[18] Freer to Hecker 30 May 1902, FGA. Pennell and Pennell, *Life*, v 2, p 206.

[19] Freer to Hecker, 13 June 1902, 3 June 1902, FGA.

[20] Freer to Hecker, 3 June 1902, 20 June 1902, FGA.

[21] Freer to Hecker, 27 June 1902, 30 June 1902, FGA.

[22] Freer to Hecker, 30 June 1902, 4 July 1902, FGA.

[23] Freer to C. Morse, 4 August 1902, 4 February 1903; Freer to Hecker, 28 July 1902, FGA. Freer to J. Whistler, 1 August 1902, BP 11, 14/24 UG.

[24] Handwritten draft of a letter to Miss Birnie-Philip, 30 October 1902; Freer Diary, 11 December 1902, FGA.

[25] *New York Times*, 3 March 1914, obituary of R. Canfield, p 1 and 6. Alexander Gardiner, *Canfield: The True Story of the Greatest Gambler* (Garden City, New York: Doubleday, Doran & Co., 1930), p 3–4.

[26] Freer to Canfield, 17 January 1903, FGA. Pennell, *Journal*, p 273, 277; Pennell, *Life*, v 2, p 292.

[27] Freer to Canfield, 1902, 17 January 1903, FGA. Pennell, *Journal*, p 279.

[28] Freer to Canfield, 17 March 1903; Freer to J. J. Cowen, 11 November 1901; Canfield to Freer, 3 March 1903, cable, 3 April 1903, FGA.

[29] Whistler to Freer, 16 June 1903, cable; Freer to Hecker, 5 July 1903, 12 July 1903; Freer to Cam Currie, 16 July 1903, FGA.

[30] Freer Diary, 17 July 1903; Freer to Hecker, 18 July 1903, FGA.

[31] Freer to Hecker, 22 July 1903, FGA. Pennell, *Journal*, p 293.

[32] Freer to Gustav Mayer, 27 January 1904; Freer to Birnie-Philip, 28 January 1904; Birnie-Philip to Freer 11 February 1904, FGA. *New York World*, 14 August 1904.

12 – Art Connoisseur

[1] Fenollosa to Freer, 4 March 1901, October 1901 (?), 26 December 1901, FGA.

[2] Fenollosa to Freer, 4 March 1901, 6 March 1901; Freer to Fenollosa, 4 April 1901, 19 April 1901, 23 November 1902, 3 January 1904; Fenollosa to Freer, 13 September 1902, 6 March 1902, 12 October 1902, 27 October 1902, FGA.

[3] Fenollosa to Freer, 12 October 1902, FGA.

[4] Fenollosa to Freer, 8 and 9 March 1903; Freer to Fenollosa, August or September 1903, FGA.

[5] Fenollosa to Freer, 8 and 9 March 1903, FGA.

[6] Fenollosa to Freer 8 March 1903; Freer to Fenollosa, 18 August 1903; Freer to Matsuki, 28 April 1904, FGA.

[7] Freer to Matsuki, 31 May 1904, 28 May 1904, November 1904; Letterbook 15:226; Freer to C. Morse, 5 December 1904; Freer to Leila Mechlin, 8 June 1906, FGA.

[8] Fenollosa, *Epochs*, p 128.

[9] Freer to Matsuki, 29 October 1902; Freer to Dewing, 17 December 1901; Freer to Fenollosa, 29 February 1904, FGA. Fenollosa, *Epochs*, v 2, p 126–135.

[10] Freer to William Burrell, 20 August 1903, FGA. Ernest Fenollosa, "The Collection of Mr. Charles Lang Freer," *Pacific Era* (November 1907), p 61.

13 – The French Circle

[1] Raymond Koechlin, "Gillot Collection," *Les Arts* (November 1903), v 23, p 17–24, English translation, p iii–vi; John La Farge, *An Artist's Letters From Japan* (New York: The Century Co., 1897), p 128, 151.

[2] Koechlin, "Gillot Collection," *Les Arts*, p iv–v.

[3] Raymond Koechlin, *Souvenirs d'un Vieil Amateur d'Art de l'Extreme-Orient* (Chalon-sur-Saone: E. Bertrand, 1930), p 19.

[4] News Clipping, Scrapbook, p 33, FGA. *Connaissance des Arts* (October 1978), p 127.

[5] Koechlin, *Souvenirs*, p 19. Gabriel P. Weisberg has written extensively on S. Bing.

[6] Raymond Koechlin, "Gaston Migeon et Le Louvre," *Notice 1ue a l'Assemblees Generale Annue1 1e de la Societe Des Amis du Louvre*, 3 March 1931, Louvre Archives: 030 268.

[7] Koechlin, *Souvenirs*, p 14.

[8] Koechlin, "Gillot Collection."

[9] Mansfield to Freer, 28 May 1896; Enrique (?) Baez to Freer, 16 March 1897; Freer to E. Morse, 13 December 1900, FGA.

[10] Voucher box, 1901, October, FGA.

[11] Freer to Hecker, 22 June 1903, FGA.

[12] Thomas W. Brunk wrote extensively on Pewabic pottery.

[13] *Kelekian as Artists See Him*, Exhibition Catalogue (New York: Durand-Ruel Galleries, October–November 1944). Raymond Koechlin, "Gaston Migeon," *Eastern Art,* 1931, v 3, p 2–3.

[14] Dikran Kelekian, *The Potteries of Persia* (Paris: H. Clarke, 1909), p 26–7. D. Kelekian to Freer, 3 February 1905; Freer to D. Kelekian, 28 December 1905; Scrapbook, p 26, unidentified news clipping dated 8 February 1910; Kelekian to Freer, 17 February 1905, 28 March 1905, FGA.

[15] Freer to Fenollosa, 11 February 1902; Freer to Hecker, 22 June 1903, 24 June 1903, FGA.

[16] Freer to Hecker, 24 June 1903, 28 June 1903; FGA.

[17] Freer to Hecker, 5 June 1904; S. Bing to Freer, 19 April 1904, FGA.

[18] Letterbook 13:108, 13 February 1904; Freer to S. Bing, 31 March 1903, 4 April 1903, 26 August 1903, FGA.

[19] Freer to C. Morse, 15 September 1904; Freer to S. Bing, 5 December 1904, 30 December 1904, FGA.

[20] Freer to Hecker, 24 May 1905, 28 June 1905, FGA.

[21] Koechlin, *Souvenirs.*

[22] Gaston Migeon, *Chefs-d'Oeuvre d'Art Japonais* (Paris: D. A. Longuet, 1905), p 2–3; Migeon, "Preface," *L'art en Chine et au Japon* by Ernest Fenollosa (Paris: Hachette et Cie., 1910), p x.

[23] Gabriel P. Weisberg et al., *Japonism, Japanese Influence on French Art 1854–1910* (Cleveland: Cleveland Museum of Art, 1975), p 12. Freer to William Burrell, 20 August 1903, FGA.

14 – Gift to the Nation

[1] Handwritten draft of the will of James Smithson, 23 October 1826, Smithsonian Institution archives. *Material Papers Relating to the Freer Gift and Bequest* (Smithsonian Institution, #2958, 8 February 1928), FGA.

[2] James A. Michener, *Japanese Prints from the Early Masters to the Modern* (Rutland, VT, Charles E. Tuttle Co., 1959), p 24.

[3] Geoffrey Drutchas has written extensively on McMillan and Moore. Freer to Samuel P. Langley, 13 December 1902, FGA.

[4] Freer to Hecker, 20 March 1903, 28 August 1903, 23 February 1905, FGA.

[5] Freer to C. Moore, 19 August 1903; Freer to William Burrell, 20 August 1903; Freer to Canfield, 20 August 1903, FGA.

[6] Frank J. Hecker, *Activities,* p 43–53. T. Roosevelt to Hecker, 16 November 1904 quoted in *Activities,* p 44.

[7] Freer to S. P. Langley, 27 December 1904, reprinted in the Smithsonian Annual Report, 1905, p xvi.

[8] Freer to Hecker, 17 January 1905 (?), 7 February 1905; Freer to C. Morse, 2 February 1905, FGA.

[9] Aline Saarinen, *The Proud Possessors*. Freer to Hecker, 23 February 1905, 13 March 1905. FGA.

[10] Freer to Rosalind Birnie-Philip, 10 March 1905; Freer to Hecker, 13 March 1905; Freer to T. Jerome, 23 December 1905; Freer to Alfred Chapman, 6 February 1906, FGA.

[11] Brunk, *Dichotomy*, p 70–77.

[12] Freer to Hecker, 6 July 1905; Freer to C. Morse, 9 December 1905; Freer to Fenollosa, 12 December 1905, FGA. Charles Moore, *Washington Past and Present* (New York: Century Co., 1929), p 24; Harrison S. Morris, *Confessions in Art* (New York: Sears Publishing, 1930), p 232–3.

[13] *Material Papers Relating to the Freer Gift and Bequest* (Smithsonian Institution, #2958, 8 February 1928), p 1–2.

[14] Theodore Roosevelt to Chief Justice Fuller, quoted in newspaper article (unidentified), 28 December 1905, Archives of American Art, Detroit, microfilm #D-45, frame 0062. Freer to the editor of *Spare Moments*, 6 February 1908; Letterbook 23:365, FGA.

[15] Freer to Hecker, 4 May 1907; Freer to W. T. Evans, 24 July 1907; Freer to Richard Rathbun, 4 December 1907, FGA.

[16] Freer to C. Morse, 30 January 1906; Note from archives; *Material Papers Relating to the Freer Gift and Bequest*, Smithsonian publication #2958, 8 February 1928, p 4-5, FGA.

[17] Freer to Keppel, 17 November 1903; Freer memo, 23 April 1906, July 1906; Freer to Matsuki, 29 June 1906; Letterbook 20:424, FGA.

[18] Freer to Tod Ford, 16 February 1906; Freer to C. Morse, 26 September 1904, 25 January 1906, 8 March 1905, 24 January 1906, 23 January 1906, 30 January 1906, FGA.

[19] Freer to Mrs. J. B. Herod, 3 October 1908; Freer to Keppel, 17 November 1903; Freer to J. H. Jordan, 5 December 1904, 5 December 1904; Letterbook 19:312; Freer to A. H. Griffith, 31 October 1908; Freer to Robert Barr, 23 July 1906; Freer to Wm. C. Weber, 14 April 1508, FGA.

[20] Freer to Tryon, 17 March 1903, 11:83, FGA. See Merrill, *An Ideal Country,* and Hobbs, *The Art of Thomas Wilmer Dewing.*

[21] Freer to Tryon, 5 July 1907, 3 August 1907; Freer to Dewing, March 1906; Freer to Montross, March 1905; Freer to Thayer, 8 October 1908; Letterbook 25:327, FGA.

[22] Freer to Dewing, 7 April 1903; Freer to Bixby, 26 December 1905; Freer to R. Knoedler, 17 January 1908, 4 March 1908; Freer to Walter P. Fearon, 7 April 1908; Freer to Truman Newberry, 22 February 1908; Freer to Saint Gaudens, 14 February 1906; Freer to F. S. Church, 23 December 1907, FGA.

[23] Freer to C. Morse, 30 January 1906, 6 April 1906; Matsuki to Freer, 23 November 1903; Fenollosa to Freer, 8 March 1903; Letterbook 20:420, 1 August 1906, 17:350,30 June 1905; Freer to D. J. R. Ushikubo, 21 October 1905; Freer to C. Morse, 9 December 1905, FGA.

[24] Freer to C. Morse, 17 October 1905, 20 October 1905; Matsuki to Freer, 23 November 1903; Freer to Matsuki, 11 December 1905; Freer to Tryon, 6 February 1906; Freer to Matsuki, 29 June 1906; Freer to Fenollosa, 17 September 1906, 27 September 1906; Freer to C. Morse, 8 November 1906; Freer to Matsuki, 26 October 1908, FGA.

[25] Freer to J. M. Kennedy, 3 October 1909; Freer to Kalebdjian Freres, 29 May 1906; Freer to Walcott, 1907, Smithsonian file, 14 January 1909; Letterbook, 23:46, 1906, 21:259, November 1906, FGA.

15 – Probing the Near East

[1] Lecture by Ernest Fenollosa delivered to the University Club under Freer's sponsorship in 1906, *Detroit Free Press,* 4 February 1906, p 20; Freer to Hecker, 11 June 1908, FGA.

[2] Freer Diary, 1906; Freer to Currie, 11 January 1907, FGA.

[3] Freer to Hecker, 3 February 1907, FGA.

[4] Ibid.

[5] Freer to Bixby, 8 January 1908; Freer Diary, 19 December 1906; Freer to Hecker, 3 February I907; Freer to F. W. Kelsey, 19 March 1908, FGA.

[6] Freer to C. Morse, 30 August 1907; Freer to Hecker, 26 September 1907; H. B. Hanna to Freer, 31 October 1907, FGA.

[7] Freer to Hecker, 16 May 1908, 20 May 1908, 26 May 1908, FGA.

[8] Freer to A. S. Depinna, 6 February 1908; Freer to Hecker, 26 May 1908; Freer to J. M. Kennedy, 20 May 1908; Freer to Hecker, 30 May 1908; Freer to F.W. Kelsey, 14 April 1908, FGA.

[9] Freer to F.W. Kelsey, 14 April 1908, FGA.

[10] Freer to Hecker, 7 May 1908, 11 June 1908, 27 June 1908, FGA.

[11] Freer to Hecker, 11 June 1908, FGA.

[12] Freer to Hecker, 27 June 1908, 20 November 1908, FGA.

[13] Freer to Hecker, 27 June 1908, FGA.

[14] Freer to Hecker, 15 August 1908, FGA.

[15] Freer to Hecker, 23 June 1909; Freer to J. M. Kennedy, 4 June 1909; Freer to Hecker, 25 June 1909, 13 July 1909, FGA.

[16] Freer to Bixby, 4 August 1909; Freer to Hecker, 12 June 1909, 24 July 1909, 28 July 1909; Maurice Nahman to Freer, 22 April 1909; *Cleveland Leader,* 2 June 1913, Scrapbook, p 8; Freer to Hecker, 28 July 1909, FGA.

[17] Letterbook 29:412, 3 March 1910, FGA. Kuhnel, *Second Presentation of the Charles Lang Freer Medal* (Freer Gallery of Art, 3 May 1960), p 15.

16 – Revisiting Japan

[1] Freer to Hecker, 3 February 1907, FGA.

[2] Freer to Migeon, 23 July 1907; news clippings enclosed in Freer to Hecker, 15 February 1907, 5 February 1907, FGA.

[3] Freer to Hecker, 21 March 1907; Freer Diary, March 1907, FGA.

[4] Freer to Hecker, 21 March 1907, FGA.

[5] Fenollosa to Freer, 12 March 1907, FGA.

[6] Freer to Hecker, 6 May 1907, FGA.

[7] Freer to Hecker, 23 April 1907, 4 May 1907, 30 May 1907, FGA.

[8] Freer to Hecker, 23 May 1907, 30 May 1907, FGA.

[9] Freer to Tryon, 7 July 1907, FGA. Christine Guth, "A Tale of Two Collectors," *Asian Art* (Fall 1991), p 29–49.

[10] Booklet, printed in Japanese, in honor of the centennial of Hara's birthday, *Hara, Centennial*; Hara to Freer, 25 May 1907, translated by Nomura, FGA.

[11] Freer to Hecker, 15 May 1907, FGA.

[12] Freer to Hecker, 6 May 1907, FGA. *Townsend Harris Memorial*, (Japan: 1937), p 12. Yoshinobu Masuda, interview with author, 8 November 1976, Sankei-in, Japan. Guth, "Masuda Don'o" *Chanoyu Quarterly*, p 29–32.

[13] Fenollosa to Freer, 12 March 1907, FGA.

[14] Freer to Hecker, 30 May 1907, 26 May 1907; Freer Diary 26 -30 May 1907; Kettaro Kaneko to Freer, 13 June 1907; Freer to H. R. Yamamoto, 16 August 1907, FGA.

[15] Freer to Hecker, 30 May 1907; Freer to Migeon 23 July 1907; Freer to Hara, 25 May 1907, FGA.

[16] Freer to Hecker, 6 May 1907, 15 June 1907, FGA.

[17] Freer to Hecker, 15 June 1907, 30 May 1907, FGA.

[18] Freer to Tryon, 7 July 1907; Freer to Morse, 21 February 1908, FGA.

[19] Freer to Hecker, 5 May 1907; memo attached to certified catalogue of ancient Korean pottery, Horace N. Allen Collection; Freer to Hecker, 30 May 1907, FGA.

[20] *Wall Street Journal*, 18 October 2017, p B18. Freer to Charles V. Lang, 21 October 1907; Freer to R. A. Rice, 12 November 1907; Freer to Nomura, March 1908; Freer to Frank O. Baldwin, 10 February 1908, FGA.

[21] Freer, Diary, 1907; Nomura to Freer, 29 November 1907; Freer to C. Morse, 21, February 1908, FGA.

[22] Freer to Holker Abbott, 22 February 1908; Freer to C. Morse, 21 February 1908; Freer to T. Masuda, 4 April 1908; Freer to Bixby, 4 March 1908, FGA.

[23] Freer to Frank G. Macomber, 11 April 1908; Freer to Mansfield, 11 April 1908; Freer to Gookin, 31 October 1910, FGA.

17 – Pioneer in China

[1] Fenollosa, *Epochs*, p 127; Koechlin, "Gillot," 1903, p iv.

[2] Freer to Marcel Bing, Letterbook 29:495; Freer to Gookin, 1 October 1910; Freer Inventory, 1906, privately printed, FGA.

[3] Freer to Hecker, 11 April 1907, FGA.

[4] Frederick W. Gookin, *Catalogue of a loan exhibition of ancient Chinese paintings, sculptures and jade objects formed by Charles Lang Freer* (Art Institute of Chicago, November 5 to December 8, 1917), p 6.

[5] Freer to Hecker, 2 September 1909, FGA.

[6] Freer to Hecker, 12 September 1909, FGA.

[7] Freer to Hecker, 27 September 1909, 11 October 1909, FGA.

[8] Freer to Hecker, 20 September 1909, FGA.

[9] Freer to Hecker, 17 September 1909; Freer to Migeon, 26 October 1908, FGA.

[10] Freer to Hecker, 11 October 1909, FGA.

[11] Freer to Hecker, 11 October 1909; Freer to S. Z. Shirae, 17 March 1914, FGA.

[12] Freer to Hecker, 11 October 1909, 27 September 1909, FGA.

[13] Freer to J. M. Kennedy, 11 November 1909, 30 September 1909; Freer to Hecker, 2 September 1909 FGA.

[14] Freer to Fritz V. Holz, 25 November 1908, FGA. *Detroit Free Press,* 30 January 1910; Freer to Hecker, 11 October 1909. FGA.

[15] Freer to A. W. Bahr, 19 January 1910; Voretzsch to Freer, 4 July 1911; Freer to Yung Hoi, 16 June 1910; Freer to Walcott, 24 January 1910; Freer to Gaston Migeon, 19 January 1910; Freer to Walcott, 17 February 1910; Nan Ming-yuen to Freer, 23 January 1910, FGA.

[16] Freer to Hecker, 19 June 1909, FGA."Detroit Explorer, Traveler Tells of Chinese Discoveries," *Buffalo Academy Notes,* v 6, no. 3, p 71.

[17] Freer to Hecker, 23 September 1910, FGA.

[18] Ibid.

[19] Freer to Hecker, 13 October 1910, FGA.

[20] Freer to Hecker, 23 September 1910, 24 October 1910; Freer to Gookin, 31 October, 1910; Freer to Hecker, 21 November 1910, 13 October 1910, FGA

[21] "Detroit Explorer," *Buffalo Academy Notes,* p 71–72.

[22] Ibid; Freer to Hecker, 21 November 1910, FGA.

[23] Freer to Hecker, 21 November 1910; Freer to Currie, 1 November 1910, FGA.

[24] "Detroit Explorer," *Buffalo Academy Notes,* p 73. *Detroit News Tribune,* 30 March 1910, Scrapbook, p 6; Freer to Gookin, 31 October 1910, FGA.

[25] Freer Lecture on Lung-men, typewritten, FGA.

[26] "Detroit Explorer," *Buffalo Academy Notes,* p 72. Freer to Hecker, 21 November 1910; Freer Lecture on Lung-men, FGA.

[27] Paul Mallon, interview with the author, November 1975, Sarthe, France.

[28] Freer to Currie, 1 November 1910, FGA.

[29] Freer to Hecker, 28 September 1910, 25 October 1910, FGA.

[30] "Detroit Explorer," *Buffalo Academy Notes*, p 71. Freer to Gookin, 31 October 1910, FGA.

[31] Freer to Hecker, 21 November 1910, FGA.

[32] Freer to Hecker, 25 December 1910, FGA.

[33] Ibid.

[34] Freer to Voretzsch, 1 September 1911; Freer to Hecker, 10 January 1911, 23 January 1911, FGA.

[35] Freer to Hecker, 23 January 1911, FGA.

[36] Freer to Hecker, 26 March 1911, FGA.

[37] *Detroit News-Tribune* and *Detroit Free Press,* 30 March 1911. Newspaper clipping, 1 October 1913, Scrapbook, p 46, FGA.

18 – Illness

[1] Freer, Diary, 28 May 1911; Freer to T. Jerome, 12 June 1911; Freer to Frederick McCormick, 3 October 1911, FGA.

[2] Freer to Mrs. Dewing, 21 September 1911, FGA.

[3] Freer to C. Walcott, n.d.; Charles L. Freer death certificate, Freer Archives, FGA.

[4] Freer Diary, summer 1911, FGA.

[5] *New York Herald,* 5 December 1997, as quoted in Hobbs, *Beauty Reconfigured,* p 66–70. Paul R. Baker, *Stanny: The Gilded Life of Stanford White* (New York: The Free Press, 1989), p 275. Freer to Currie, 16 July 1903, FGA.

[6] Freer to Tryon, 17 July 1907, FGA. Nelson C. White Papers, Archives of American Art, as quoted in Glazer, *Freer,* p 60. Freer to C. Morse, 31 July 1906; Freer to Currie, 16 July 1903. FGA.

[7] Agnes Meyer, "Charles L. Freer and His Gallery" (Washington, D.C., Freer Gallery of Art, 1970), p 18.

[8] Freer to Mrs. Dewing, 21 Sept 1911; Freer to Dattari, 31 August 1911, FGA.

[9] Freer to Dewing, 11 November 1911; Freer to T. Jerome, 1 December 1911; Freer Diary, November 1911, FGA.

[10] Freer to T. Jerome, 1 December 1911, FGA. Freer to A. Meyer, 8 September 1913, Box 13, A. Meyer MSS, Library of Congress (LC).

[11] Exhibition Catalogue, New Building, 24 March 1912, Government Printing Office.

[12] Julian L Street, *Abroad at Home* (New York: Century Co., 1914), p 103. Freer to T. Jerome, 1 December 1911, 13 December 1912, FGA.

[13] Freer to Bixby, 14 March 1913; Freer to Currie, 20 September 1913, FGA.

19 – Life in New York City

[1] Freer to F. McCormick, 20 December 1912; Boston Fine Arts Museum file, letter dated April 1912, FGA.

[2] American School in China file; Freer to McCormick, 20 December 1912; McCormick to Freer, 26 December 1912, FGA.

[3] *Washington Evening Star*, 5 and 6 January 1913. *New York Tribune*, 8 January 1913, 22 April 1913. Freer to F. W. Mann, 15 May 1914; Kelsey to Freer, 28 January 1915; Warner to Freer, 15 April 1913; Walcott to Freer, 17 April 1913; Freer to Warner, 18 April 1913; Warner to Walcott, 12 April 1913, FGA; Warner file, Box 135, Cleveland Museum of Art Archives (CMAA). "The Asiatic Institute of New York City, Plunder and Destruction of Antiquities in China, 1914," *The Evening Post*, New York City, 10 March 1914.

[4] Paul Mallon, interview with author, November 1975.

[5] L. Warner to Whiting, 7 July 1916, #135, CMAA. Agnes Meyer, "Freer," p 16. Freer Diary, 7 March 1917, FGA. Freer to E. Meyer, 6 March 1917, E. Meyer MSS, #122; Freer to A. Meyer, 2 October 1917, A. Meyer MSS, #15, Library of Congress (LC).

[6] McCormick to Paul S. Reinsch at the American Legation in Peking, 23 June 1914; McCormick to Freer, 30 June 1914, FGA. Warner to Frederick

Whiting, September 1914, 7 February 1914, 19 November 1916, Warner file, #135, CMAA.

[7] McCormick to Freer, 23 January 1915; Freer to E. Meyer, 26 October 1914; McCormick to Freer, 2 July 1914, 12 October 1914; Freer to McCormick, 8 July 1914; Freer to T. Hara, 24 August 1914, FGA.

[8] J. R. Kennedy to E. Meyer, 13 February 1913, E. Meyer MSS, #131; Freer to E. Meyer, 18 February 1913, E. Meyer MSS, #23, LC. Freer to Currie, 31 July 1916; E. Meyer to Freer, 23 October 1914, FGA. Freer to E. Meyer, 7 January 1913, E. Meyer MSS, #23, LC.

[9] A. Meyer, "Freer," p 3–4.

[10] Ibid. Freer to E. Meyer, 7 May 1913, E. Meyer MSS, #122, LC. Freer Diary, 14 May 1913, FGA.

[11] Freer to E. Meyer, 7 June 1913, E. Meyer MSS, #122, LC. E. Meyer to Freer, 13 October 1914, FGA.

[12] Freer to Currie, 9 January 1914; Freer to T. Jerome, 14 January 1914; Freer to Bixby, 29 May 1914, FGA.

[13] Canfield to Freer, 12 June 1913, 18 February 1914; Freer to Canfield, 11 March 1914; Canfield to Freer, 11 March 1914, 12 March 1914, FGA. Jean Strouse, *Morgan: American Financier* (New York: Random House, 1999) p 688. *New York Times*, 3 March 1914, p 1 and 6.

[14] Freer to Whiting, 1 May 1914, #108, CMAA. Freer to Dewing, 11 November 1911, 13 July 1911, FGA. Freer to E. Meyer, n.d. E. Meyer MSS, Box #122, LC. Freer to Voretzsch 29 April 1913, FGA.

[15] Ferguson to Freer, 26 May 1914; Freer to Ferguson, 7 July 1914, FGA.

[16] Freer to E. Meyer, 3 April 1914, E. Meyer MSS, #23, LC. A. Meyer to Freer, 13 July 1914, 14 November 1914, FGA.

[17] William M. Milliken, *Born Under the Sign of Libra: An Autobiography* (Cleveland: Western Reserve Historical Society, 1977), p 43. Belle Greene to A. Meyer, 21 February 1914, E. Meyer MSS, #122, LC. R. W. B. Lewis, *Edith Wharton* (New York: Harper & Row, 1975), p 294.

[18] Bernard Berenson to E. Meyer, 27 February 1914; A. Meyer to Freer, 20 November 1914, 25 November 1914, E. Meyer MSS, #122; A. Meyer to Freer, 25 November 1914, E. Meyer, MSS; Freer to A. Meyer, 21 December 1914, A. Meyer MSS, LC.

[19] Freer to A. Meyer, 21 December 1914; A. Meyer to Freer, 10 October 1914; Freer to A. Meyer, 12 December 1914; A. Meyer to Freer, 30 March 1915; A. Meyer MSS, LC; Freer to A. Meyer, 2 May 1915, #122, E. Meyer MSS LC.

[20] Freer to Marie Meyer-Riefstahl, 17 March 1914, FGA, quoted in Warren I. Cohen, *East Asian Art and American Culture* (New York: Columbia University Press, 1992), p 54. Freer to A. Meyer, 28 April 1914, 19 June (1917), A. Meyer MSS #16, LC. T. Hara to Freer, 4 December 1916; Nomura to Freer, 13 June 1915; Shojiro Abe to Freer, 3 April 1913; Nomura to Freer, 21 December 1912; Freer to T. Masuda, 1 September 1914, FGA.

[21] Nomura to Freer, 13 June 1915; Freer to T. Masuda, 7 May 1918; Freer to Bixby, 30 April 1919; Koechlin to Freer, 16 July 1915, 27 September 1916, 30 December 1915, 13 August 1916; Gaston Migeon to Freer, 26 July 1918; Freer to S. T. Peters, 10 September 1914; M. Bing to Freer, 6 January 1916; Freer to M. Bing, 2 February 1916, FGA.

[22] Freer to Ida Franke, 19 January 1915; Freer to Currie, 17 May 1917, FGA.

20 – Collector Revitalized

[1] Freer to Ida Franke, 27 January 1915, FGA. Whiting to L. Warner n.d., #108 and #135 CMAA.

[2] Freer to A. Meyer, 22 January 1915, A. Meyer MSS, #15, LC.

[3] *Detroit News*, 29 April 1911; *Boston Transcript*, 15 July 1915.

[4] "Necrologie de C. T. Loo," typewritten, from Mme. Pierre Emanuel, daughter of C. T. Loo, Paris, interview with author, November 1975. *American Art News*, 20 March 1915. Freer to P'ang Tszu-cheng, 16 March 1915, FGA.

[5] Freer to P'ang Yuan-chi, February 1912; Ferguson to Freer, 3 March 1915, FGA; Freer to A. Meyer, 22 March 1915, 30 March 1915. #15, A. Meyer MSS, LC.

[6] Freer to E. Meyer, 1 May 1915, E. Meyer MSS, #122, LC. Freer to George Alger, 30 April 1915, FGA.

[7] A. Meyer to Freer, 12 July 1915, A. Meyer MSS, #15, LC.

[8] Freer to S. T. Peters, 24 February 1914; Freer to McCormick, 23 March. I914, FGA.

[9] Fenollosa to Freer, 25 September 1906; Freer to C. Morse, 17 September 1906; Fenollosa to Freer, 12 March 1907, FGA. Louisine Havemeyer, *Sixteen to Sixty; Memoirs of a Collector* (New York: privately printed,1961), p 24.

[10] A. Meyer to Freer, 30 March 1915, 18 April 1915, A. Meyer MSS #15; E. Meyer to Freer 30 April 1915, E. Meyer MSS, #23; Freer to E. Meyer, n.d. from Plaza Hotel, A. Meyer MSS, #16, LC.

[11] Freer to Whiting, 29 March 1915, #108, CMAA.

[12] Tomita to Arthur MacLean, 16 February 1917, #2, CMAA; Warner to Whiting, 26 August 1916, #135; Freer to Whiting, 10 October 1913, #108, CMAA.

[13] Henry W. Kent to Freer, 15 December 1915, MMAA; Freer to Whiting, 28 June 1915, #108, CMAA; Freer to A. Meyer, 30 June 1915, A. Meyer MSS, #15, LC; Freer to Bosch-Reitz, 19 August 1915, 2 January 1916, 15 January 1918, 24 January 1918 #3, Metropolitan Museum of Art Archives (MMAA); *Boston Evening Transcript*, 4 February 1916; Curator (MacLean) to Ralph King, 22 January 1916, #139, CMAA.

[14] Whiting to Freer, 21 July 1914, 26 May 1914, 23 December 1914, 26 June 1915; Freer to Whiting, 25 May 1914, 28 May 1914, 7 June 1915, 29 March 1915, 29 May 1914; Freer to Saunders, 28 June 1915, #108, CMAA.

[15] Joseph Breck to Freer, 15 December 1915, 19 February 1917; Freer to Bixby, 30 April 1919, 24 May 1919 FGA; Freer to A. Meyer, 18 February, A. Meyer MSS, #15, LC; Freer to George Draper, 11 February 1918; Freer to Nathan H. Dole, 18 June 1906; Freer to Bixby, 7 November 1900; Bixby to Freer, 24 May 1919; Freer to Bixby 30 April 1919, FGA.

[16] Peters-Freer correspondence 1913–1914; Freer to Fenollosa, 2 December 1902; Freer to Frank Gari Macomber, 11 March 1904, FGA; Christopher Benfey, "Tea with Okakura," *New York Review of Books*, 25 May 2000, p 46; Freer to J. T. Coolidge, 16 November 1903, 20 June 1904, FGA; L. Warner to Whiting, 17 March 1914, # 135, CMAA; see also *Hara Centennial.*

[17] Whitehall, Walter Muir, *Museum of Fine Arts, Boston: A Centennial History* (Boston: Museum of Fine Arts, January 1, 1970), 2 v, p 355, p 440, p 36.

[18] Freer to M. Bing, 2 February 1916; Freer to Currie, 22 March 1915, FGA.

[19] P'ang Lai ch'en to Freer, n.d.; P'ang Tszu-cheng to Freer 26 January 1918; Freer to Bixby, 30 April 1919; Freer to Yue, 5 July 1919, 16 and 8 January 1918, 12 December 1917; Freer to K. T. Wong, 1 February 1918; Yue to Freer, 21 November 1917, FGA; Freer to Ralph King, 19 January 1917, #139, CMAA.

[20] Warner to Whiting, 22 April 1915, #135, CMAA; Freer to A. Meyer, 30 June 1915, 3 January 1917, A. Meyer MSS, #15, LC; Freer to Bixby, 21 January 1918; K. T. Wong to Freer, 17 October 1916, FGA.

[21] Freer to Gookin, 10 March 1916, FGA.

[22] Freer to A. Meyer, 3 January 1917, A. Meyer MSS, #15, LC; Freer to George B. Gordon, 10 November 1918, FGA.

21 – Final Pursuits

[1] Freer to A. Meyer, 24 August 1915, A. Meyer MSS, #15, LC; Freer to Ida Franke, 8 September 1915, FGA.

[2] Freer to E. Meyer, 17 October 1915, E. Meyer MSS, #122, LC; Freer, Diary, 17 October 1915, FGA.

[3] Freer to A. Meyer, 18 November 1915, A. Meyer MSS, #15, LC.

[4] Mansfield, "Freer," *Parnassus*, p 17; Freer to B. Berenson, 11 August 1917, FGA; Freer to A. Meyer, 14 May 1917, A. Meyer MSS, #15, LC.

[5] Freer to A. Meyer, 28 April 1916, A. Meyer MSS, #15, LC; Freer Diary 1915 –1916, FGA; A. Meyer, "Freer," p 18.

[6] Freer to Seth Marshall, 28 January 1916, FGA; Freer to A. Meyer, 11 November 1915, A. Meyer MSS, #15, LC; Seth Marshall to Freer, 18 November 1915, FGA.

[7] Author's interviews with Harvey Buchanan, Draper's son-in-law, November 1975, and Dr. John Caughey, Draper's student, December 1975, Cleveland, Ohio. Draper to Freer, 27 December 1916, FGA.

[8] Freer to Currie, 31 July 1916, FGA.

[9] Freer to Draper, 21 September 1917, FGA.

[10] Freer to Draper, 21 September 1917, 3 September 1917, 5 October 1917, 15 October 1917, FGA.

[11] Warner to Whiting, 7 July 1916, #135, CMAA; A. Meyer, *Freer*, p 16; Freer Diary, March 7, 1917, FGA; Freer to E. Meyer, 6 March 1917, E. Meyer MSS, #122; Freer to A. Meyer, 2 October 1917, A. Meyer MSS, #15, LC.

22 – The Freer Gallery of Art

[1] Freer to Saint Gaudens, 26 February 1906; Freer to C. F. McKim, 25 June 1906, FGA.

[2] Freer to Walcott, 21 April 1908, FGA.

[3] Freer to Hecker, 26 June 1909, 8 July 1909, FGA.

[4] Katsuji Makino to Freer, 18 May 1913; Freer to Thayer, 12 August 1912. FGA.

[5] Freer to A. Meyer, 26 August 1917, 29 July 1917, A. Meyer MSS, #15. LC.

[6] Freer, Diary, 1 March 1916, FGA; Freer to A. Meyer, 12 September 1916, A. Meyer MSS, #15, LC; Walcott to Freer, 13 February 1917, FGA.

[7] Freer to Draper, 15 October 1917, 11 February 1918, FGA. A. Meyer to Freer, 11 March 1918, 1 May 1918, A. Meyer MSS, #15, LC.

[8] Freer's will, 13 May 1918, *Material Papers Relating to the Freer Gift and Bequest*, Smithsonian publication #2958, 8 February 1928, FGA.

[9] Freer to Draper, 15 October 1917; Walcott memo, 2 June 1918, confirmed the choice of Draper as curator, Smithsonian Institute file, FGA.

[10] Freer to Draper, 30 August 1918, FGA.

[11] Katharine Rhoades to Agnes Meyer, 1 March 1918, A. Meyer MSS, #15, LC.

[12] A . Meyer, "Freer," p 19. A. Meyer, diary, 30 November 1917, A. Meyer MSS, Box 1-6, LC.

[13] Freer Diary, 2 February 1918; Freer to Hecker, 13 October 1910; Freer to Currie, 17 May 1917; Freer to Harrie Ledyard, 29 November (1916); Freer to Truman Newberry, 13 December 1917; Alanson S. Brooks to Freer, 15 January 1918, FGA.

[14] For example, see J. M. Kennedy to Freer, 23 May 1917, FGA.

[15] Agnes Meyer, Diary, 4 February 1919, A. Meyer MSS, #1-6, LC.

[16] Louisine W. Havemeyer, "The Freer Museum of Oriental Art with Personal Recollections of the Donor," *Scribner's Magazine* (May 1923), p 539. Freer, Diary, 28 April 1919, 9 May 1919, FGA.

[17] Freer to Watson Freer, 30 May 1919, box was in storage in California, per David Hogge, former archivist, FGA.

[18] Freer's will, 4 May 1919, *Material Papers*, p 14.

[19] Freer Diary; Freer to Lodge, 27 May 1919, 4 June 1919; Lodge to Freer, 7 June 1919, FGA.

[20] Freer to Lodge, 12 June 1919; Advisory Committee proposal, n.d., E. Meyer MSS, #122, LC.

[21] Freer's will, 13 May 1918, *Material Papers*; Walcott to Freer, 13 February 1917, FGA.

[22] Freer to A. Meyer, 25 January 1919, A. Meyer MSS, #15, LC.

[23] A. Meyer, "Freer," p 121. E. Meyer to Freer, 15 August 1919, E. Meyer MSS,#122, LC.

[24] Freer to Emory W. Clark, 4 August 1919, FGA.

[25] Freer Diary, 12 September 1919, FGA.

[26] K. Rhoades, "An Appreciation of Charles Lang Freer," *Ars Orientalis*, v 2, 1957, p 4.

Epilogue

[1] Langdon Warner, "The Freer Gift of Eastern Art to America," *Asia*, August 1923, v 23, p 592.

[2] Katharine Rhoades, "Charles Lang Freer," typewritten, 20 March 1923; *Material Papers*, p 25, FGA. Berthold Laufer, "The Freer Art Treasures: A Gift to the People of the United States," *Oriental Review* (February 1913), v 3, p 263. Paul Brocket, "The National Gallery of Art," *The Sketch Book* (November 1907), v 6, p 270.

[3] Warner, "Freer Gift," p 590.

[4] Osvald Siren, "Address," *First Presentation of the Charles Lang Freer Medal*, (Freer Gallery of Art, 25 February 1956), p 13–14, 25, 26.

[5] See Rhoades–A. Meyer correspondence, A. Meyer MSS, #16, LC.

[6] Warner, "Freer Gift," pp 590, 612. Siren, *First Freer Medal*, p 20. L. Ashton, "The Opening Exhibition at the Freer Gallery, Washington," *Jahrbuch der Asiatischen Kunst*, 1924, p 239–240.

[7] Laurence Sickman, "Address of Acceptance," *Fifth Presentation of the Charles Lang Freer Medal*, (Freer Gallery of Art, 11 September 1973), p 15.

[8] J. Olivier Curwood, "Charles Lang Freer, an American Art Collector," *International Studio*, supplement (June 1905), p 76–78. Brocket, "National Gallery," p 270. "Art in America," *Burlington Magazine* (April 1906), p 68. Wilfred B. Shaw, "The Relation of Modern American Art to That of China and Japan: Demonstrated at the Recent Exhibition at Ann Arbor" (August 1910), v 18, p 522. "The Freer Collection," *Art and Progress* (June 1912), v 3, p 615.

IMAGE CREDITS

Front cover. Charles Lang Freer Papers. Freer Gallery of Art and Arthur M. Sackler Gallery Archives. Smithsonian Institution, Washington, D.C. Gift of the estate of Charles Lang Freer, FSA.01_12.01.2.7

Front and back cover. Freer Gallery of Art, Smithsonian Institution, Washington, D.C.: Gift of Charles Lang Freer, F1903.309

1. Charles Lang Freer Papers. Freer Gallery of Art and Arthur M. Sackler Gallery Archives. Smithsonian Institution, Washington, D.C. Gift of the estate of Charles Lang Freer, FSA_A.01_12.01.4.01
2. Freer Gallery of Art, Smithsonian Institution, Washington, D.C.: Gift of Charles Lang Freer, F1893.12a-b
3. Freer Gallery of Art, Smithsonian Institution, Washington, D.C.: Gift of Charles Lang Freer, F1906.66a
4. Charles Lang Freer Papers. Freer Gallery of Art and Arthur M. Sackler Gallery Archives. Smithsonian Institution, Washington, D.C. Gift of the estate of Charles Lang Freer, FSA_A.01_12.02.1.07
5. Freer Gallery of Art, Smithsonian Institution, Washington, D.C.: Gift of Charles Lang Freer, F1898.389
6. Freer Gallery of Art, Smithsonian Institution, Washington, D.C.: Gift of Charles Lang Freer, F1903.89
7. Freer Gallery of Art, Smithsonian Institution, Washington, D.C.: Gift of Charles Lang Freer, F1892.23a-b
8. Freer Gallery of Art, Smithsonian Institution, Washington, D.C.: Gift of Charles Lang Freer, F1906.229
9. Freer Gallery of Art, Smithsonian Institution, Washington, D.C.: Gift of Charles Lang Freer, F1897.38
10. Charles Lang Freer Papers. Freer Gallery of Art and Arthur M. Sackler Gallery Archives. Smithsonian Institution, Washington, D.C. Gift of the estate of Charles Lang Freer, FSA_A.01_12.01.6.2
11. Freer Gallery of Art, Smithsonian Institution, Washington, D.C.: Gift of Charles Lang Freer, F1903.120
12. Freer Gallery of Art, Smithsonian Institution, Washington, D.C.: Gift of Charles Lang Freer, F1902.92

13. Freer Gallery of Art, Smithsonian Institution, Washington, D.C.: Gift of Charles Lang Freer, F1905.268

14. Freer Gallery of Art, Smithsonian Institution, Washington, D.C.: Gift of Charles Lang Freer, F1909.345a-h

15. Freer Gallery of Art, Smithsonian Institution, Washington, D.C.: Gift of Charles Lang Freer, F1914.53

16. Freer Gallery of Art, Smithsonian Institution, Washington, D.C.: Gift of Charles Lang Freer, F1917.183

17. Freer Gallery of Art, Smithsonian Institution, Washington, D.C.: Gift of Charles Lang Freer, F1911.338

18. Freer Gallery of Art, Smithsonian Institution, Washington, D.C.: Gift of Charles Lang Freer, F1917.179

19. Freer Gallery of Art, Smithsonian Institution, Washington, D.C.: Gift of Charles Lang Freer, F1913.21

20. © 2019 The Estate of Edward Steichen / Artists Rights Society (ARS), New York

21. Charles Lang Freer Papers. Freer Gallery of Art and Arthur M. Sackler Gallery Archives. Smithsonian Institution, Washington, D.C. Gift of the estate of Charles Lang Freer, FSA_A.01_12.01.7.07

22. Smithsonian Institution Archives. Image # AI-29413.

INDEX

ACKNOWLEDGMENTS

My PhD dissertation, *Charles Lang Freer, Pioneer Collector of Oriental Art*, was the genesis of this biography. New research and editing hopefully have resulted in a life-story worthy of that remarkable man. My thanks to Morris Rossabi for starting me on this journey, and to the late Sherman E. Lee for his early guidance.

I received unstinting support from the staff of the Freer Gallery of Art. James Ulak gave me valuable insights, as did J. Keith Wilson. Kathryn Philips and Mike Smith unearth information with uncanny skill. To the retired archivist David Hogge, I owe a special thanks. Retired curator Susan A. Hobbs proffered wise advice. Lee Glazer and Katherine Roeder also volunteered their assistance.

Detroit historians, the late Thomas W. Brunk and Geoffrey G. Drutchas, shared their research, as did William Colburn of The Freer House. At the Detroit Institute of Art, the library staff and Kenneth Myers provided valuable information.

Publishing can be as daunting as writing. I am grateful to Carolyn Hanson, Jennifer Berry, Nina Spahn, and Lauren Kanne for smoothing the process.

Needless to say, any mistakes made in *West Meets East* are mine.

Closer to home, good friends and family armed me with welcome support. My thanks to Lynne Feldman, Brigitte Hautelet, the Dahs, Vicki Nielsen, tennis friends, and Camille Nebeker.

To my extraordinary grandchildren: Lucy, Emma, Tom, Sam, Will, Sara, and Madeleine—my eternal thanks to you all for years of joy. Finally my deepest gratitude and love go to my children: Allan "John" Tomlinson, Laura Barton, and Will Tomlinson for enabling me to complete this writing journey. They spur me on; from them I constantly learn.